This is the last page.

Kakuriyo: Bed & Breakfast for Spirits has been printed in the original Japanese format to preserve the orientation of the artwork.

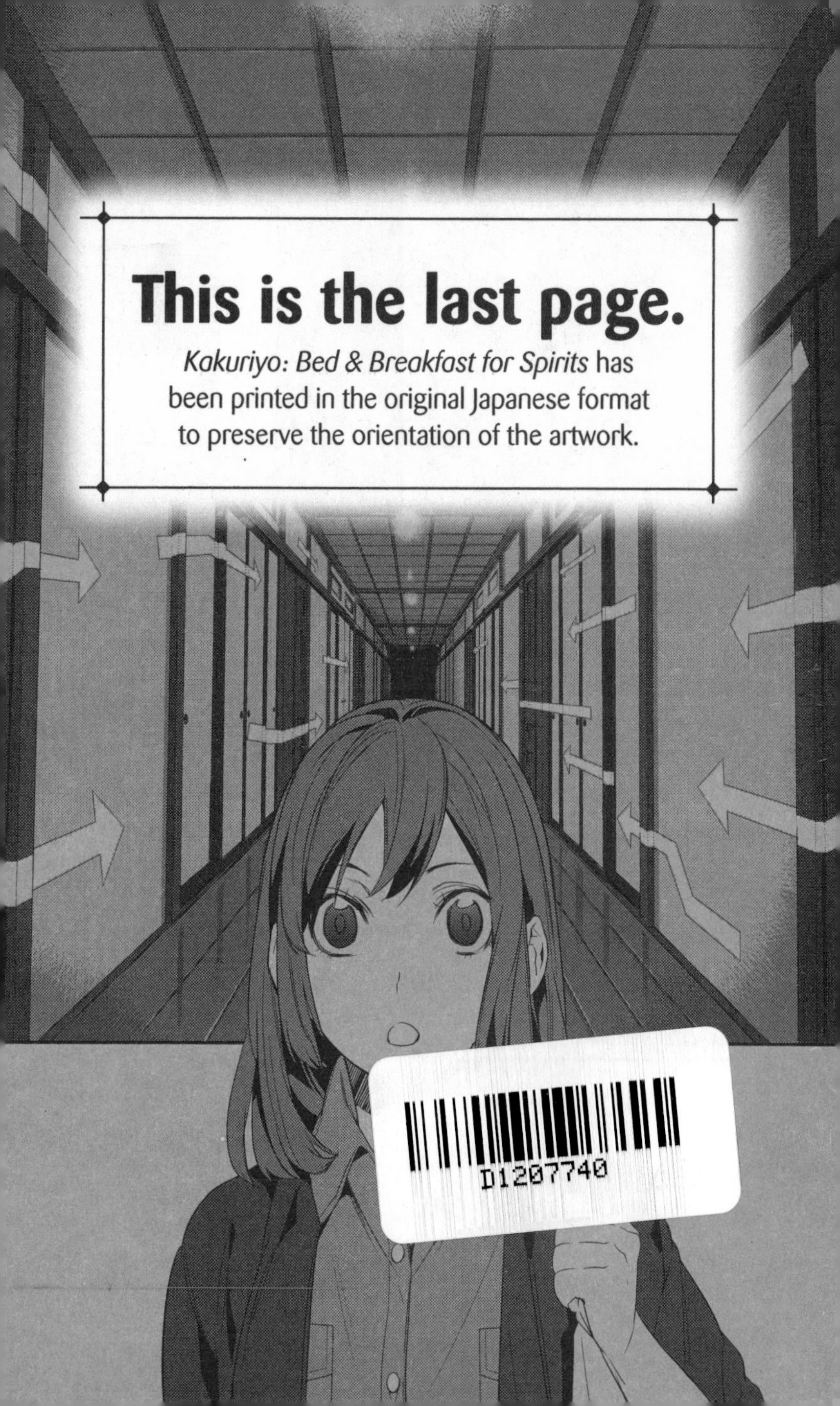

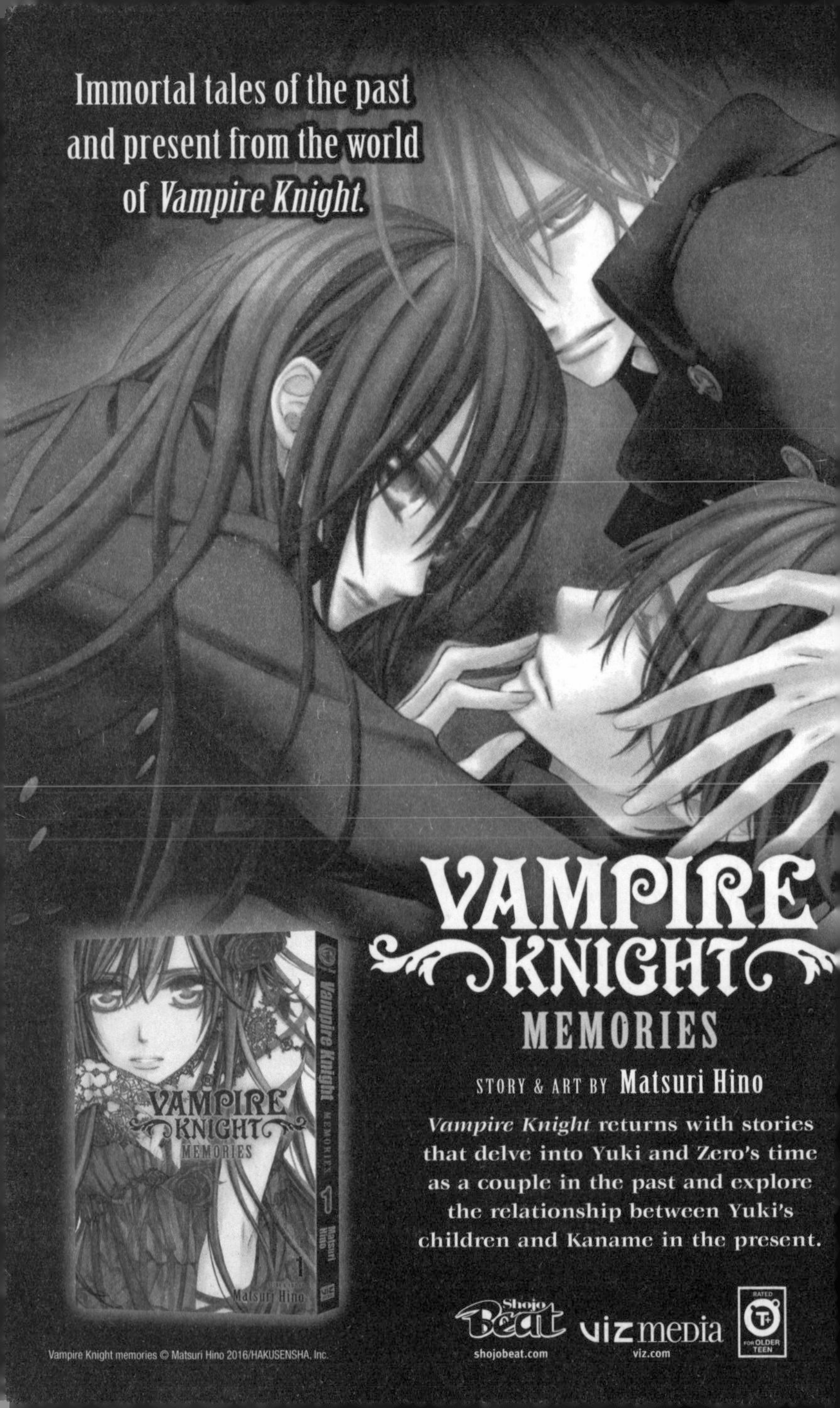

Immortal tales of the past and present from the world of *Vampire Knight*.
VAMPIRE KNIGHT
MEMORIES
STORY & ART BY Matsuri Hino
Vampire Knight returns with stories that delve into Yuki and Zero's time as a couple in the past and explore the relationship between Yuki's children and Kaname in the present.
Vampire Knight MEMORIES 1 Matsuri Hino
VAMPIRE KNIGHT MEMORIES
1
Matsuri Hino
Shojo Beat
shojobeat.com
viz media
viz.com
RATED T+ FOR OLDER TEEN
Vampire Knight memories © Matsuri Hino 2016/HAKUSENSHA, Inc.

Black Bird

STORY AND ART BY
KANOKO SAKURAKOUJI

There is a world of **myth** and **magic** that intersects ours, and only a special few can see it. Misao Harada is one such person, and she wants nothing to do with magical realms. She just wants to have a normal high school life and maybe get a boyfriend.

But she is the bride of demon prophecy, and her blood grants incredible powers, her flesh immortality. Now the demon realm is fighting over the right to her hand...or her life!

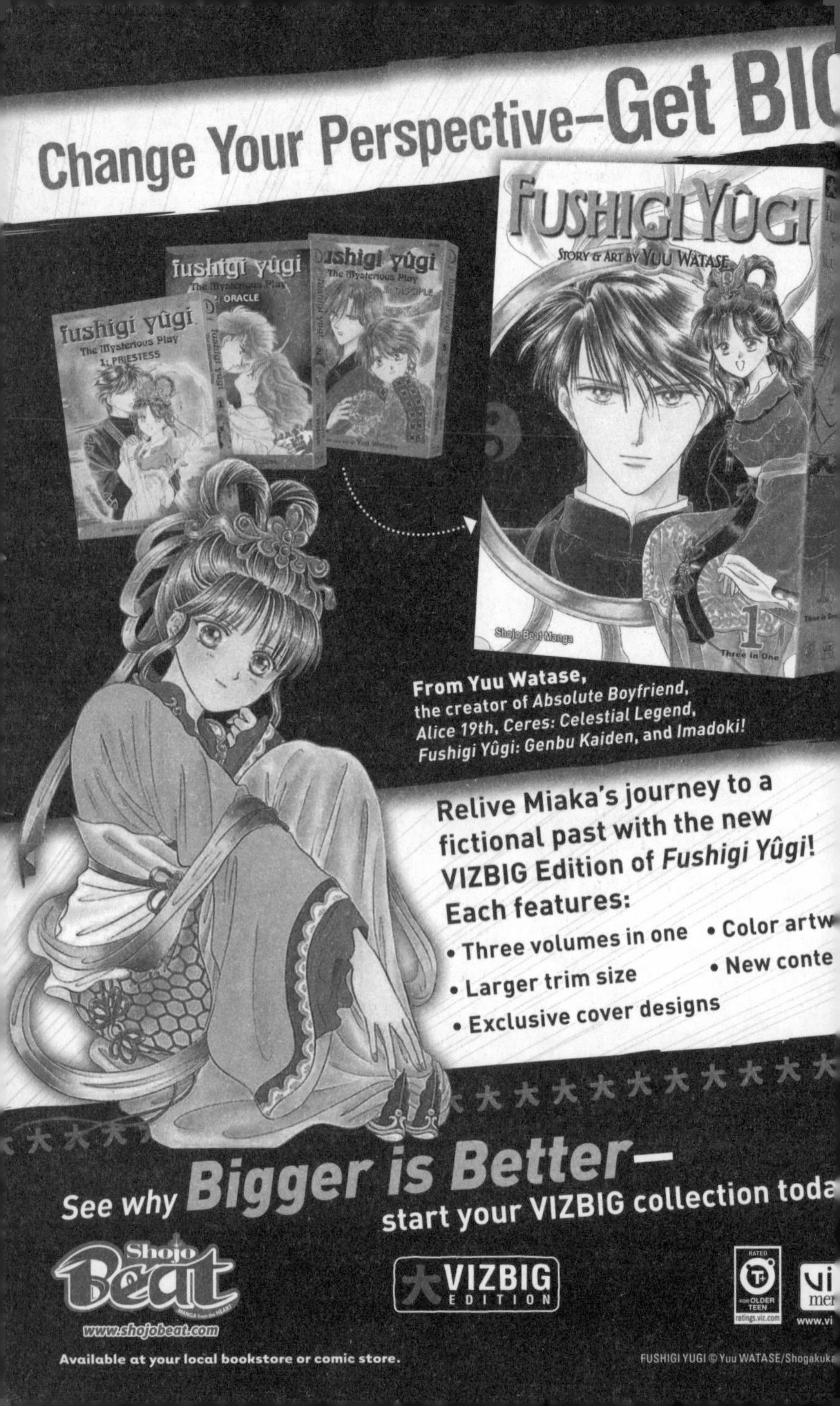
Change Your Perspective–Get BIG
FUSHIGI YÛGI
STORY & ART BY YUU WATASE
Shojo Beat Manga
1
Three in One
fushigi yûgi
The Mysterious Play
1: PRIESTESS
fushigi yûgi
The Mysterious Play
2: ORACLE
fushigi yûgi
The Mysterious Play
3: DISCIPLE
From Yuu Watase,
the creator of Absolute Boyfriend,
Alice 19th, Ceres: Celestial Legend,
Fushigi Yûgi: Genbu Kaiden, and Imadoki!
Relive Miaka's journey to a fictional past with the new VIZBIG Edition of Fushigi Yûgi!
Each features:
• Three volumes in one
• Larger trim size
• Exclusive cover designs
• Color artw
• New conte
See why Bigger is Better–
start your VIZBIG collection toda
Shojo Beat
MANGA from the HEART
www.shojobeat.com
VIZBIG EDITION
RATED T+ FOR OLDER TEEN
ratings.viz.com
Available at your local bookstore or comic store.
FUSHIGI YUGI © Yuu WATASE/Shogakuka

Kakuriyo
Bed & Breakfast for Spirits

6

SHOJO BEAT EDITION

Art by **Waco Ioka**
Original story by **Midori Yuma**
Character design by **Laruha**

English Translation & Adaptation **Tomo Kimura**
Touch-up Art & Lettering **Joanna Estep**
Design **Francesca Truman**
Editor **Pancha Diaz**

KAKURIYO NO YADOMESHI AYAKASHIOYADO NI YOMEIRI SHIMASU. Vol. 6
©Waco Ioka 2019
©Midori Yuma 2019
©Laruha 2019
First published in Japan in 2019 by KADOKAWA CORPORATION, Tokyo.
English translation rights arranged with KADOKAWA CORPORATION, Tokyo.

Printed in Canada

Published by VIZ Media, LLC.
P.O. Box 77010
San Francisco, CA 94107

10 9 8 7 6 5 4 3 2 1
First printing, September 2020

viz.com

shojobeat.com

Kakuriyo

**Bed & Breakfast
for Spirits**

Kakuriyo

Bed & Breakfast
for Spirits

6

Art by

Waco Ioka

Original Story by **Midori Yuma**
Character Design by **Laruha**

CONTENTS

Chapter 24

RRRRMBLE

FLASH

DON'T GO OUTSIDE.

PRETEND LIKE NO ONE LIVES HERE.

DON'T OPEN THE DOOR EVEN IF SOMEONE KNOCKS.

DON'T SAY A WORD.

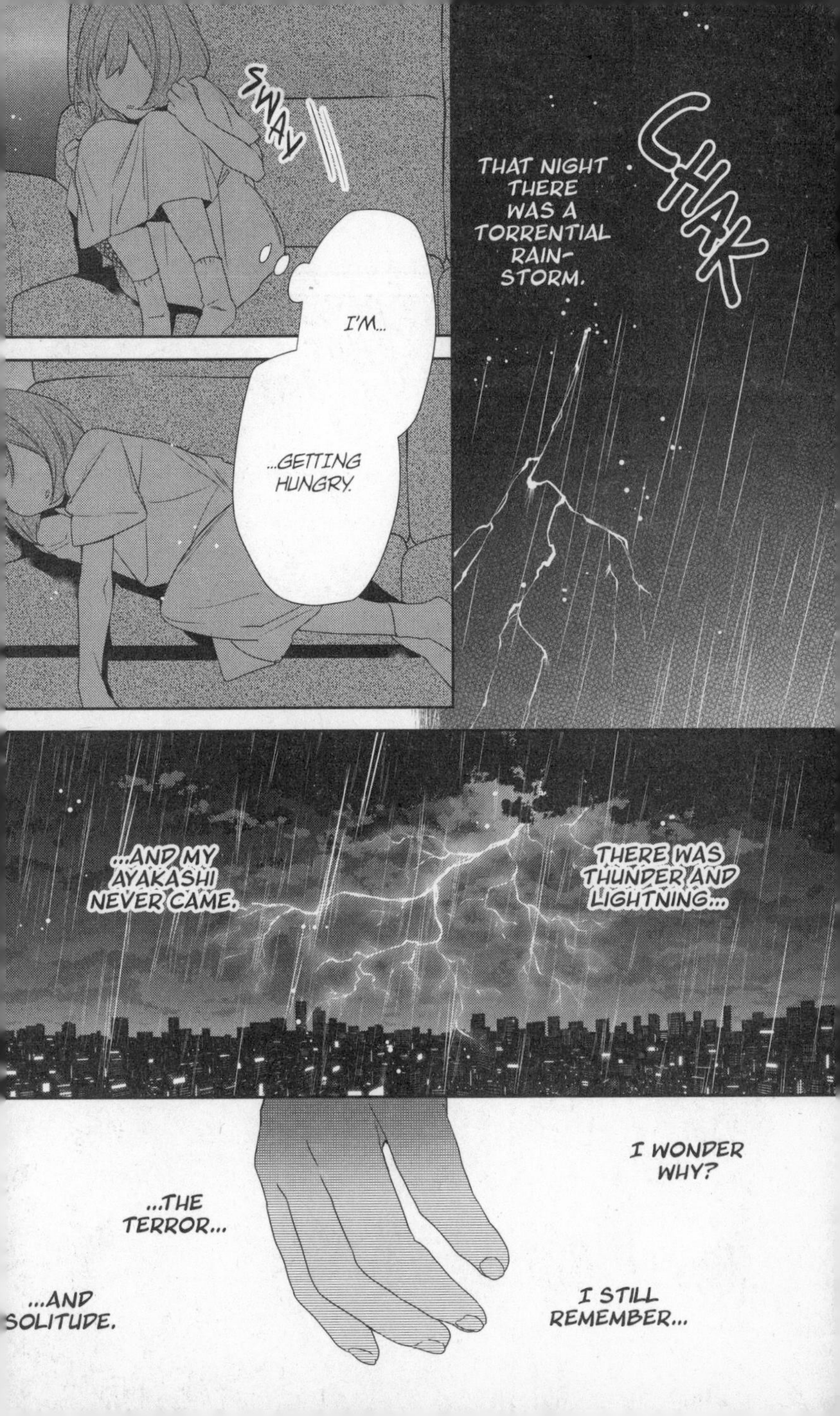
CHAK
THAT NIGHT THERE WAS A TORRENTIAL RAIN-STORM.
SWAY
I'M...
...GETTING HUNGRY.
THERE WAS THUNDER AND LIGHTNING...
...AND MY AYAKASHI NEVER CAME.
I WONDER WHY?
I STILL REMEMBER...
...THE TERROR...
...AND SOLITUDE.

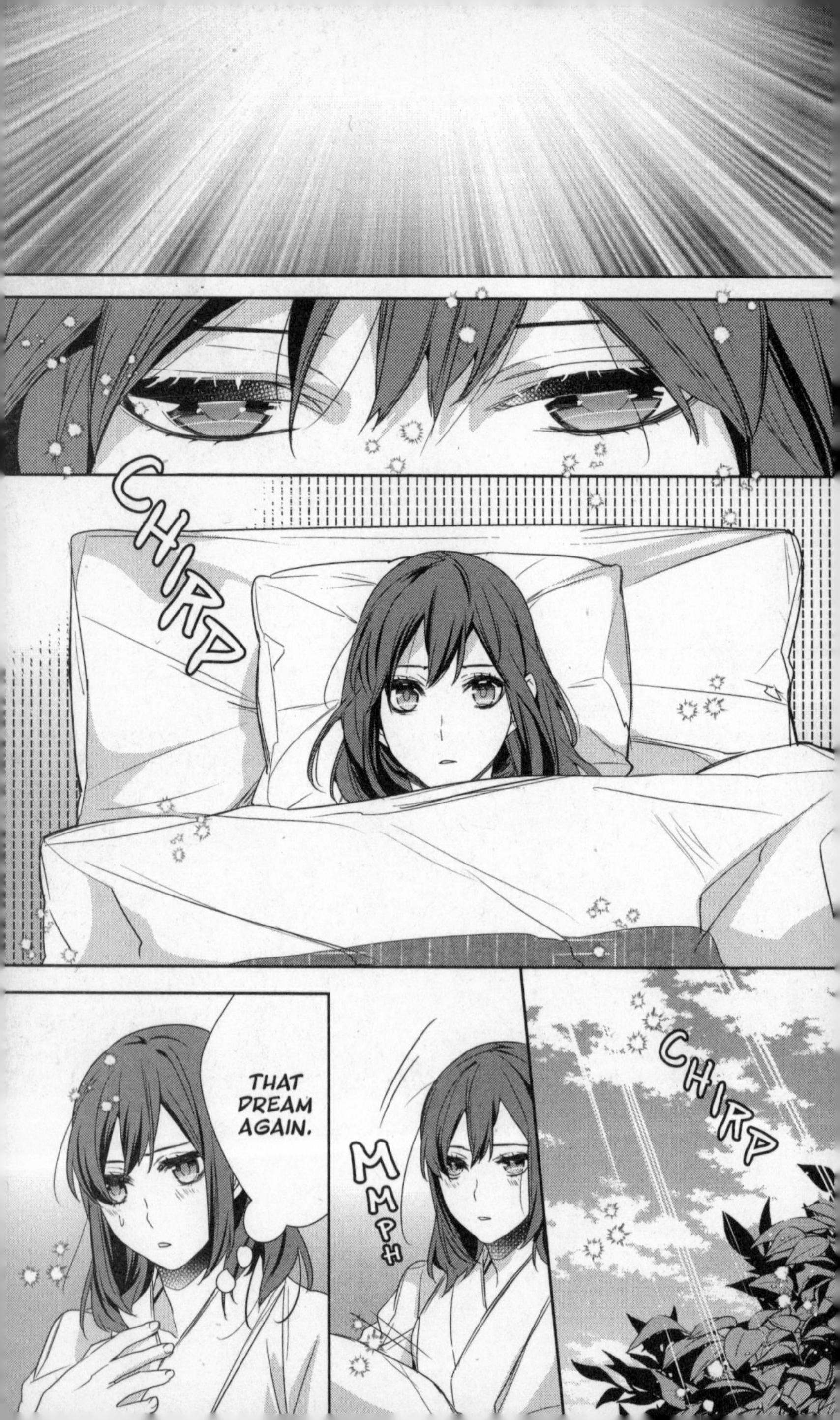
CHIRP
CHIRP
MMPH
THAT DREAM AGAIN.

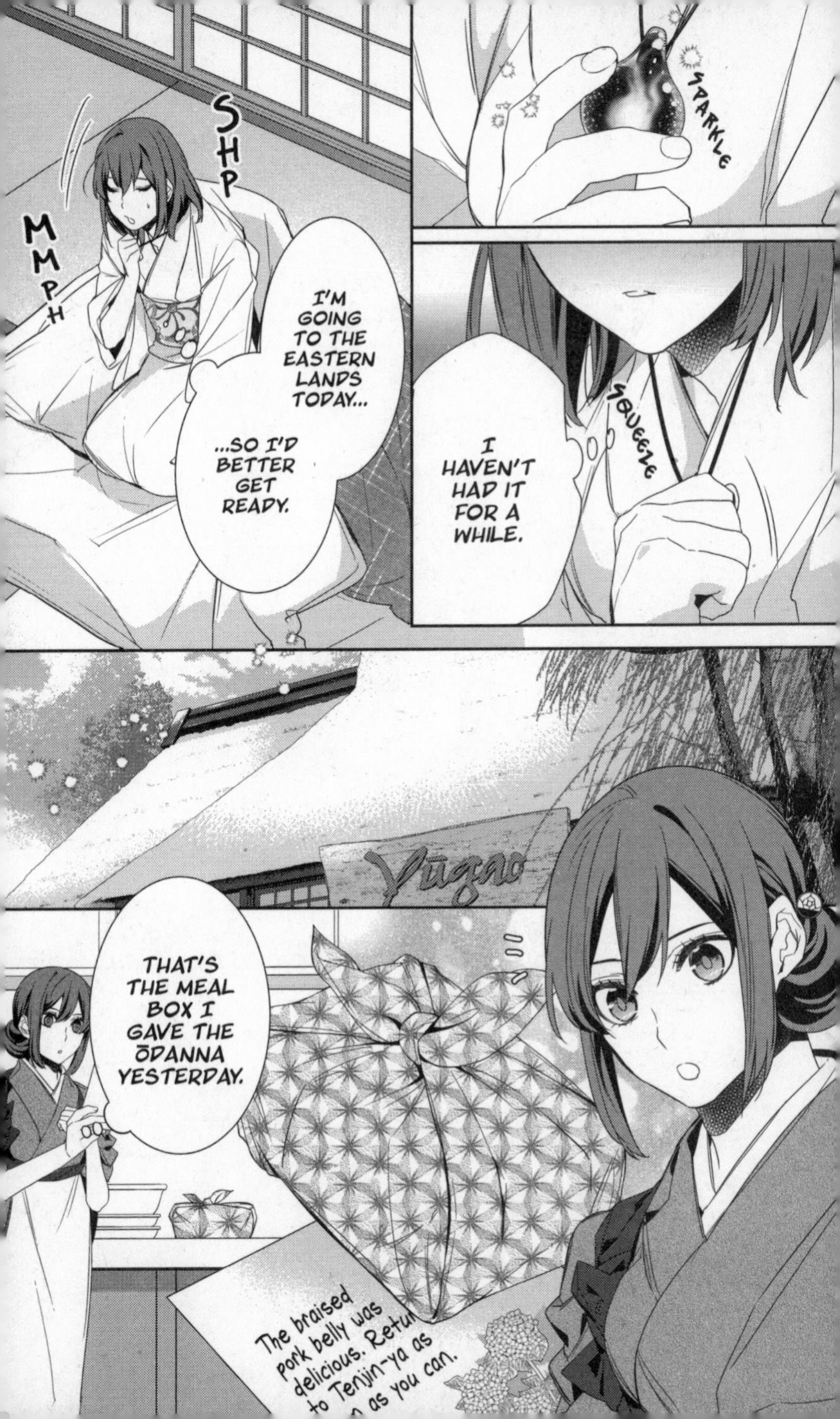
SPARKLE
SQUEEZE
I HAVEN'T HAD IT FOR A WHILE.
SHP
MMPH
I'M GOING TO THE EASTERN LANDS TODAY...
...SO I'D BETTER GET READY.
Yūgao
THAT'S THE MEAL BOX I GAVE THE ŌDANNA YESTERDAY.
The braised pork belly was delicious. Retu to Tenjin-ya as n as you can.

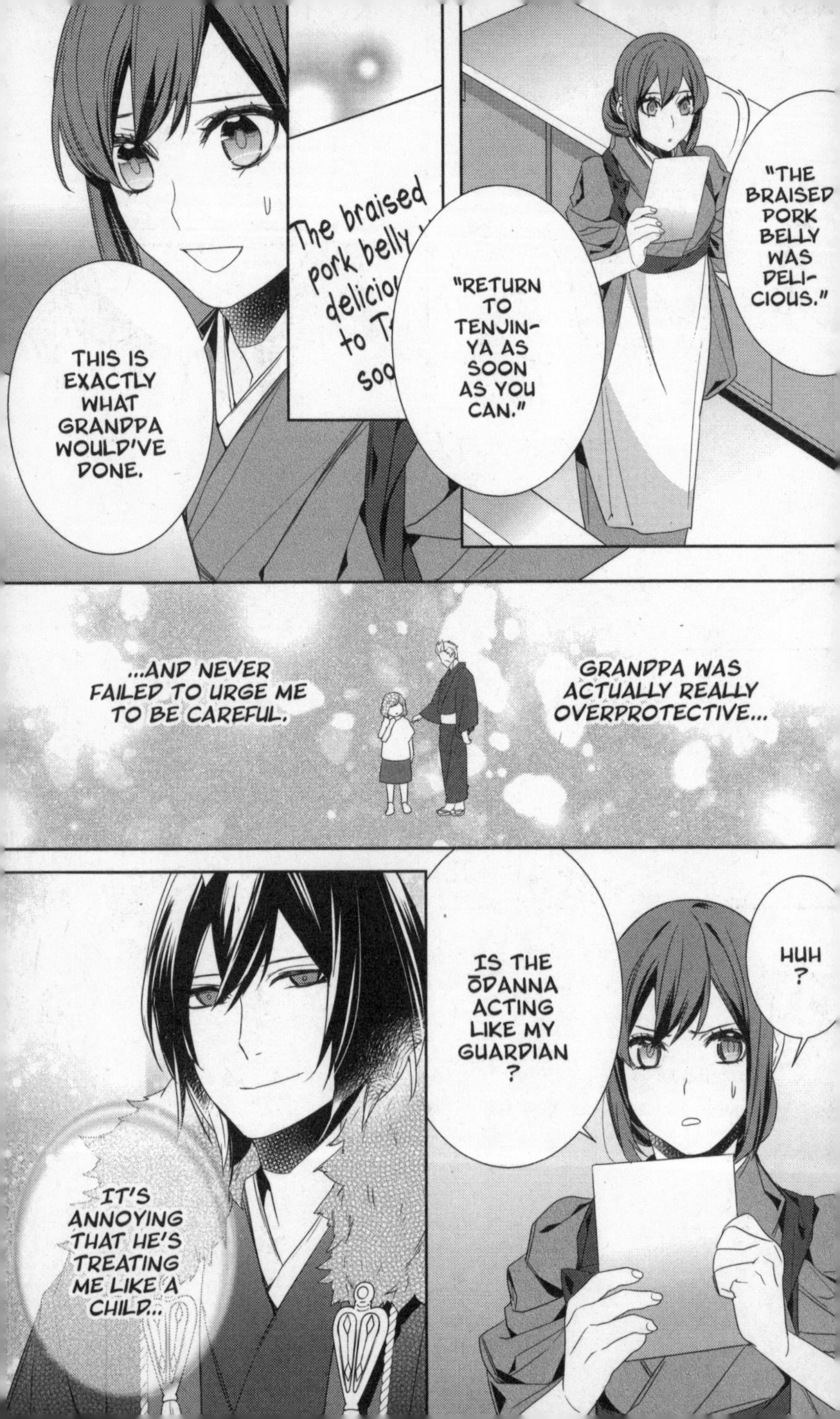
"THE BRAISED PORK BELLY WAS DELICIOUS."
"RETURN TO TENJIN-YA AS SOON AS YOU CAN."
The braised pork belly
THIS IS EXACTLY WHAT GRANDPA WOULD'VE DONE.
GRANDPA WAS ACTUALLY REALLY OVERPROTECTIVE...
...AND NEVER FAILED TO URGE ME TO BE CAREFUL.
HUH?
IS THE ŌDANNA ACTING LIKE MY GUARDIAN?
IT'S ANNOYING THAT HE'S TREATING ME LIKE A CHILD...

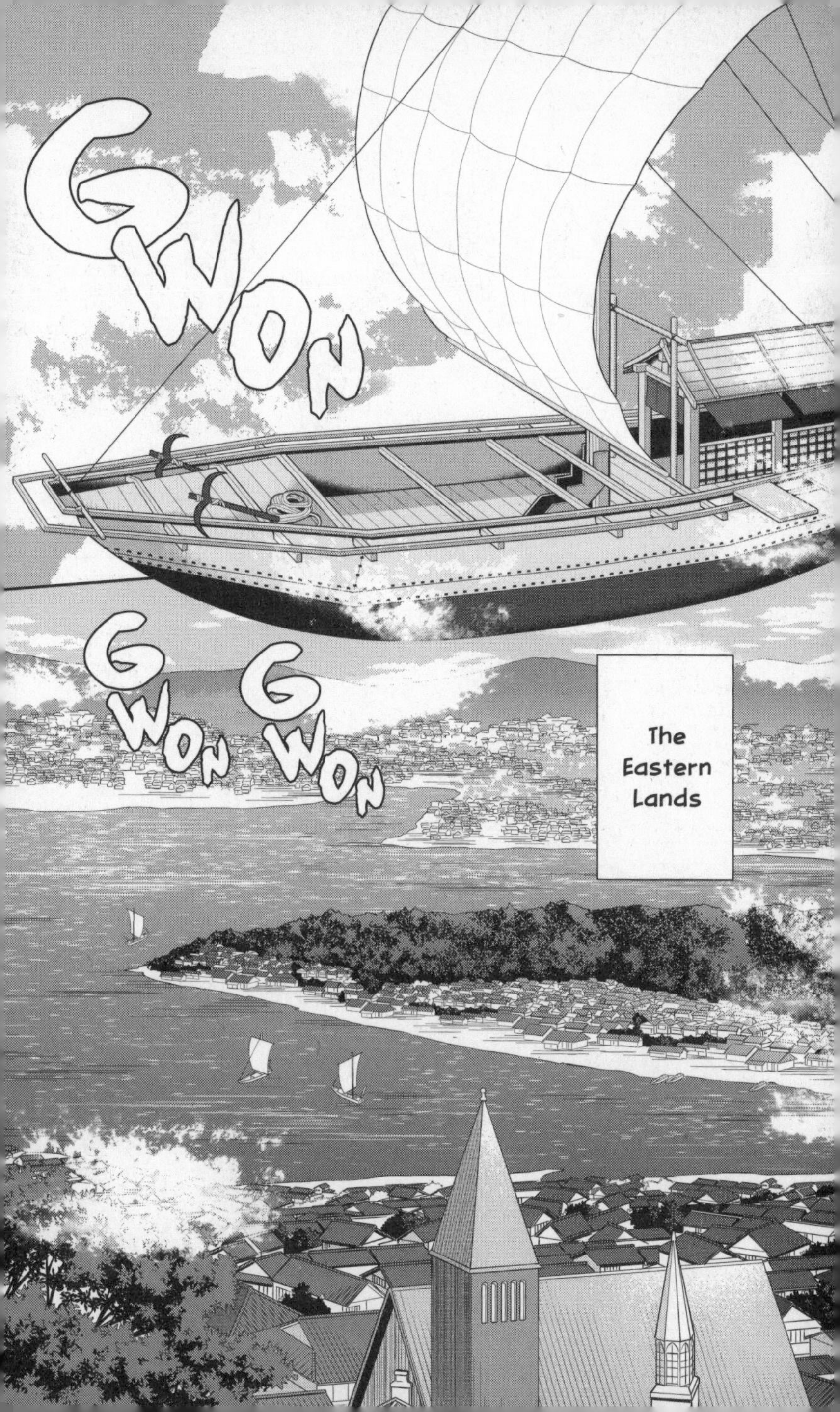
GWON
The Eastern Lands
GWON GWON

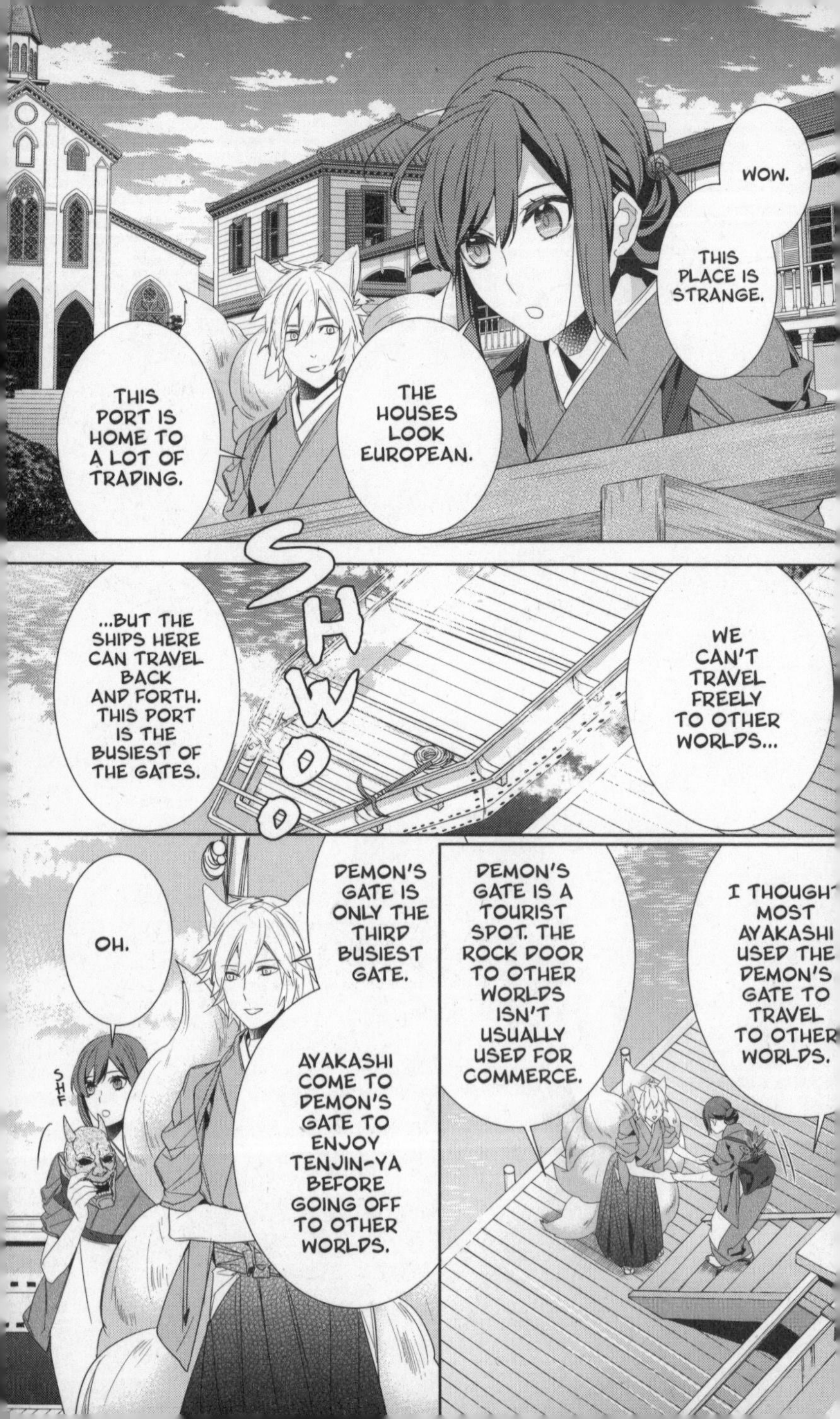
WOW.
THIS PLACE IS STRANGE.
THE HOUSES LOOK EUROPEAN.
THIS PORT IS HOME TO A LOT OF TRADING.
WE CAN'T TRAVEL FREELY TO OTHER WORLDS...
SHWOO
...BUT THE SHIPS HERE CAN TRAVEL BACK AND FORTH. THIS PORT IS THE BUSIEST OF THE GATES.
I THOUGHT MOST AYAKASHI USED THE DEMON'S GATE TO TRAVEL TO OTHER WORLDS.
DEMON'S GATE IS A TOURIST SPOT. THE ROCK DOOR TO OTHER WORLDS ISN'T USUALLY USED FOR COMMERCE.
DEMON'S GATE IS ONLY THE THIRD BUSIEST GATE.
OH.
AYAKASHI COME TO DEMON'S GATE TO ENJOY TENJIN-YA BEFORE GOING OFF TO OTHER WORLDS.
SHF

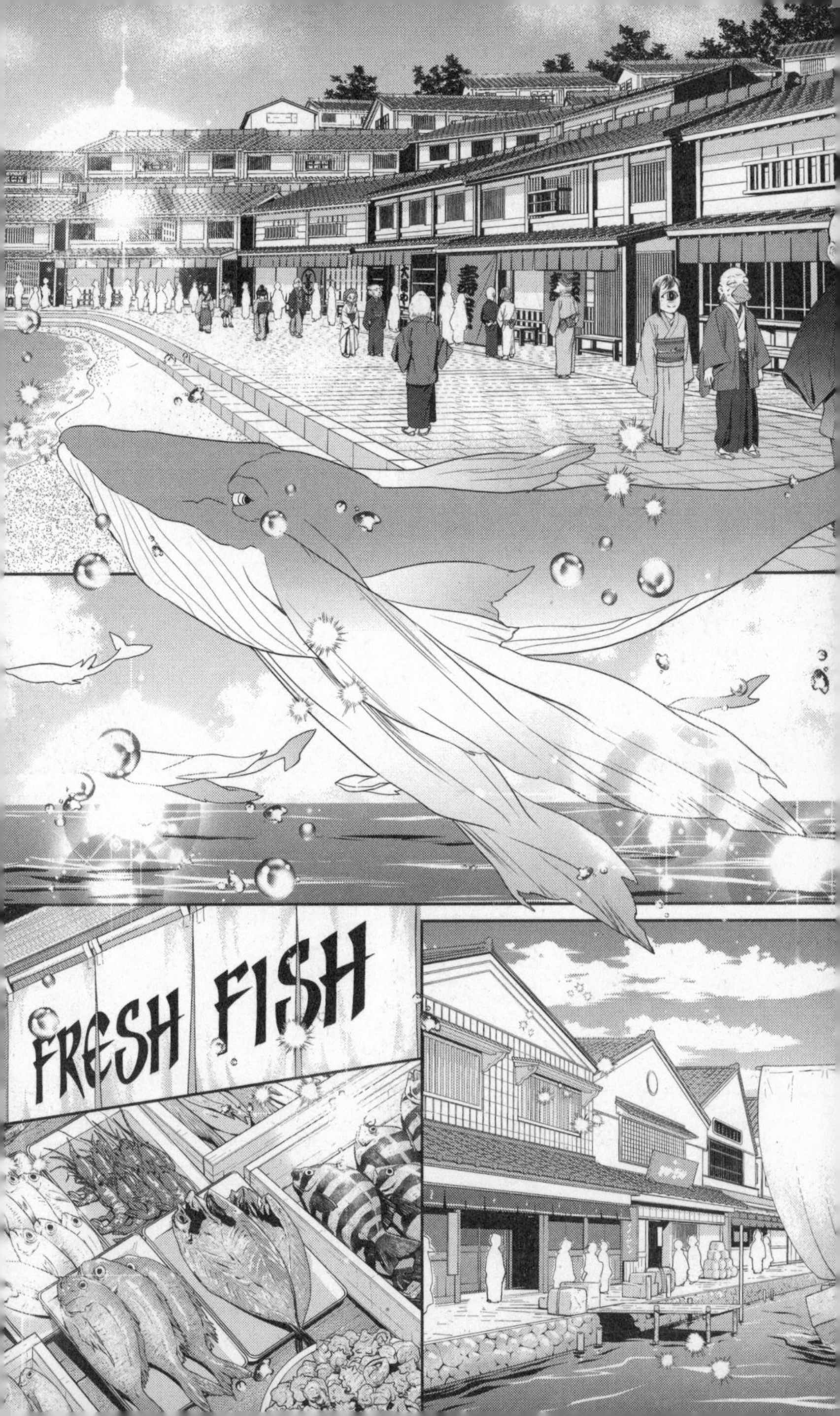
FRESH FISH

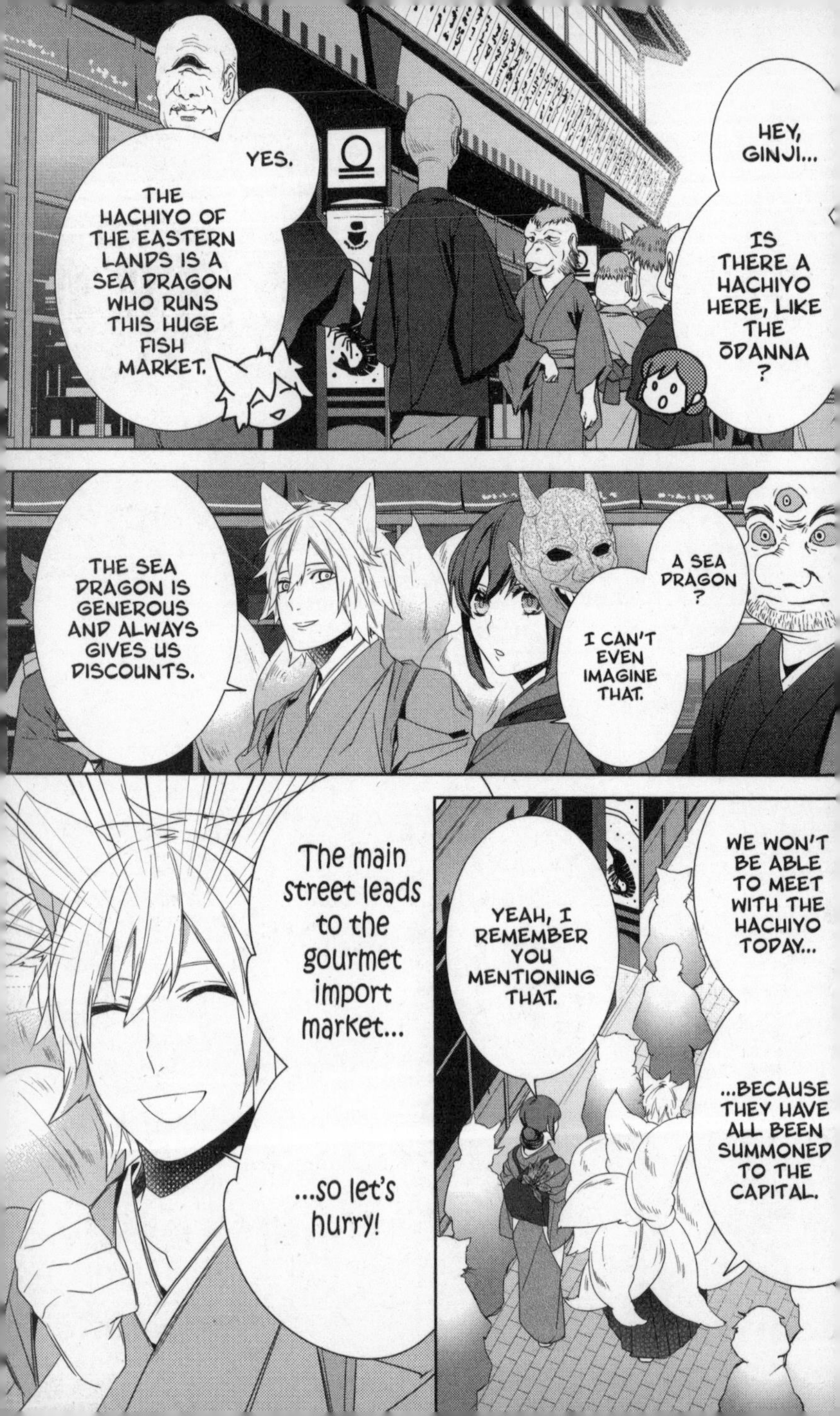
HEY, GINJI...
IS THERE A HACHIYO HERE, LIKE THE ŌDANNA?
YES.
THE HACHIYO OF THE EASTERN LANDS IS A SEA DRAGON WHO RUNS THIS HUGE FISH MARKET.
A SEA DRAGON?
I CAN'T EVEN IMAGINE THAT.
THE SEA DRAGON IS GENEROUS AND ALWAYS GIVES US DISCOUNTS.
WE WON'T BE ABLE TO MEET WITH THE HACHIYO TODAY...
...BECAUSE THEY HAVE ALL BEEN SUMMONED TO THE CAPITAL.
YEAH, I REMEMBER YOU MENTIONING THAT.
The main street leads to the gourmet import market...
...so let's hurry!

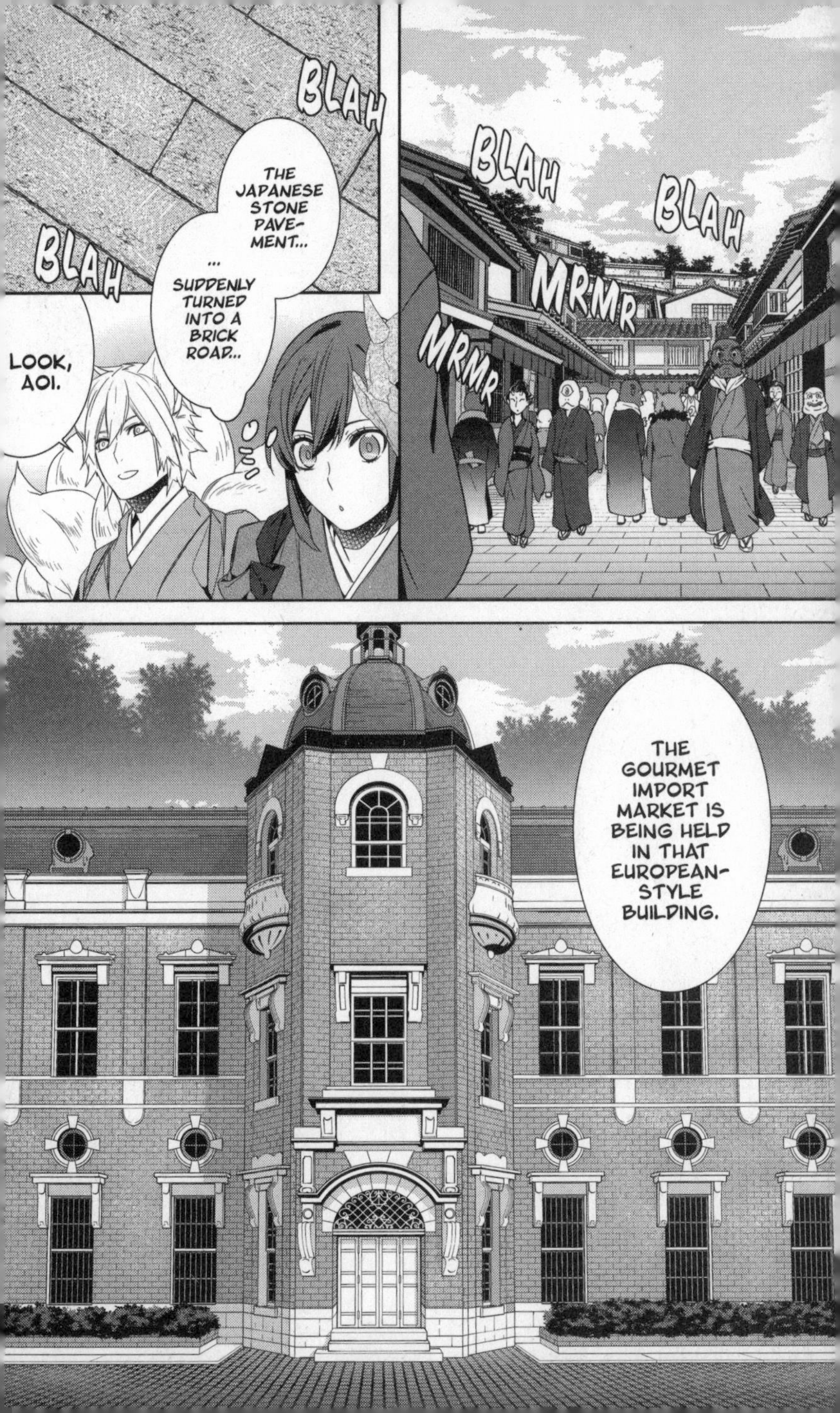

BLAH
BLAH
MRMR
MRMR
BLAH
THE JAPANESE STONE PAVEMENT...
... SUDDENLY TURNED INTO A BRICK ROAD...
BLAH
LOOK, AOI.
THE GOURMET IMPORT MARKET IS BEING HELD IN THAT EUROPEAN-STYLE BUILDING.

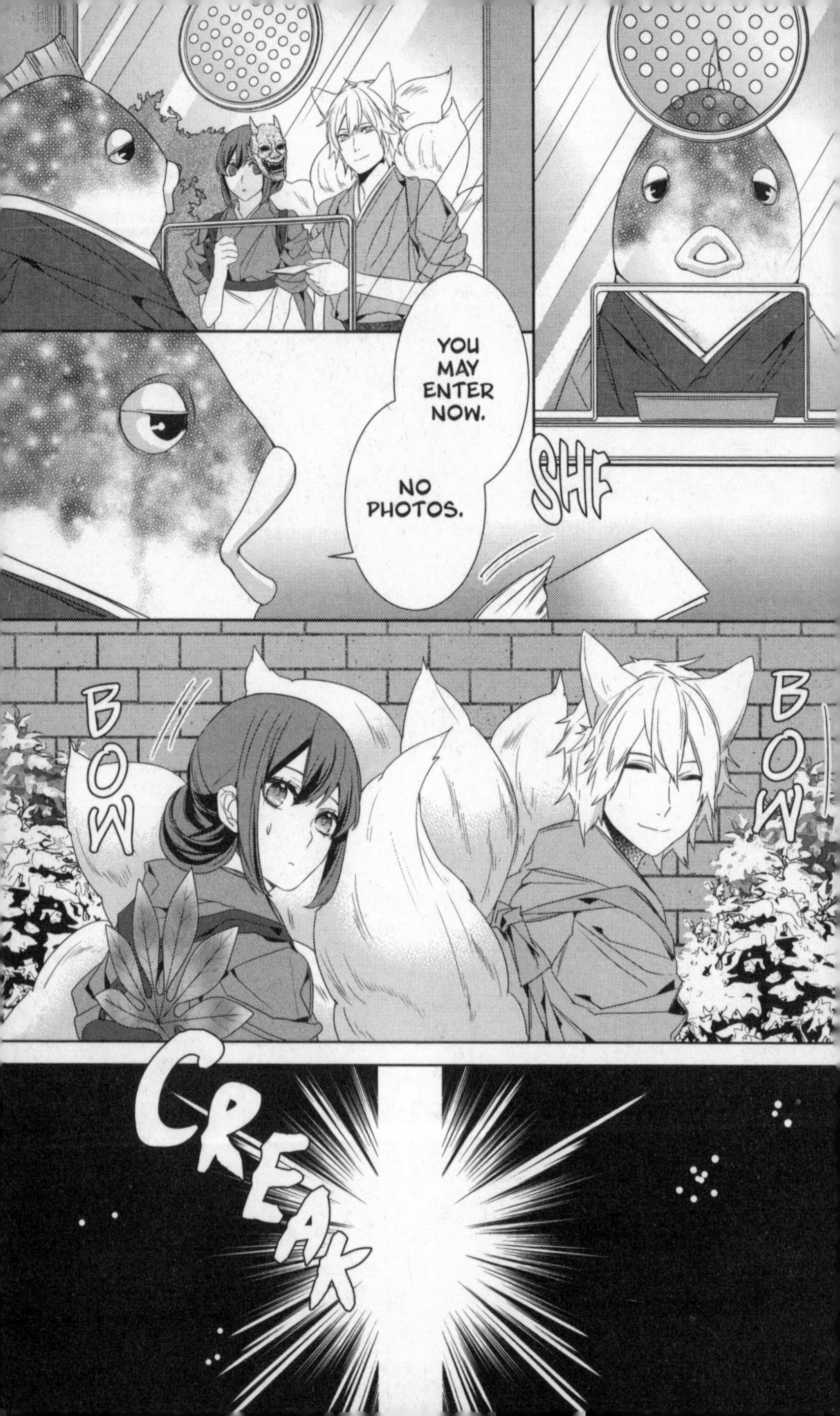
YOU MAY ENTER NOW.
NO PHOTOS.
SHF
BOW
BOW
CREAK

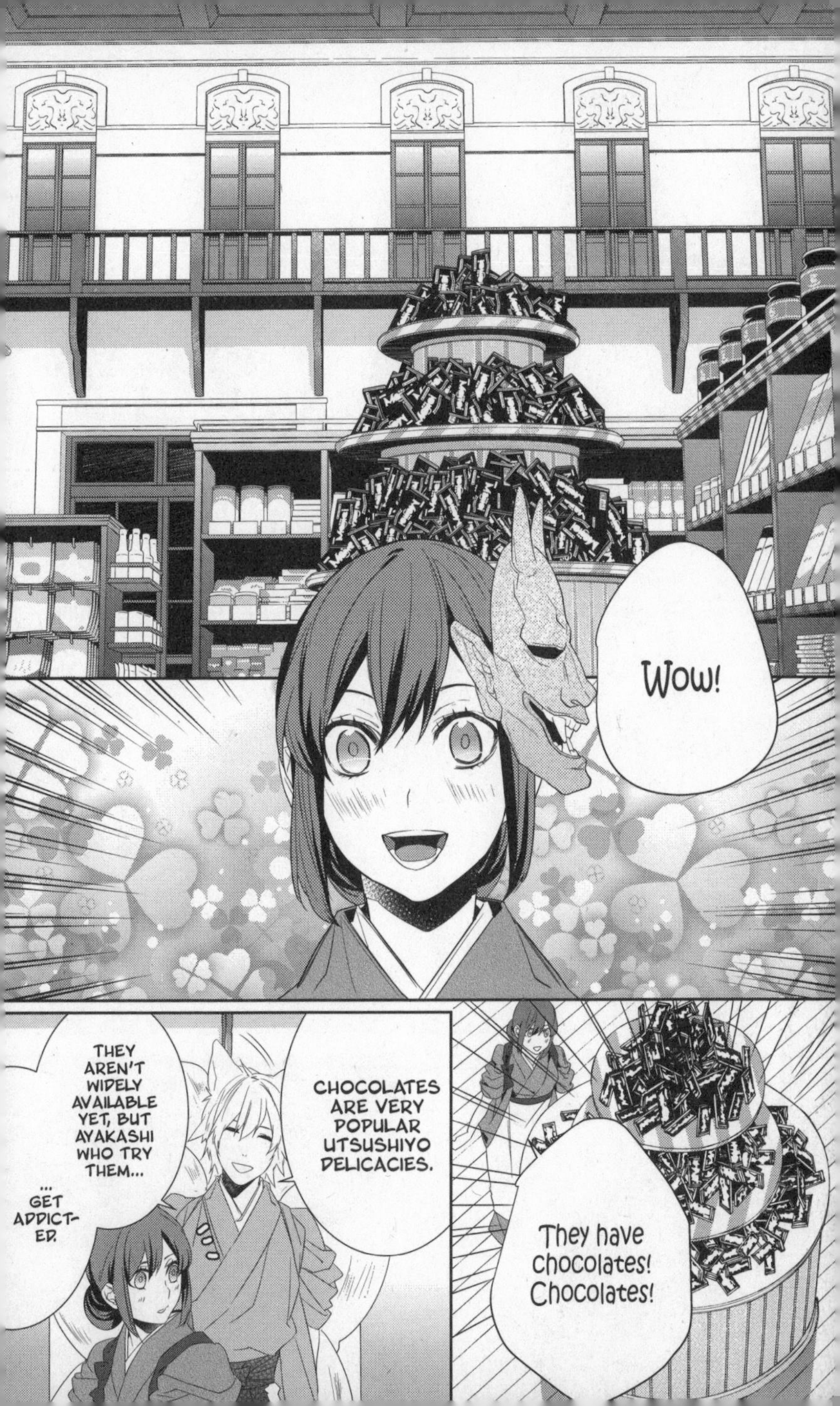
Wow!
They have chocolates! Chocolates!
CHOCOLATES ARE VERY POPULAR UTSUSHIYO DELICACIES.
THEY AREN'T WIDELY AVAILABLE YET, BUT AYAKASHI WHO TRY THEM...
...GET ADDICT-ED.

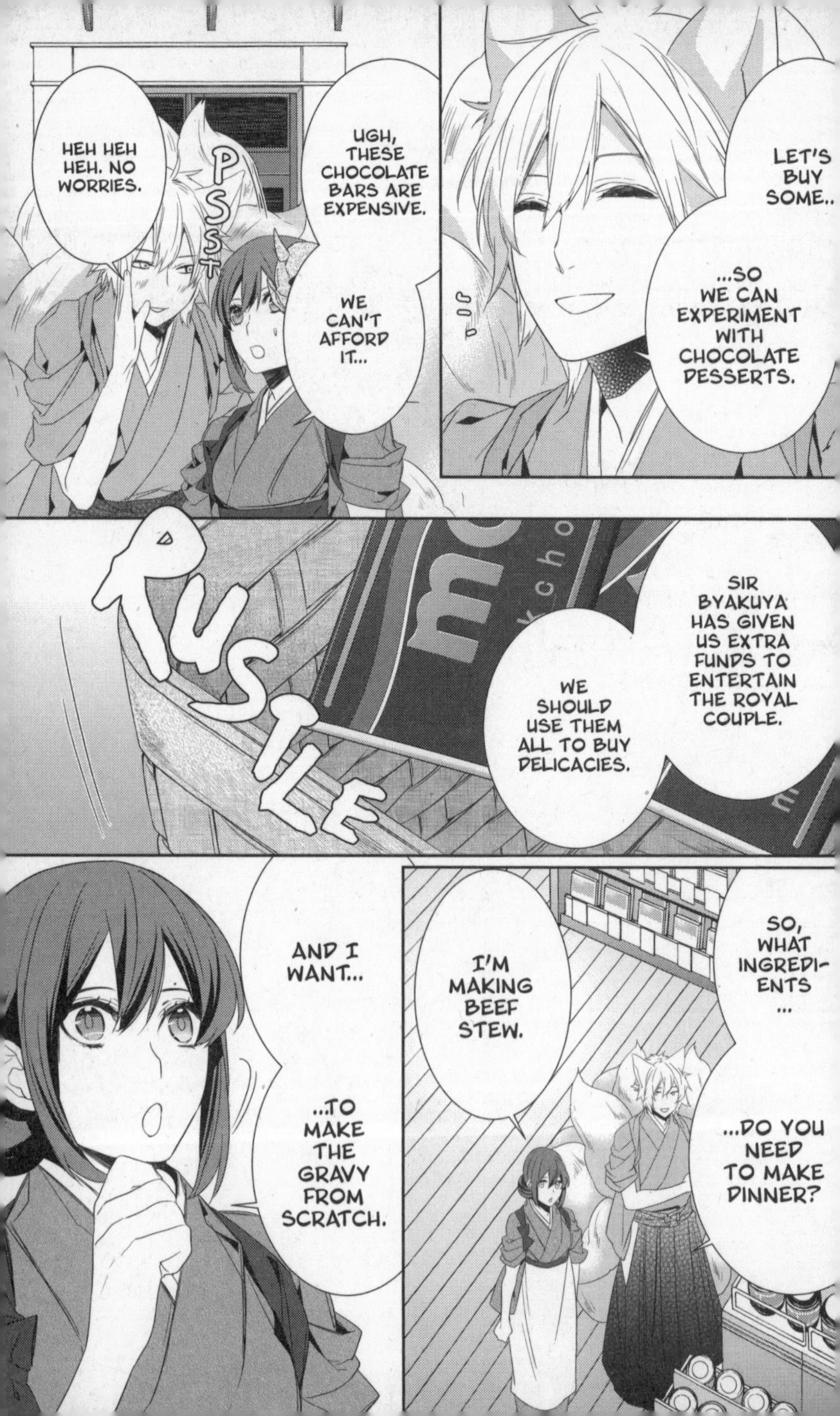
LET'S BUY SOME..
...SO WE CAN EXPERIMENT WITH CHOCOLATE DESSERTS.
UGH, THESE CHOCOLATE BARS ARE EXPENSIVE.
WE CAN'T AFFORD IT...
HEH HEH HEH. NO WORRIES.
PSST
SIR BYAKUYA HAS GIVEN US EXTRA FUNDS TO ENTERTAIN THE ROYAL COUPLE.
WE SHOULD USE THEM ALL TO BUY DELICACIES.
RUSTLE
SO, WHAT INGREDI- ENTS ...
...DO YOU NEED TO MAKE DINNER?
I'M MAKING BEEF STEW.
AND I WANT...
...TO MAKE THE GRAVY FROM SCRATCH.

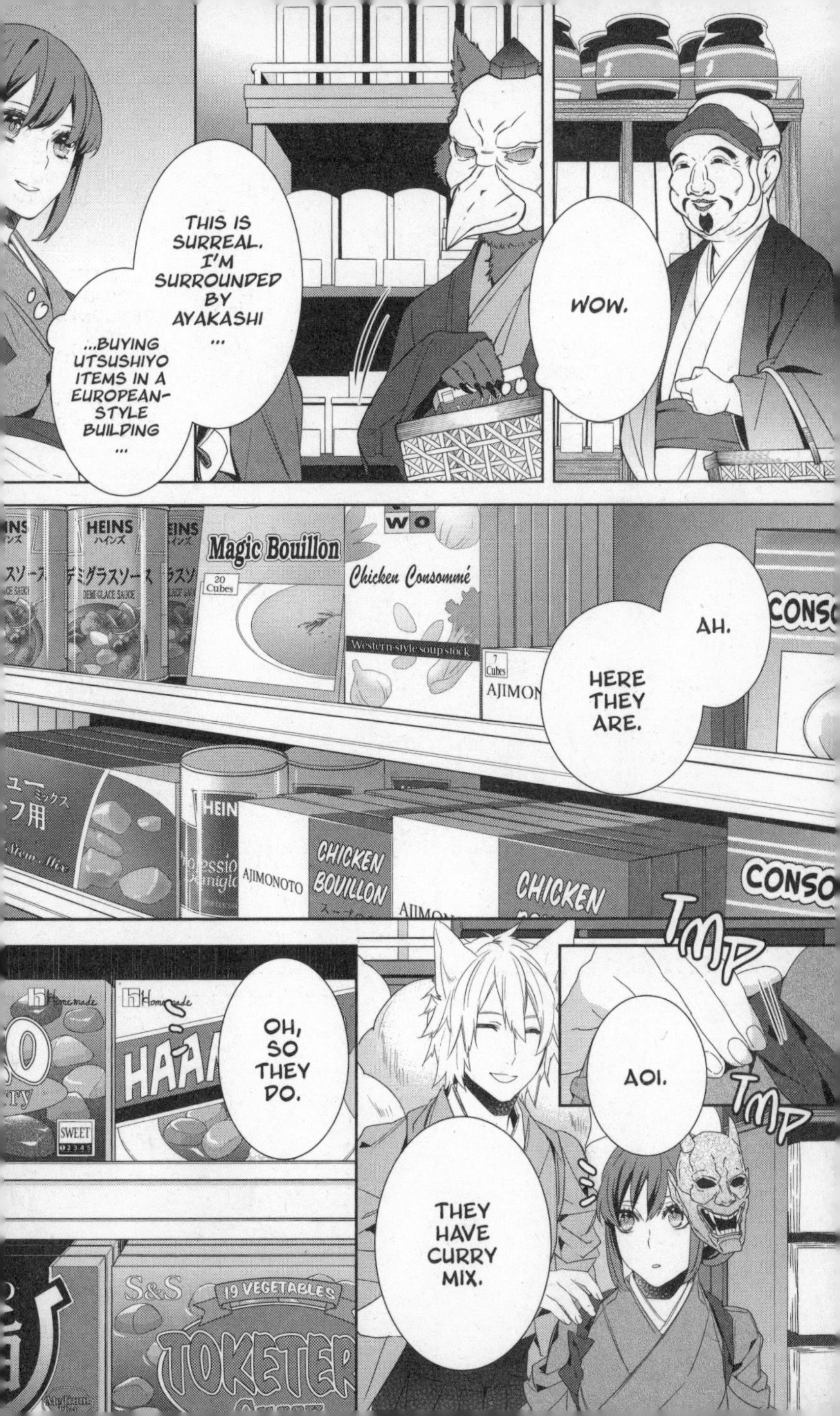
WOW.
THIS IS SURREAL. I'M SURROUNDED BY AYAKASHI ...
...BUYING UTSUSHIYO ITEMS IN A EUROPEAN-STYLE BUILDING ...
AH.
HERE THEY ARE.
HEINS
DEMI-GLACE SAUCE
Magic Bouillon
20 Cubes
Chicken Consommé
Western-style soup stock
7 Cubes
AJIMONOTO
CHICKEN BOUILLON
CHICKEN
TMP
TMP
AOI.
THEY HAVE CURRY MIX.
OH, SO THEY DO.
Homemade
SWEET
S&S
19 VEGETABLES
TOKETER

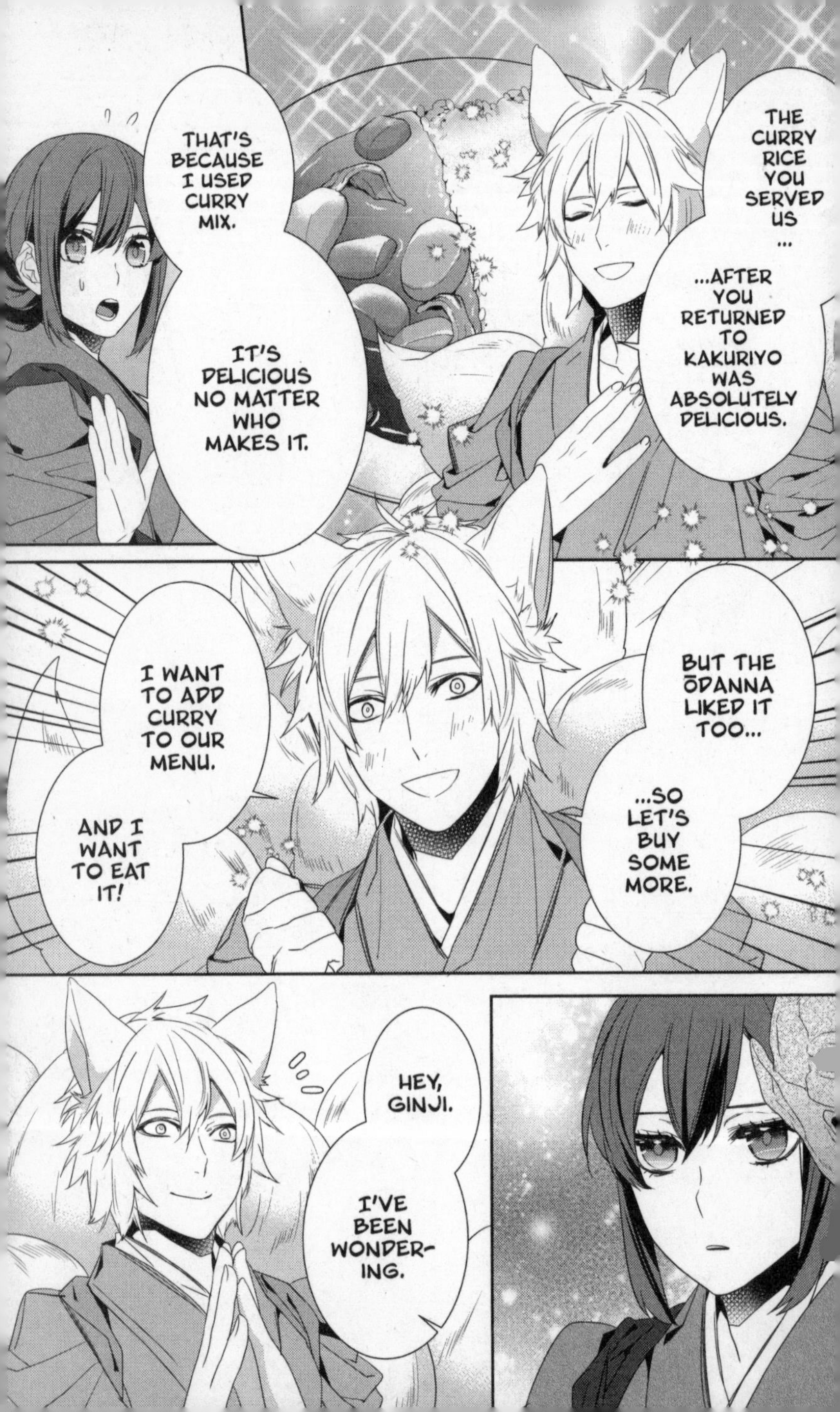
THE CURRY RICE YOU SERVED US ...
...AFTER YOU RETURNED TO KAKURIYO WAS ABSOLUTELY DELICIOUS.
THAT'S BECAUSE I USED CURRY MIX.
IT'S DELICIOUS NO MATTER WHO MAKES IT.
BUT THE ŌDANNA LIKED IT TOO...
...SO LET'S BUY SOME MORE.
I WANT TO ADD CURRY TO OUR MENU.
AND I WANT TO EAT IT!
HEY, GINJI.
I'VE BEEN WONDER-ING.

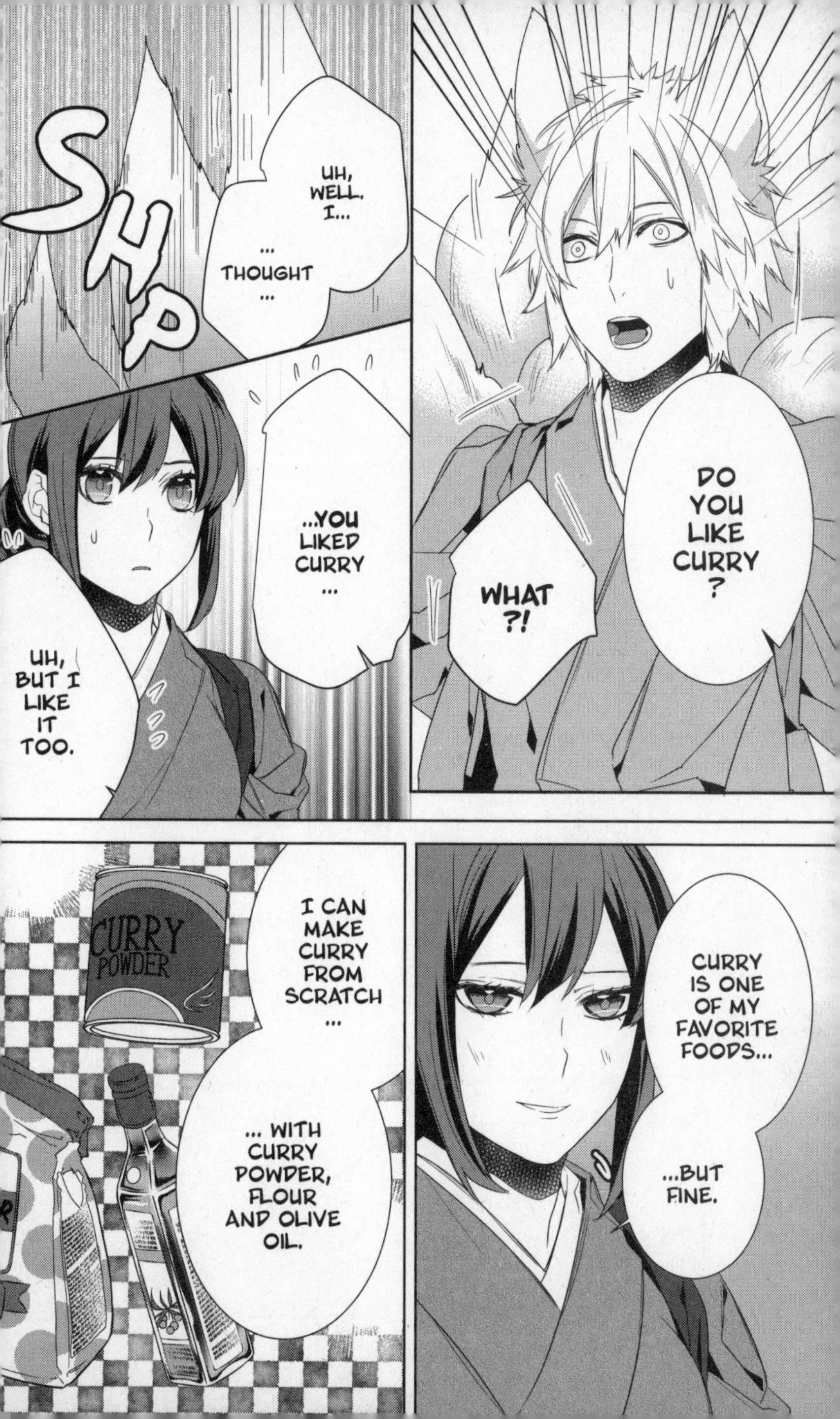
DO YOU LIKE CURRY?
WHAT?!
SHP
UH, WELL. I... ... THOUGHT ...
...YOU LIKED CURRY ...
UH, BUT I LIKE IT TOO.
CURRY IS ONE OF MY FAVORITE FOODS...
...BUT FINE.
I CAN MAKE CURRY FROM SCRATCH ...
... WITH CURRY POWDER, FLOUR AND OLIVE OIL.
CURRY POWDER

Kakuriyo
Bed & Breakfast
for Spirits

Kakuriyo
Bed & Breakfast
for Spirits

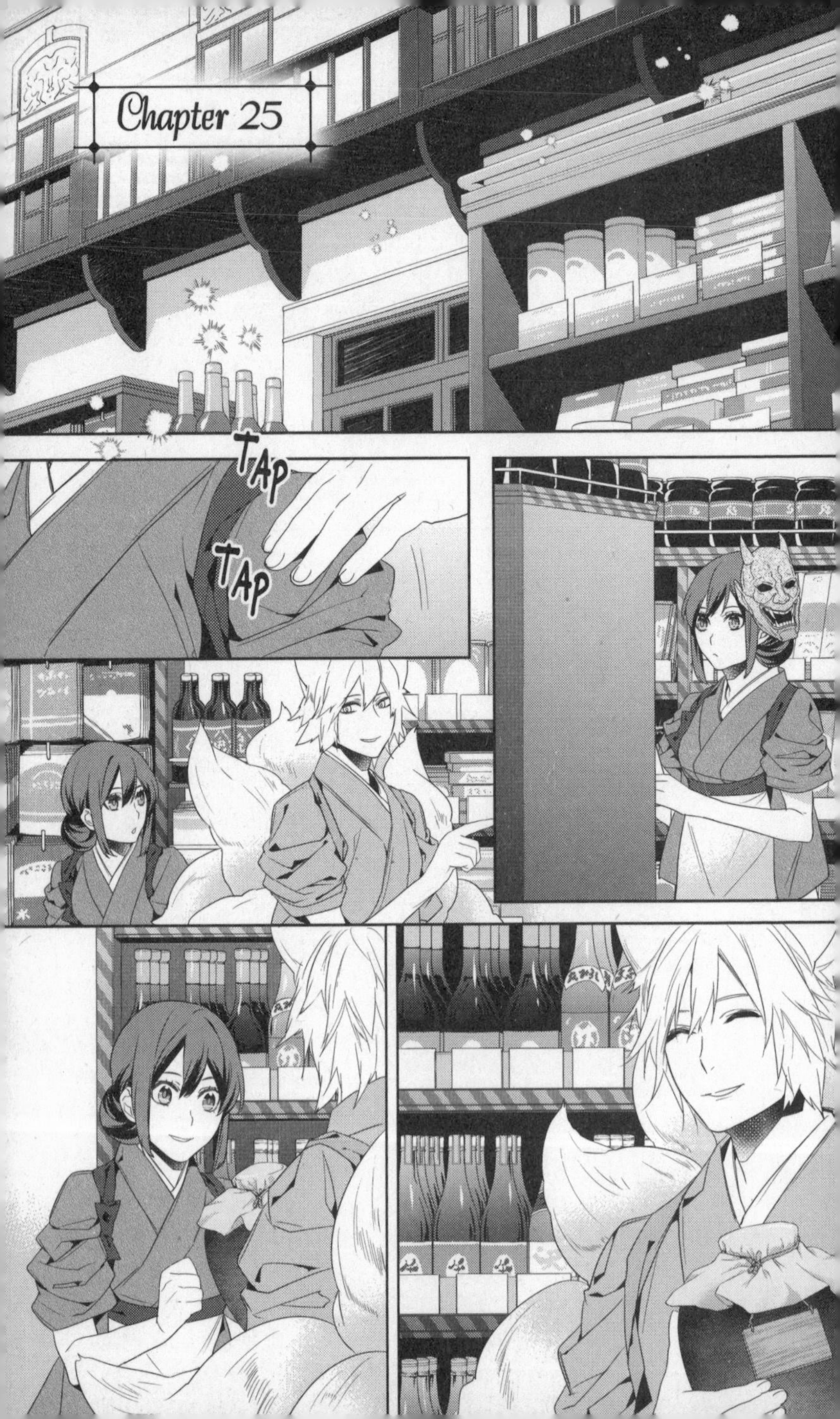
Chapter 25
TAP
TAP

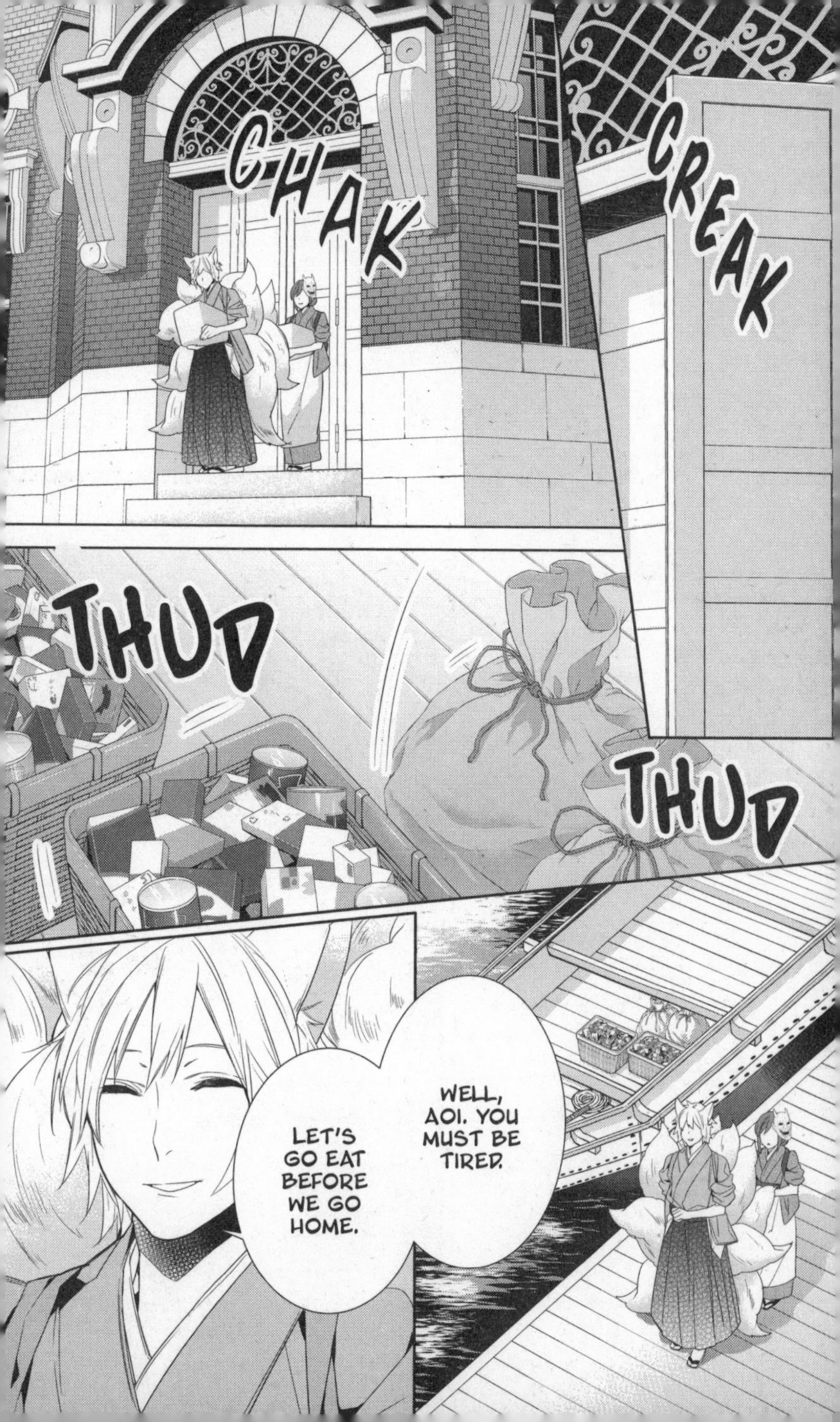
CREAK
CHAK
THUD
THUD
WELL, AOI. YOU MUST BE TIRED.
LET'S GO EAT BEFORE WE GO HOME.

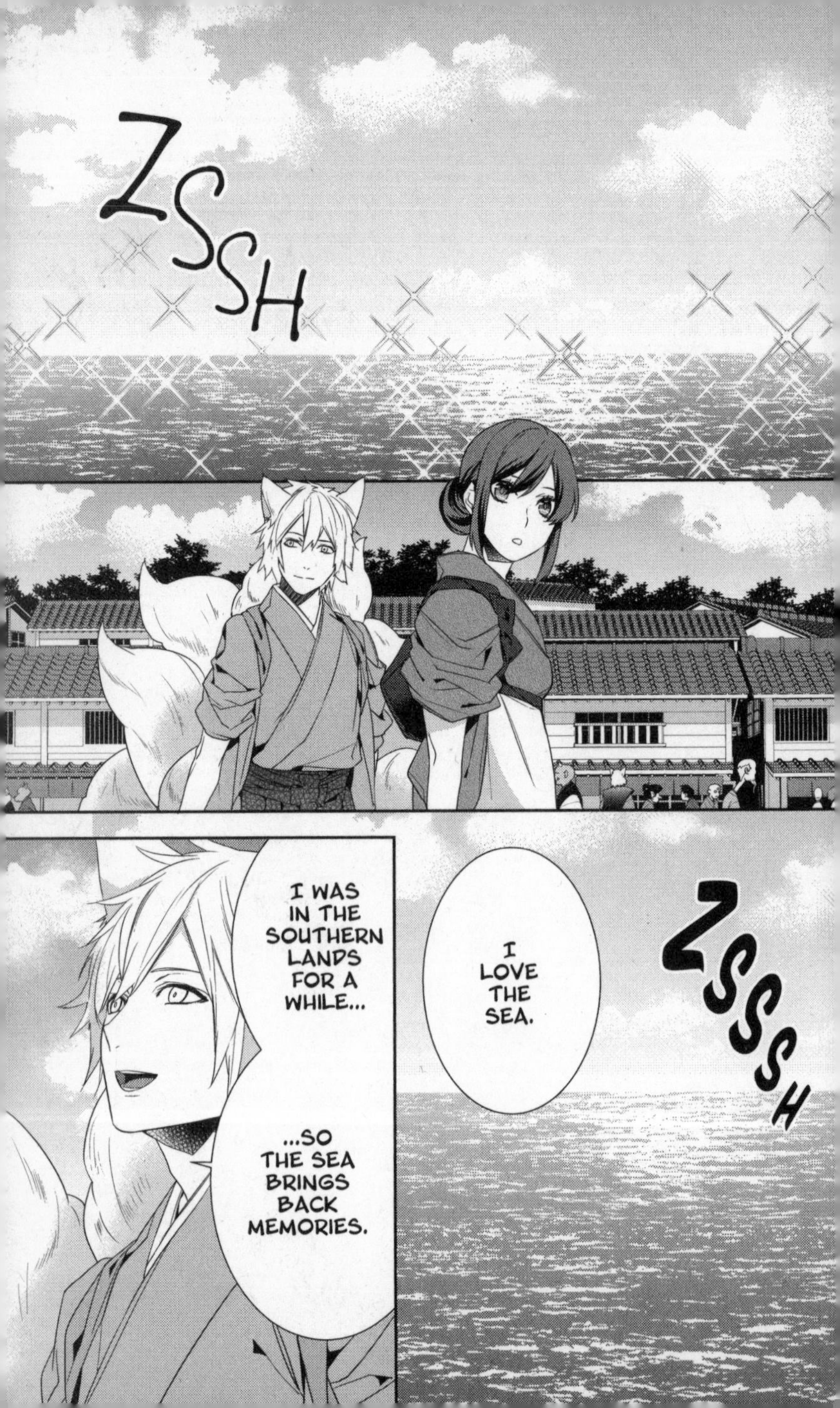
ZSSH
ZSSSH
I LOVE THE SEA.
I WAS IN THE SOUTHERN LANDS FOR A WHILE...
...SO THE SEA BRINGS BACK MEMORIES.

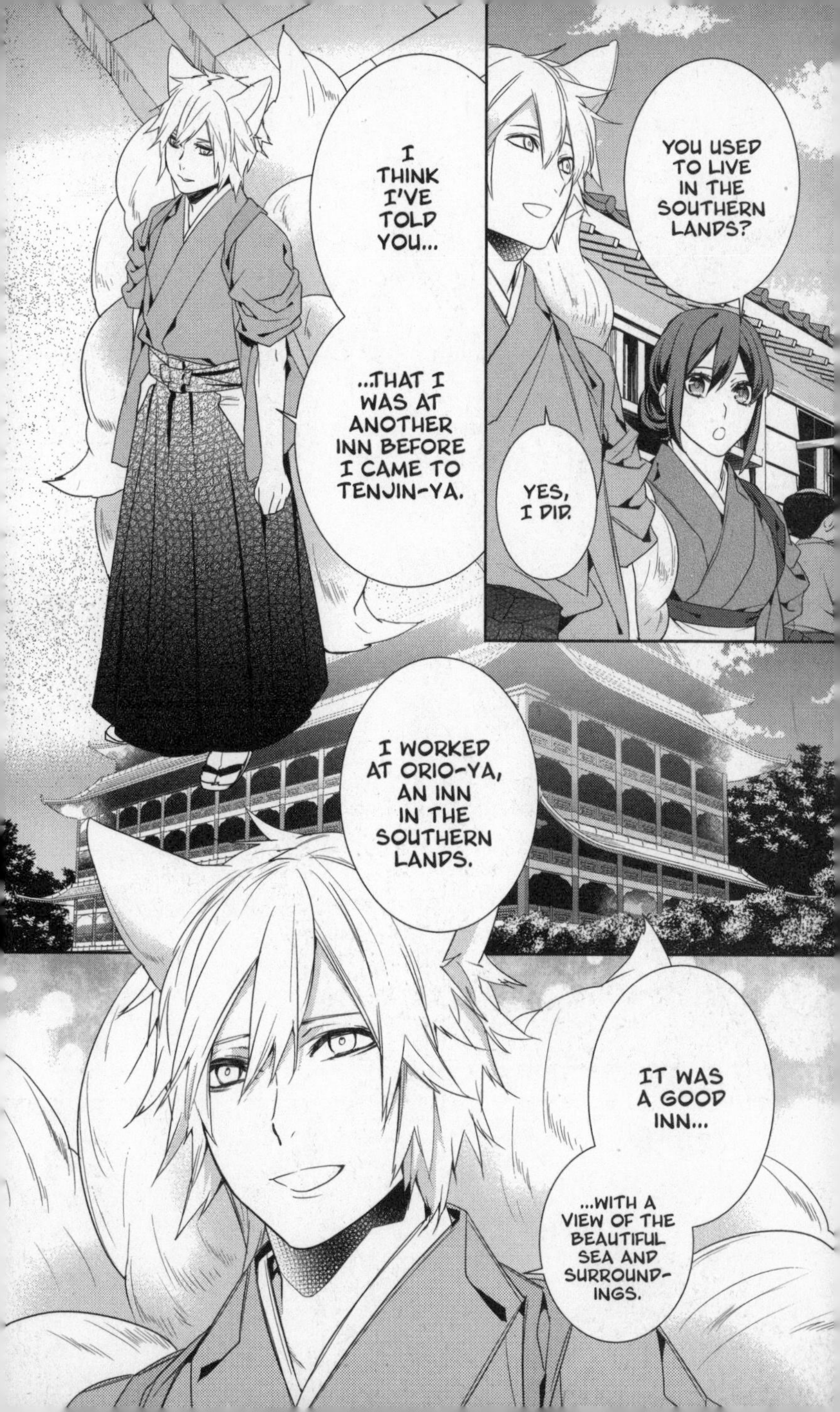
YOU USED TO LIVE IN THE SOUTHERN LANDS?
YES, I DID.
I THINK I'VE TOLD YOU...
...THAT I WAS AT ANOTHER INN BEFORE I CAME TO TENJIN-YA.
I WORKED AT ORIO-YA, AN INN IN THE SOUTHERN LANDS.
IT WAS A GOOD INN...
...WITH A VIEW OF THE BEAUTIFUL SEA AND SURROUND-INGS.

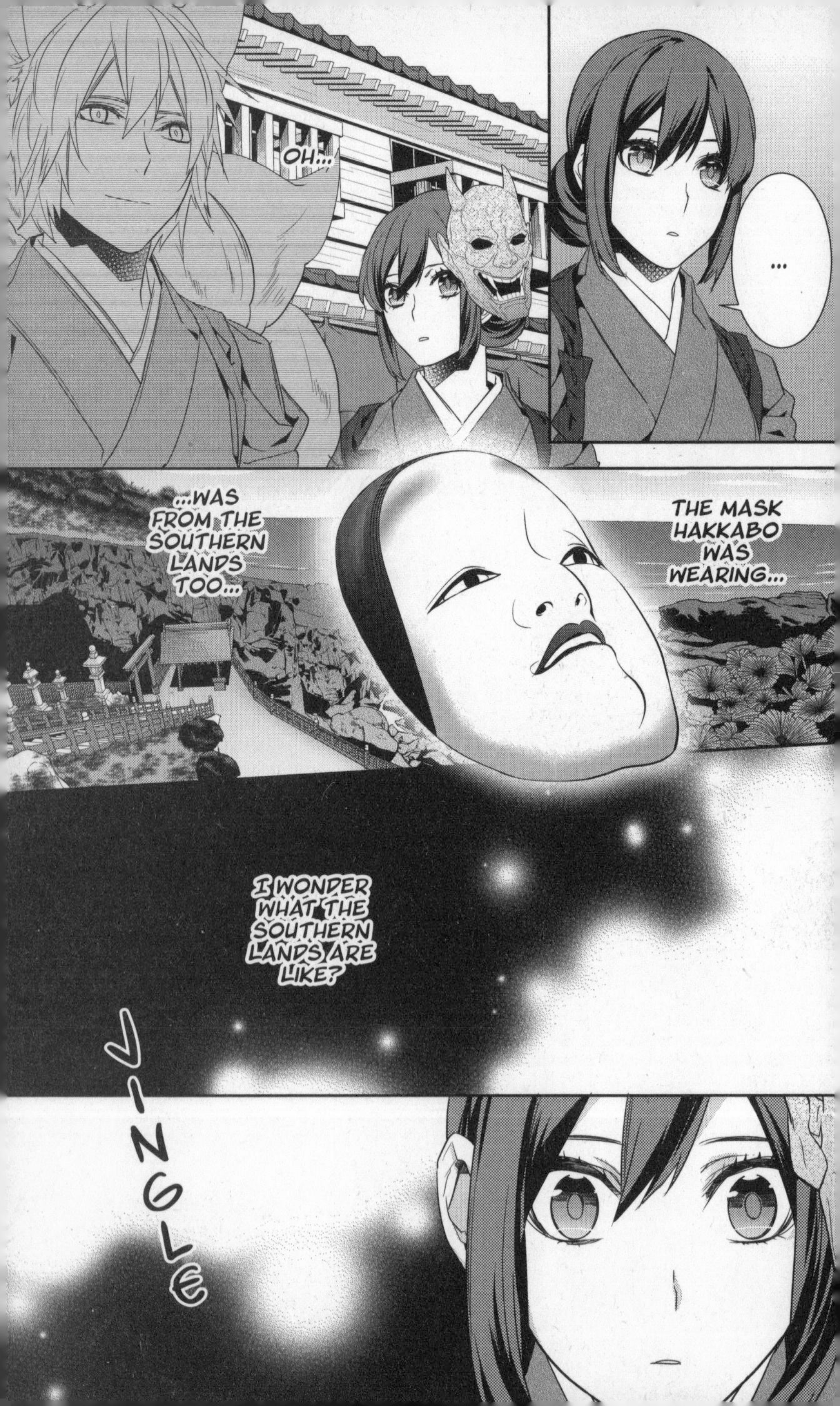
...
OH...
THE MASK HAKKABO WAS WEARING...
...WAS FROM THE SOUTHERN LANDS TOO...
I WONDER WHAT THE SOUTHERN LANDS ARE LIKE?
JINGLE

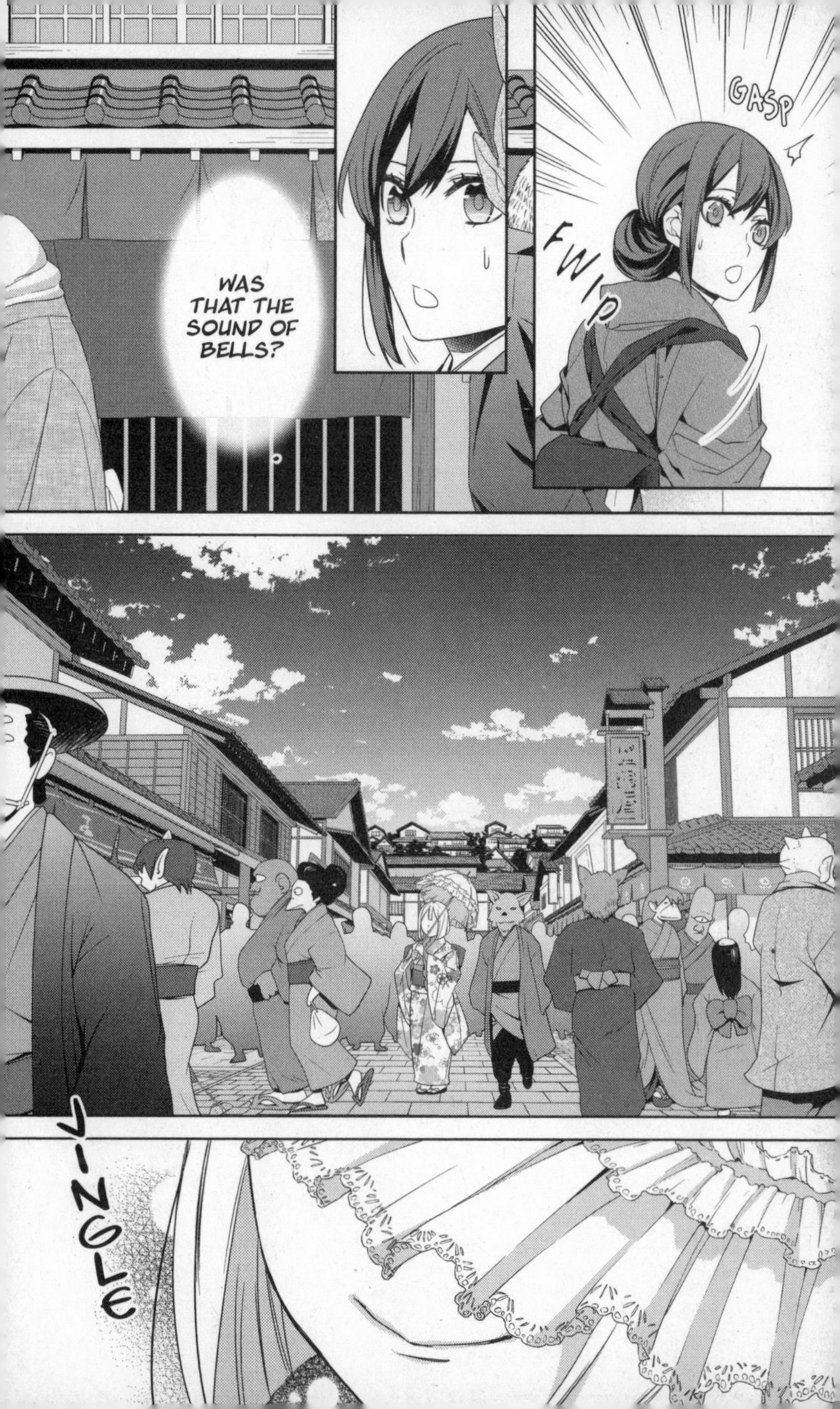
GASP
FWIP
WAS THAT THE SOUND OF BELLS?
JINGLE

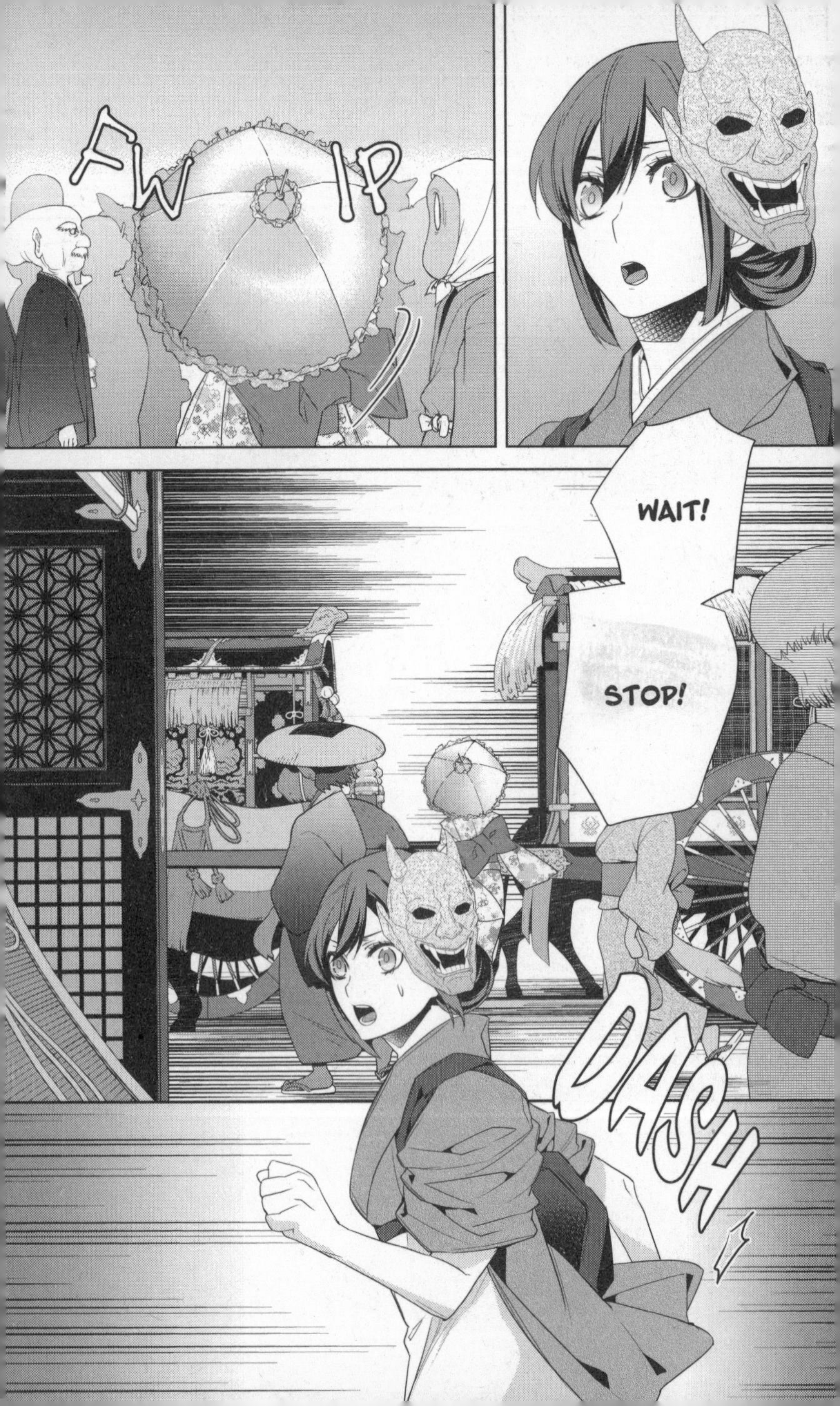
FWIP
WAIT!
STOP!
DASH

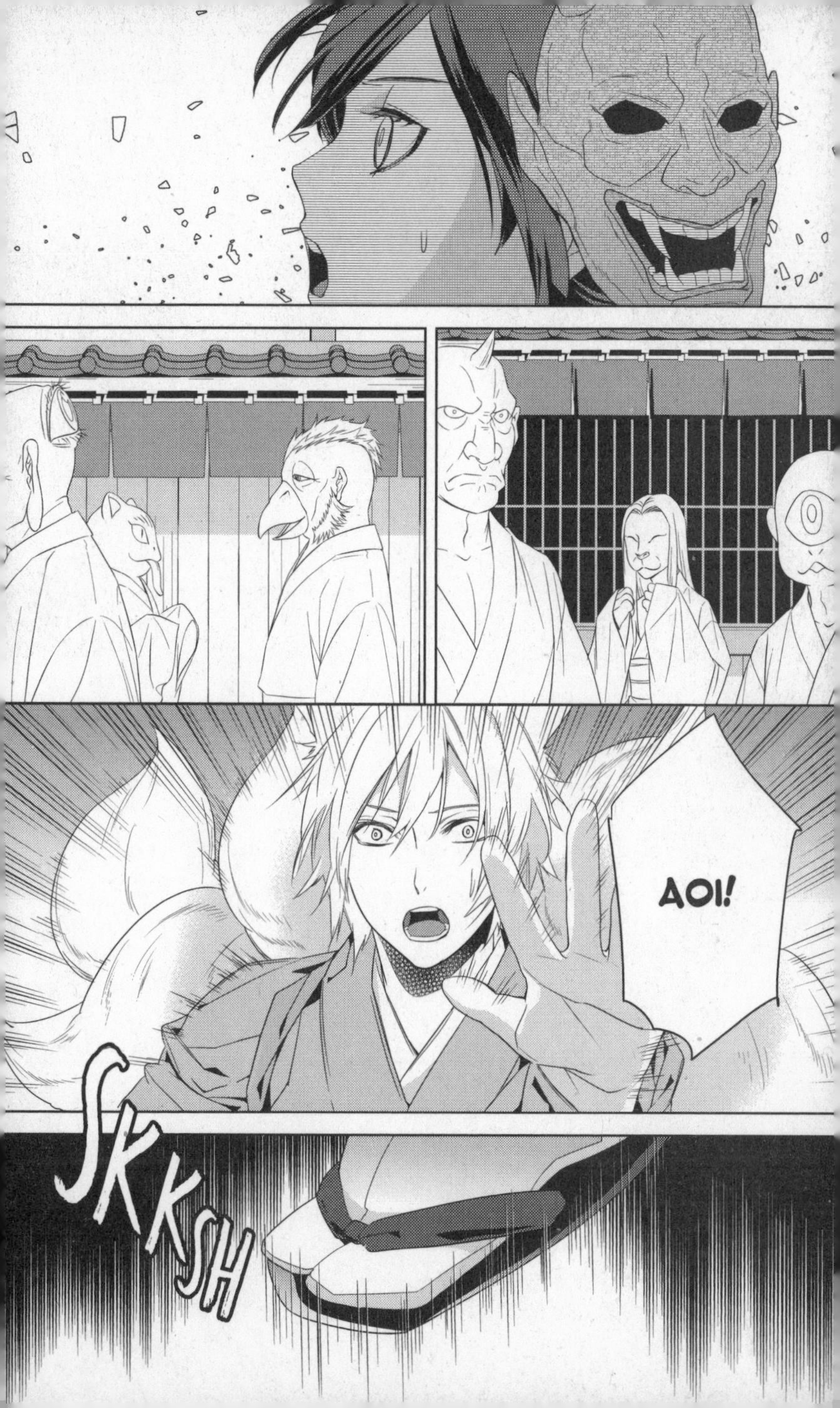
AOI!
SKKSH

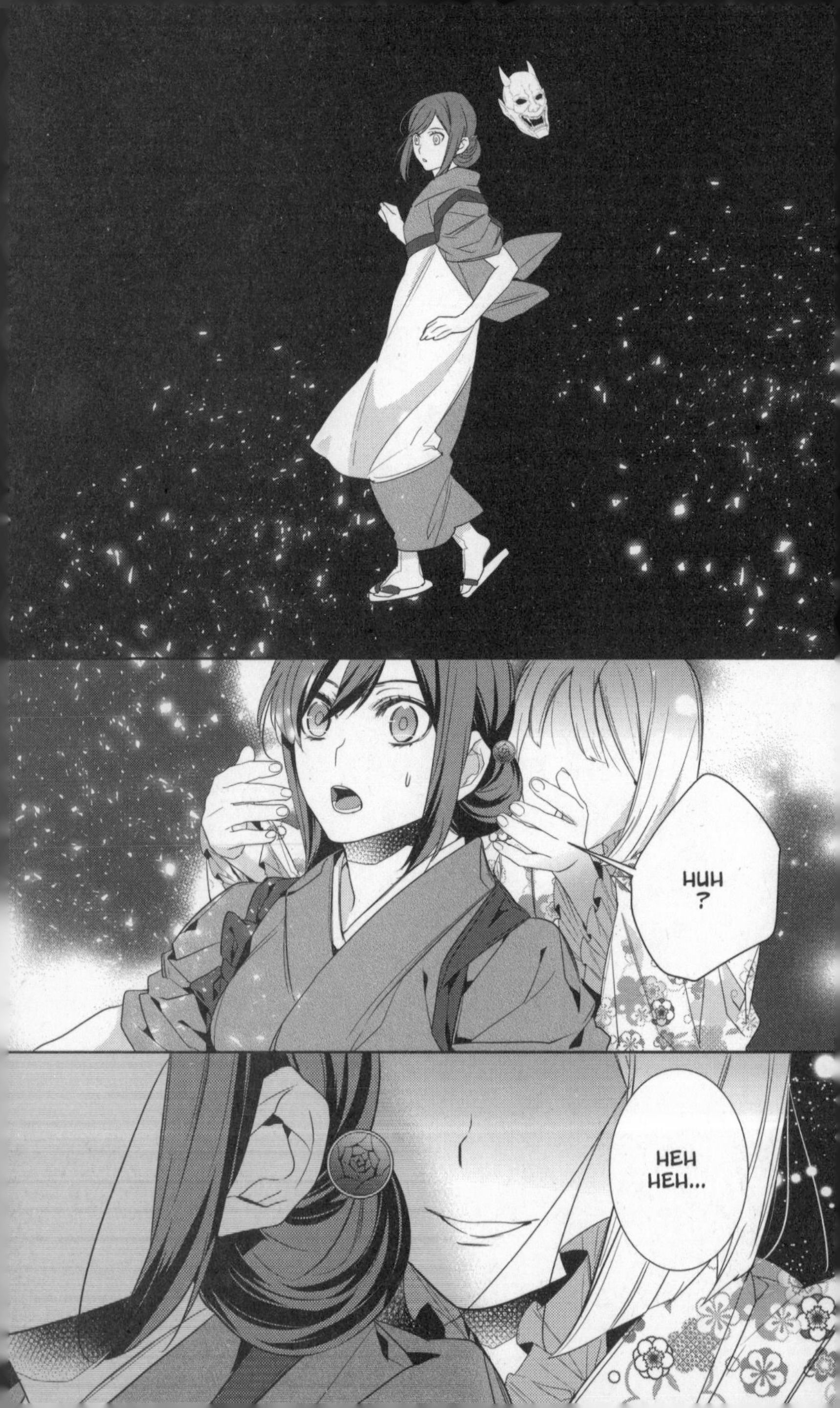
HUH?
HEH HEH...

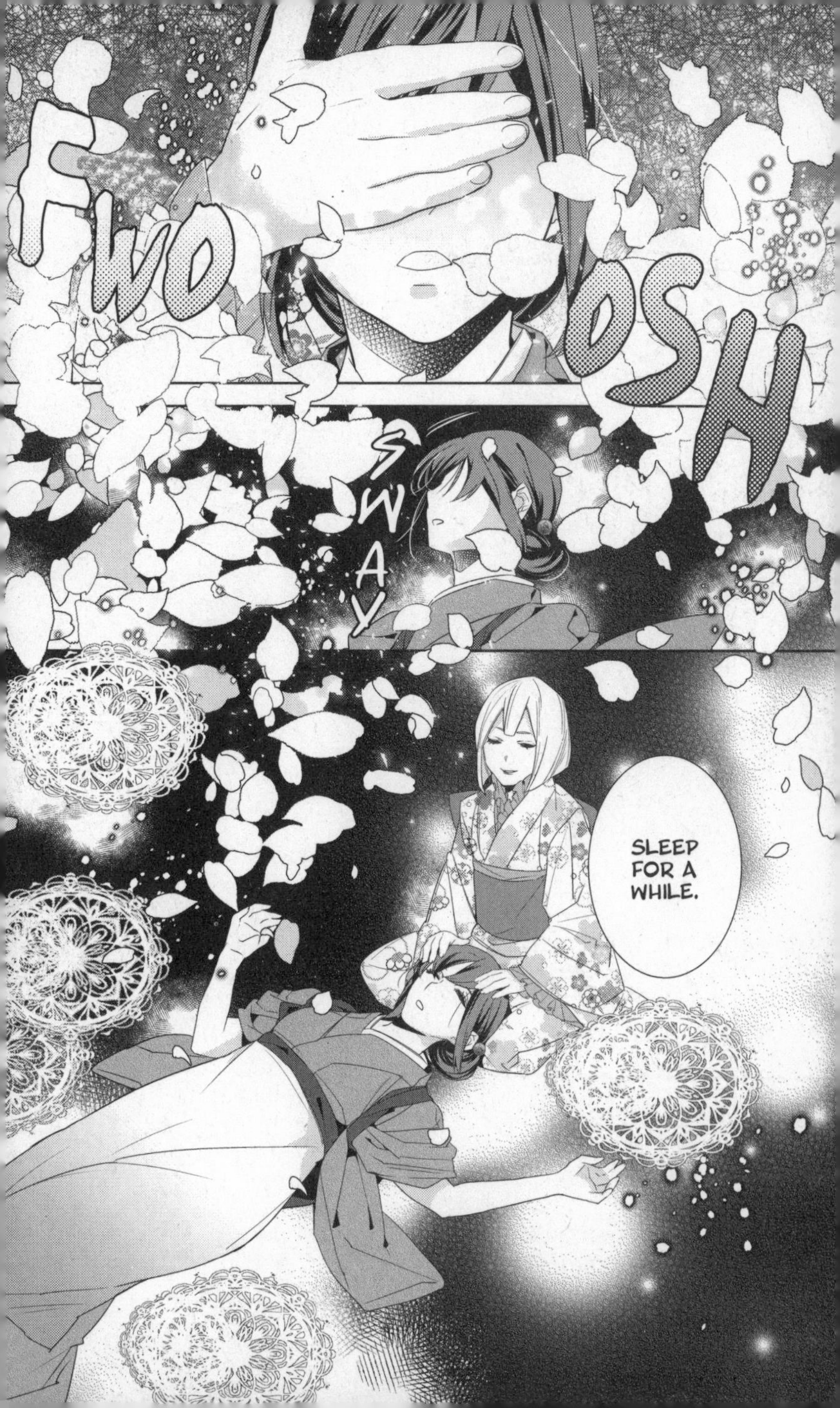
FWOOSH
SWAY
SLEEP FOR A WHILE.

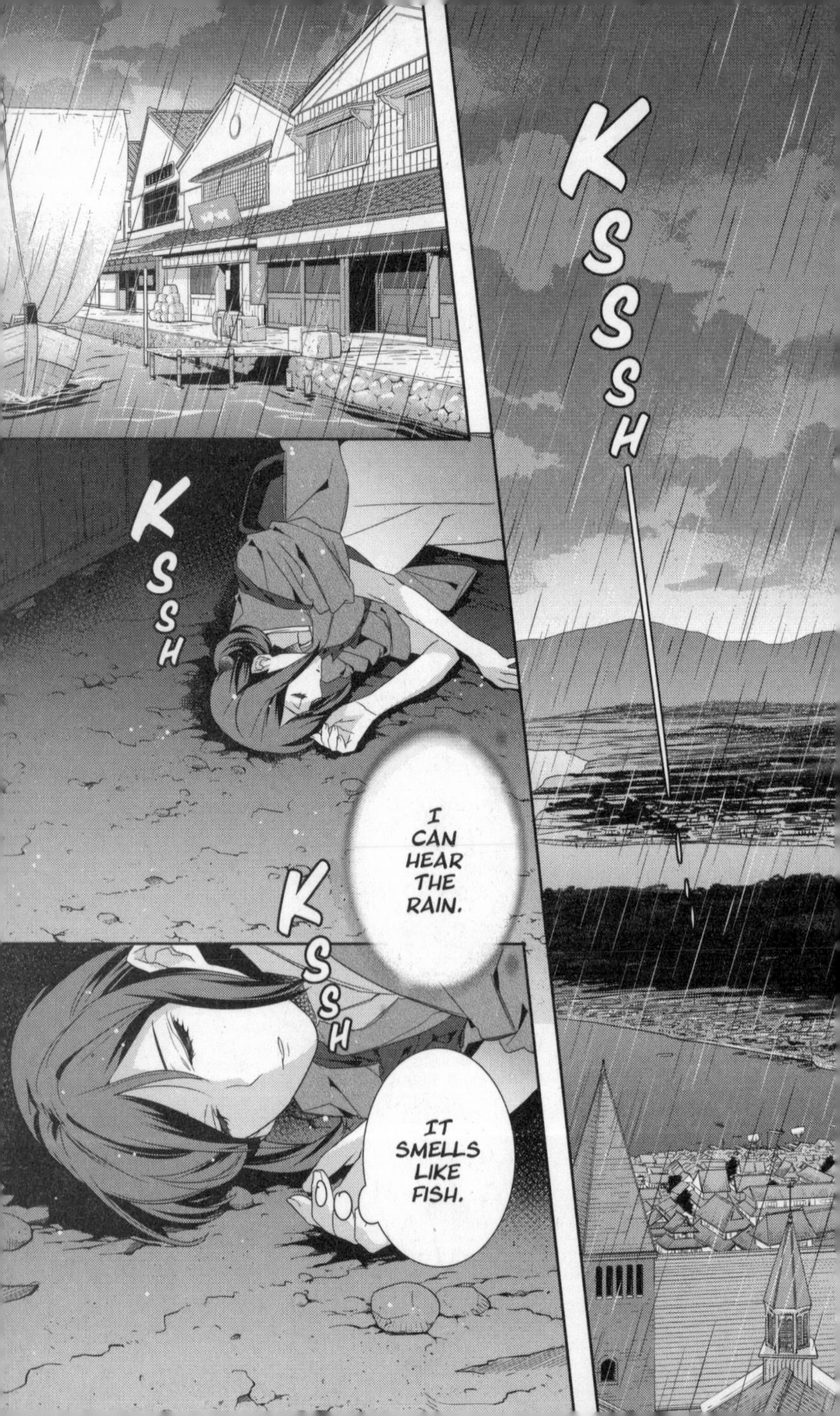
KSSSH
KSSH
I CAN HEAR THE RAIN.
KSSH
IT SMELLS LIKE FISH.

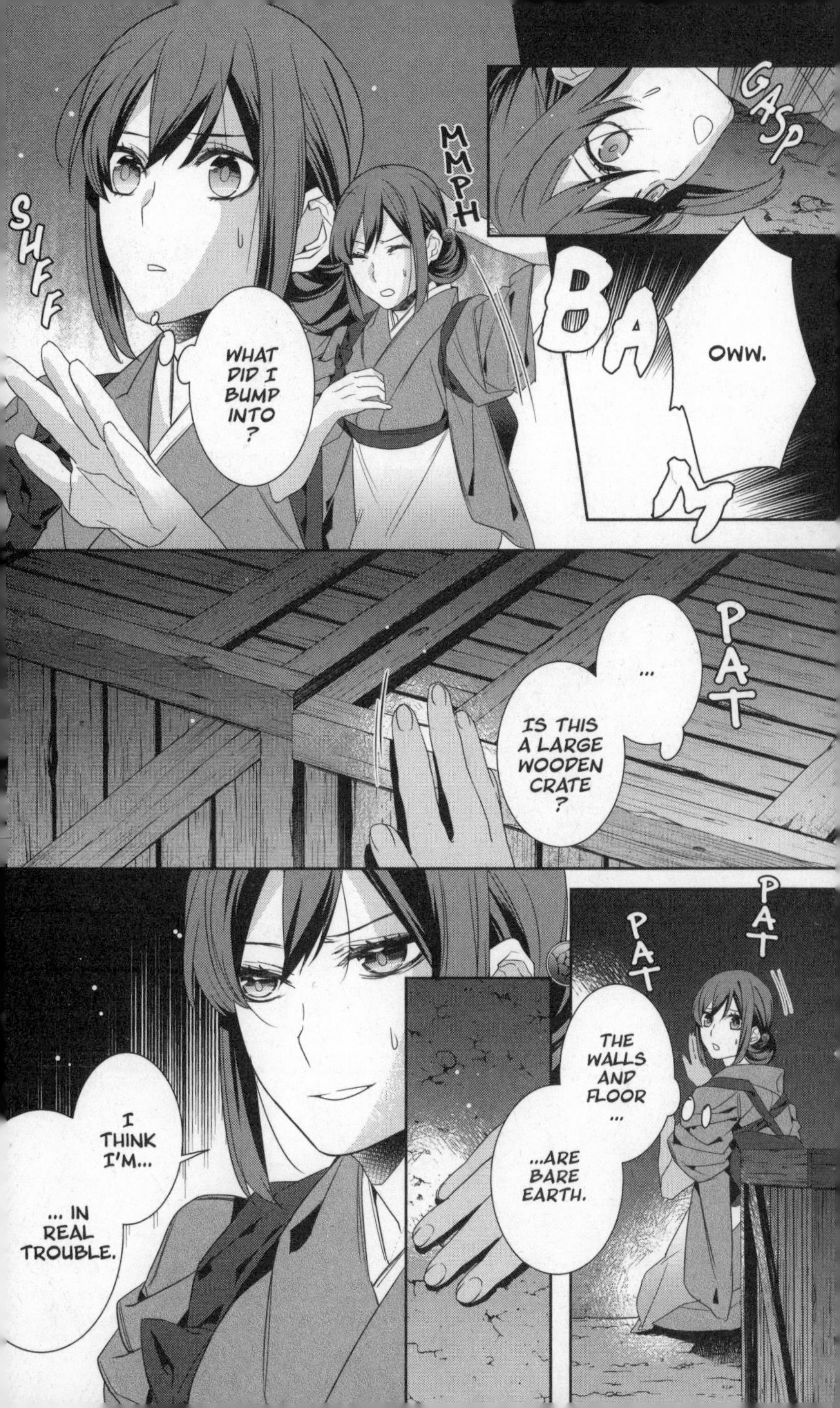
GASP
BAM
OWW.
MMPH
SHFF
WHAT DID I BUMP INTO?
PAT
...
IS THIS A LARGE WOODEN CRATE?
PAT PAT
THE WALLS AND FLOOR...
...ARE BARE EARTH.
I THINK I'M...
... IN REAL TROUBLE.

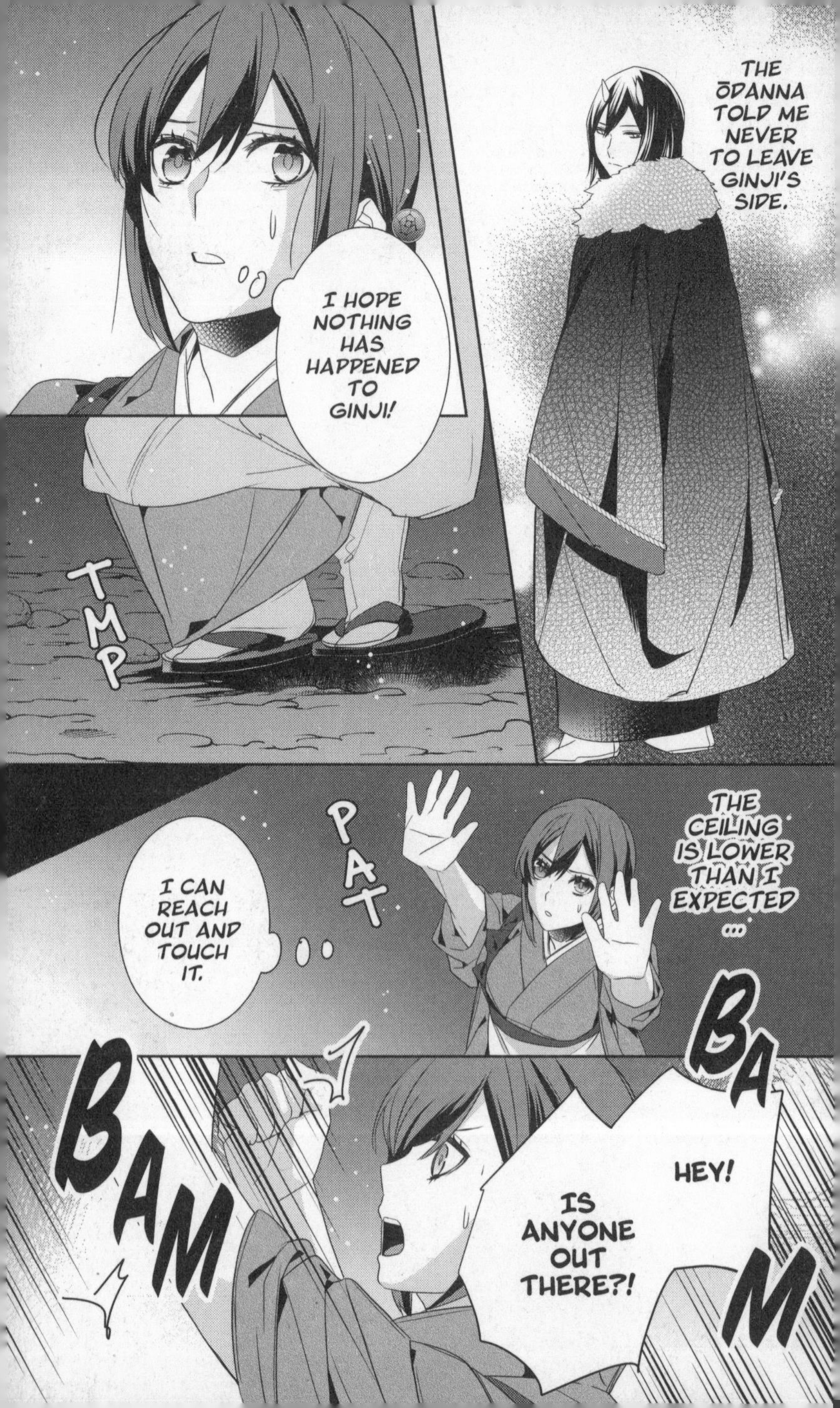
THE ŌDANNA TOLD ME NEVER TO LEAVE GINJI'S SIDE.
I HOPE NOTHING HAS HAPPENED TO GINJI!
TMP
THE CEILING IS LOWER THAN I EXPECTED...
PAT
I CAN REACH OUT AND TOUCH IT.
BAM
HEY!
IS ANYONE OUT THERE?!
BAM

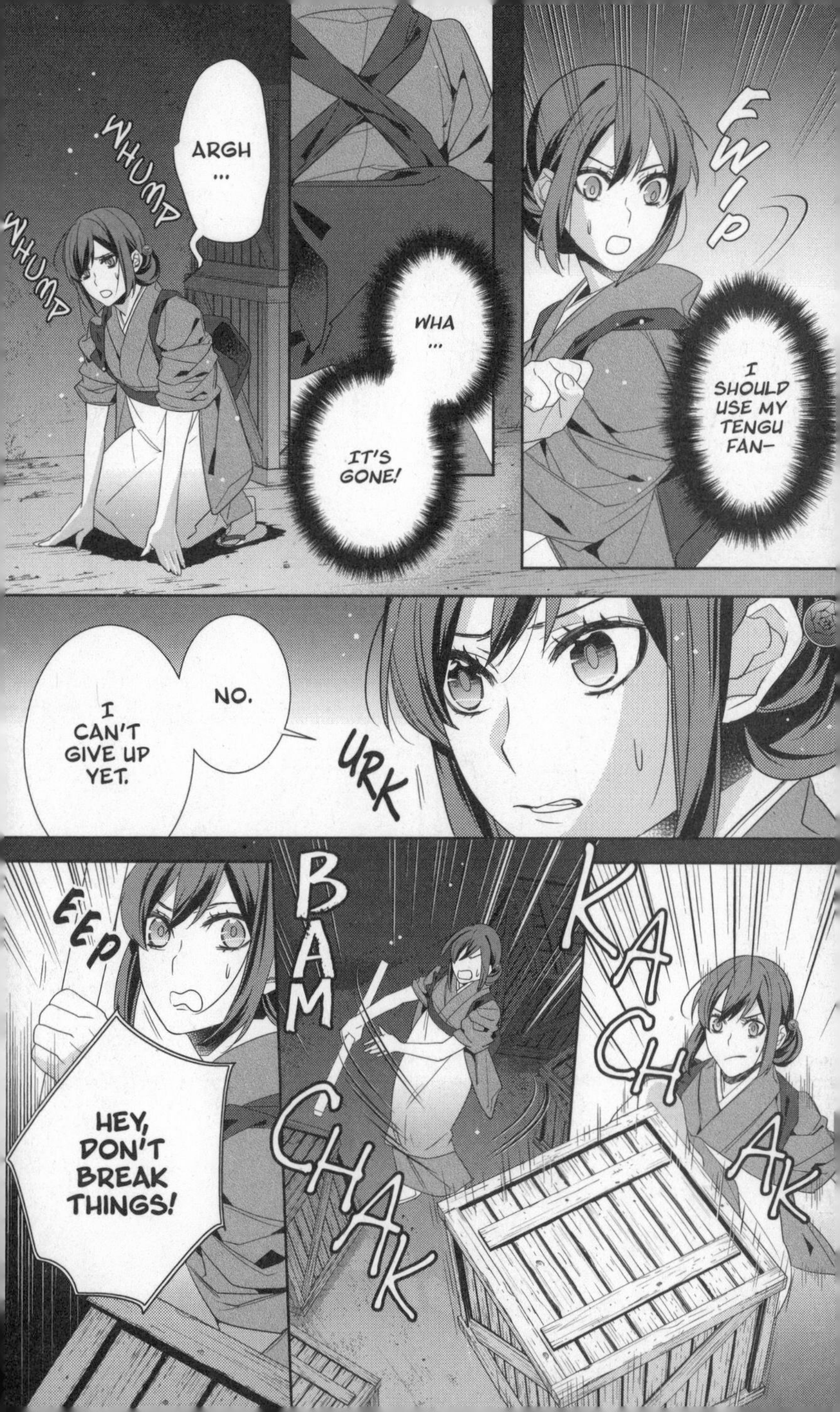
FWIP
I SHOULD USE MY TENGU FAN—
WHA ...
IT'S GONE!
WHUMP
WHUMP
ARGH ...
NO.
I CAN'T GIVE UP YET.
URK
KACHAK
BAM
CHAK
EEP
HEY, DON'T BREAK THINGS!

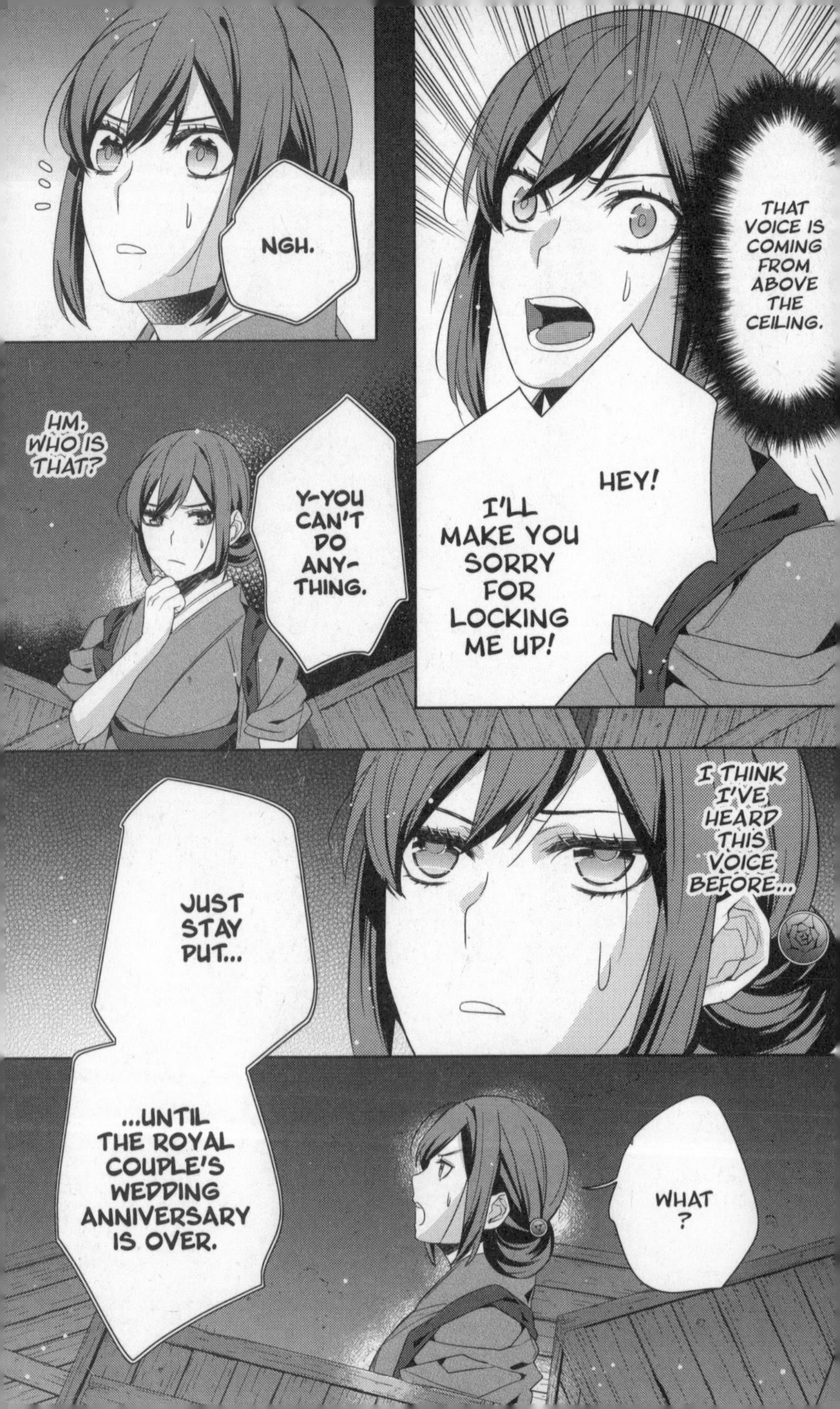
THAT VOICE IS COMING FROM ABOVE THE CEILING.
HEY!
I'LL MAKE YOU SORRY FOR LOCKING ME UP!
NGH.
Y-YOU CAN'T DO ANY-THING.
HM. WHO IS THAT?
I THINK I'VE HEARD THIS VOICE BEFORE...
JUST STAY PUT...
...UNTIL THE ROYAL COUPLE'S WEDDING ANNIVERSARY IS OVER.
WHAT?

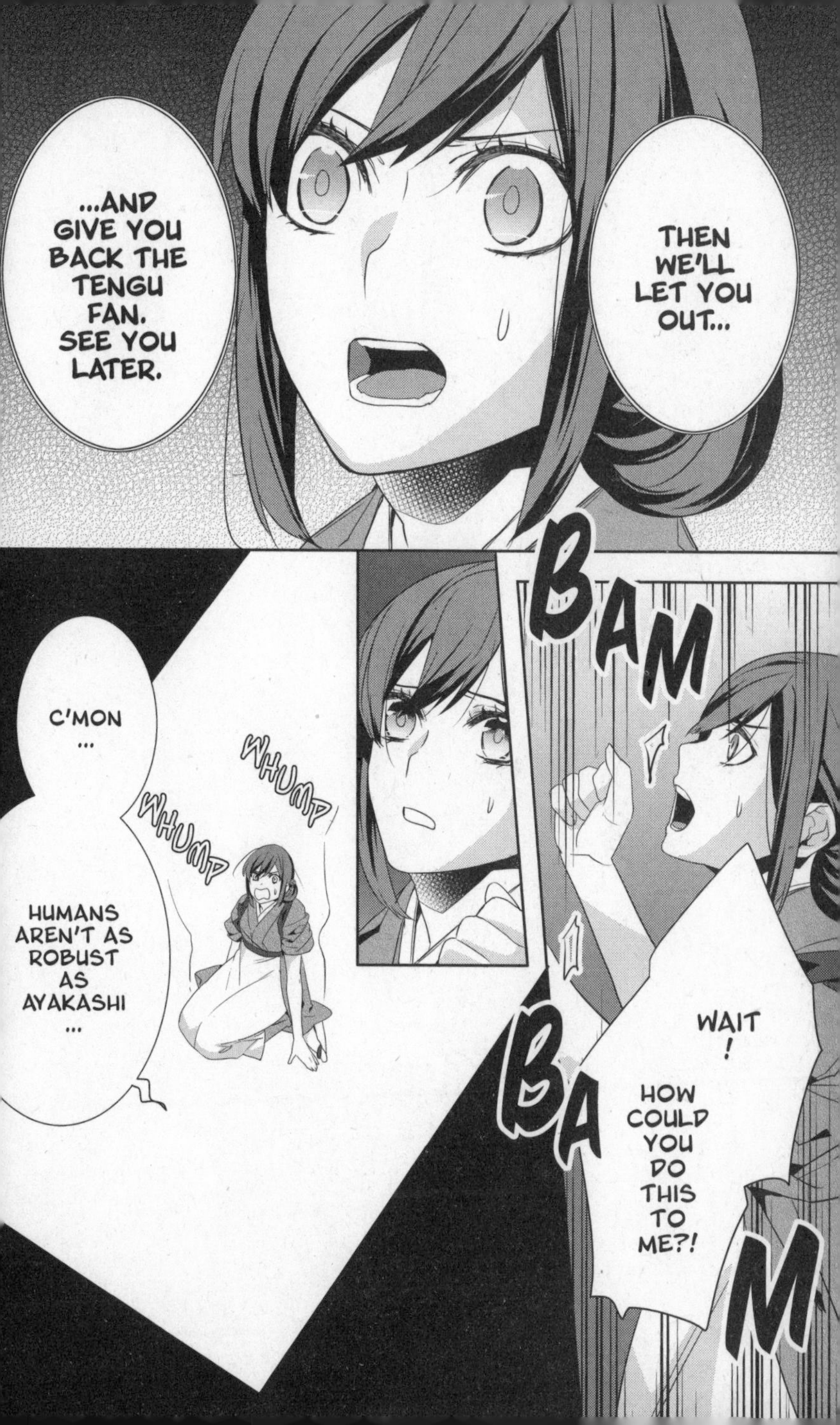
THEN WE'LL LET YOU OUT...
...AND GIVE YOU BACK THE TENGU FAN. SEE YOU LATER.
BAM
WAIT! HOW COULD YOU DO THIS TO ME?!
BAM
WHUMP
WHUMP
C'MON...
HUMANS AREN'T AS ROBUST AS AYAKASHI...

Kakuriyo
Bed & Breakfast
for Spirits

Kakuriyo
Bed & Breakfast
for Spirits

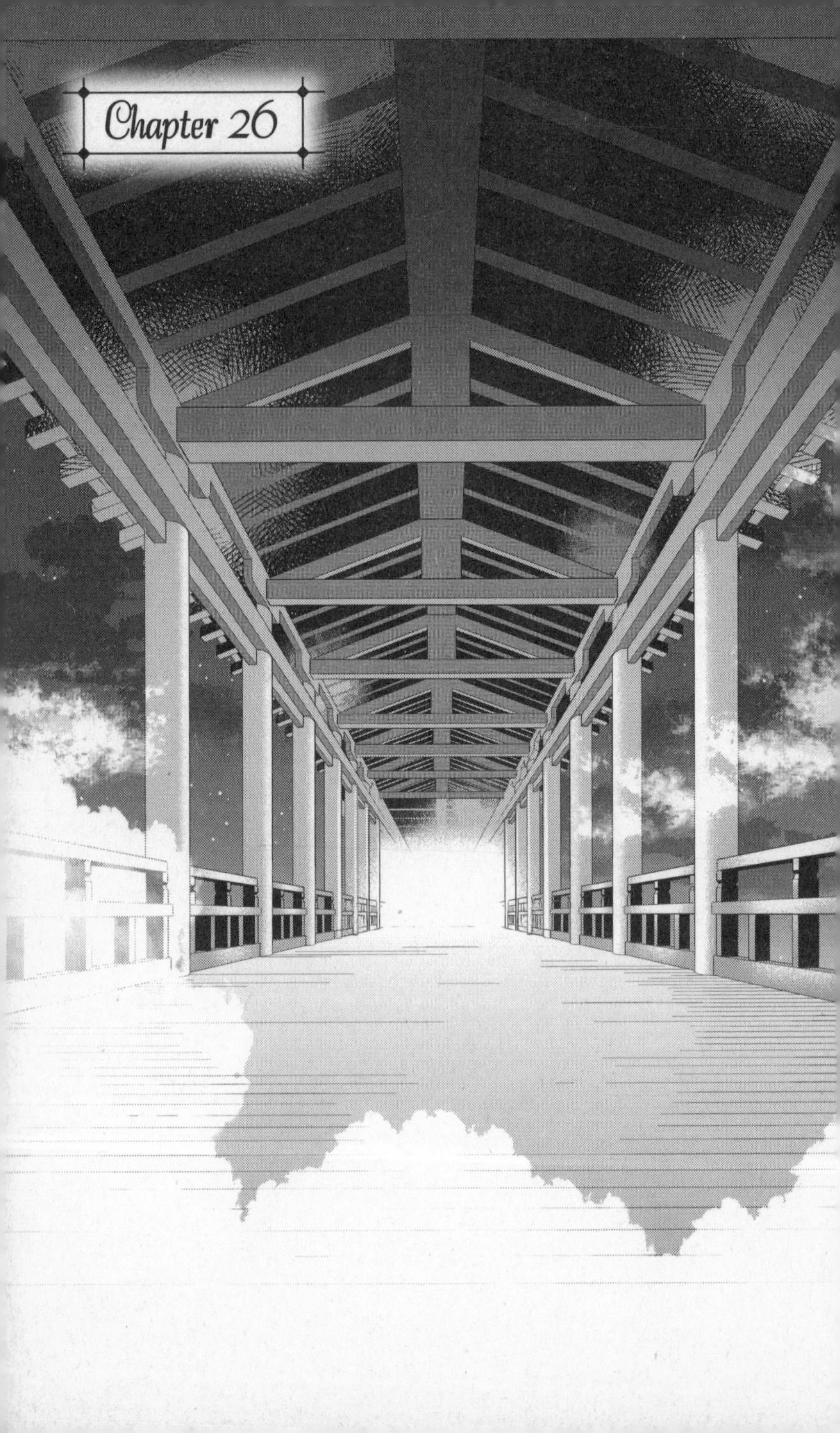
Chapter 26

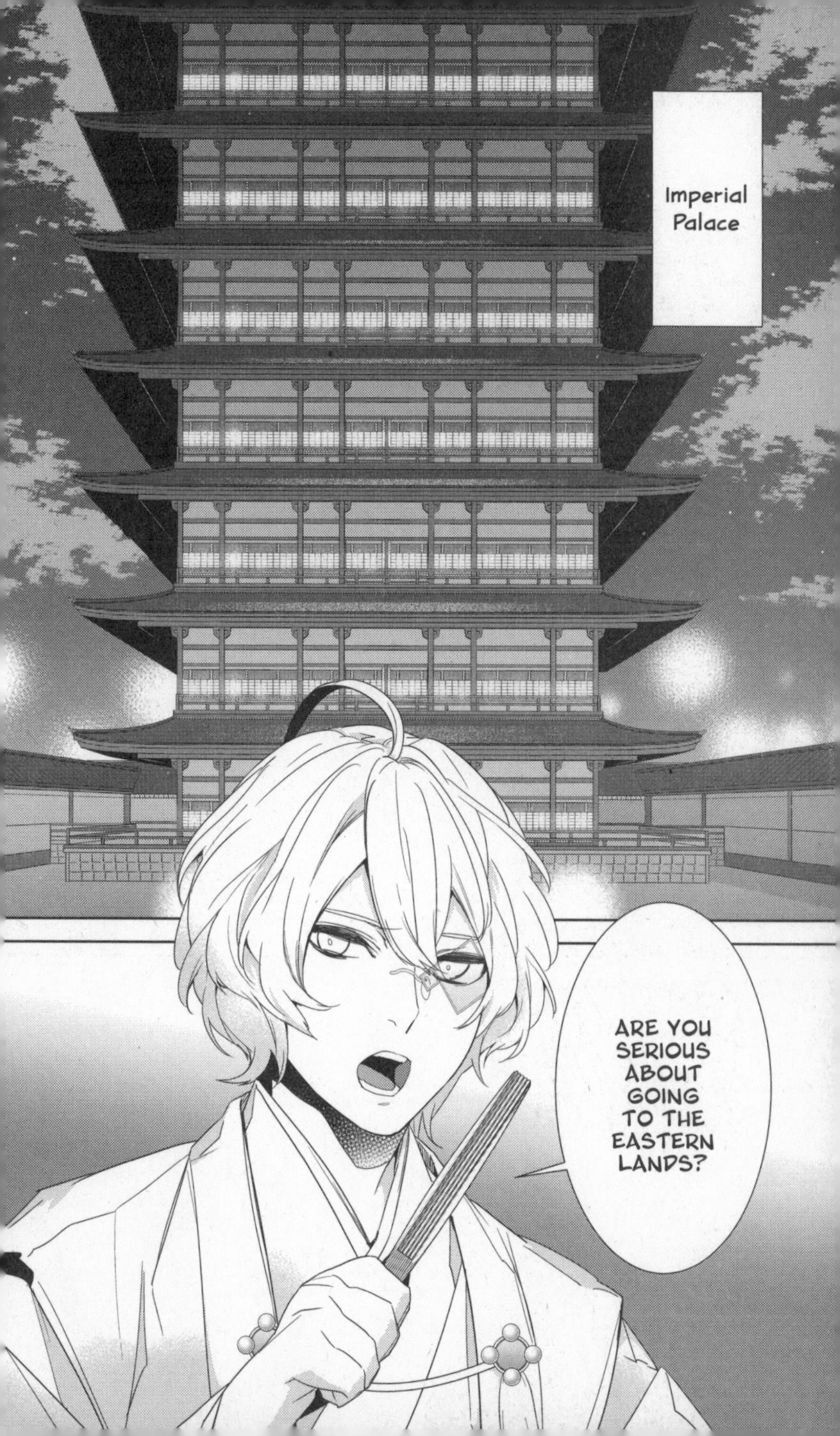
Imperial Palace
ARE YOU SERIOUS ABOUT GOING TO THE EASTERN LANDS?

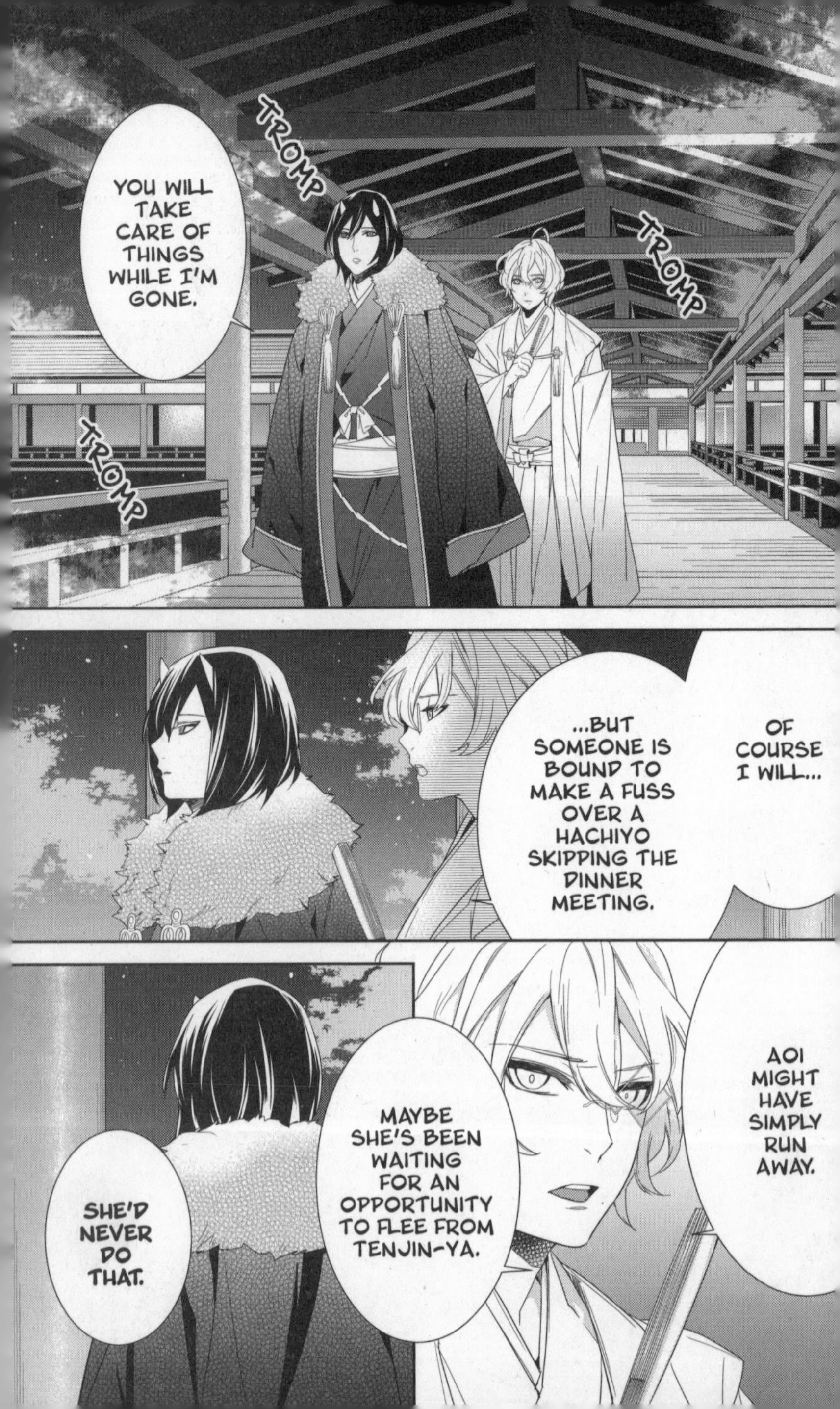
TROMP
TROMP
YOU WILL TAKE CARE OF THINGS WHILE I'M GONE.
TROMP
OF COURSE I WILL...
...BUT SOMEONE IS BOUND TO MAKE A FUSS OVER A HACHIYO SKIPPING THE DINNER MEETING.
AOI MIGHT HAVE SIMPLY RUN AWAY.
MAYBE SHE'S BEEN WAITING FOR AN OPPORTUNITY TO FLEE FROM TENJIN-YA.
SHE'D NEVER DO THAT.

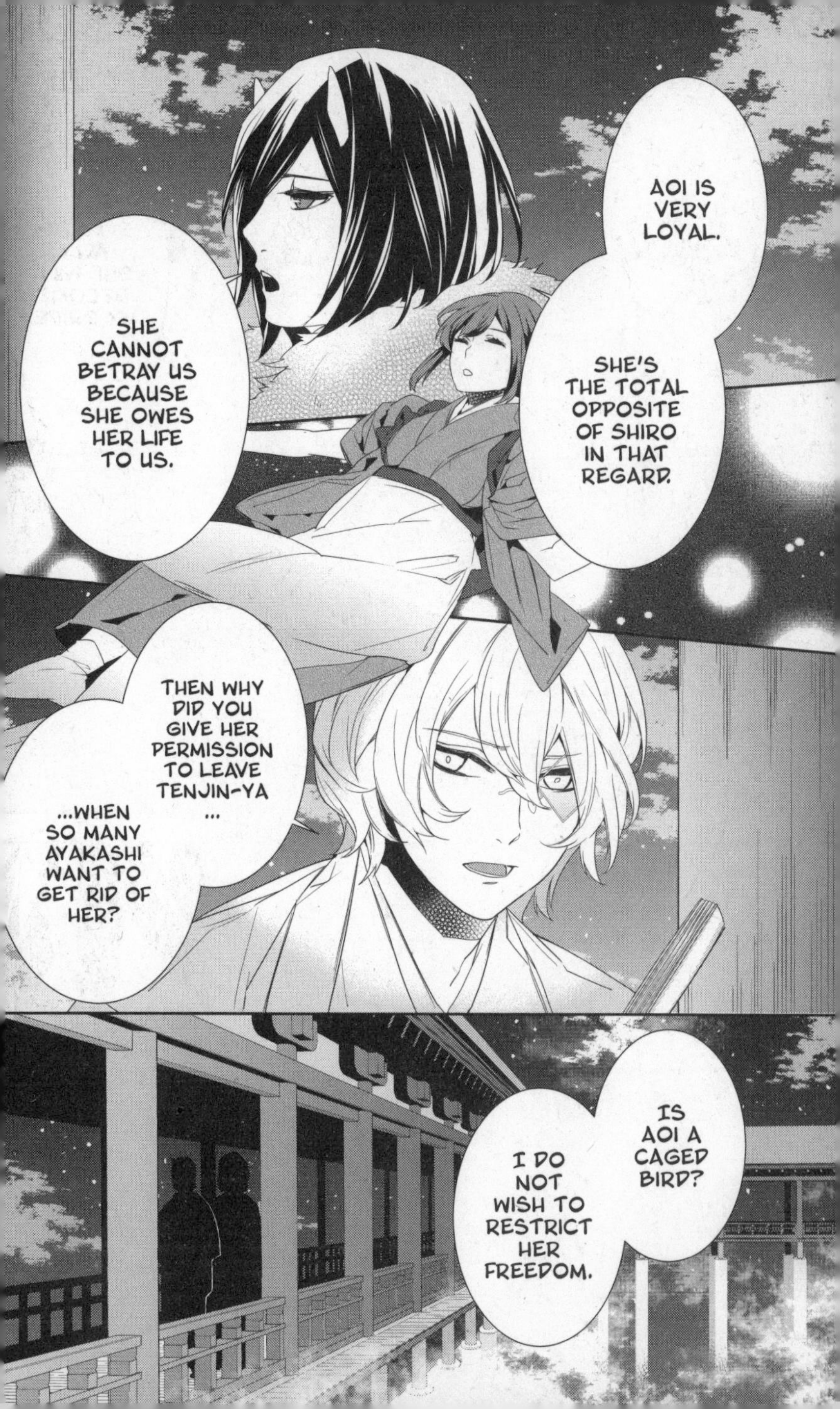
AOI IS VERY LOYAL.
SHE'S THE TOTAL OPPOSITE OF SHIRO IN THAT REGARD.
SHE CANNOT BETRAY US BECAUSE SHE OWES HER LIFE TO US.
THEN WHY DID YOU GIVE HER PERMISSION TO LEAVE TENJIN-YA ...
...WHEN SO MANY AYAKASHI WANT TO GET RID OF HER?
IS AOI A CAGED BIRD?
I DO NOT WISH TO RESTRICT HER FREEDOM.

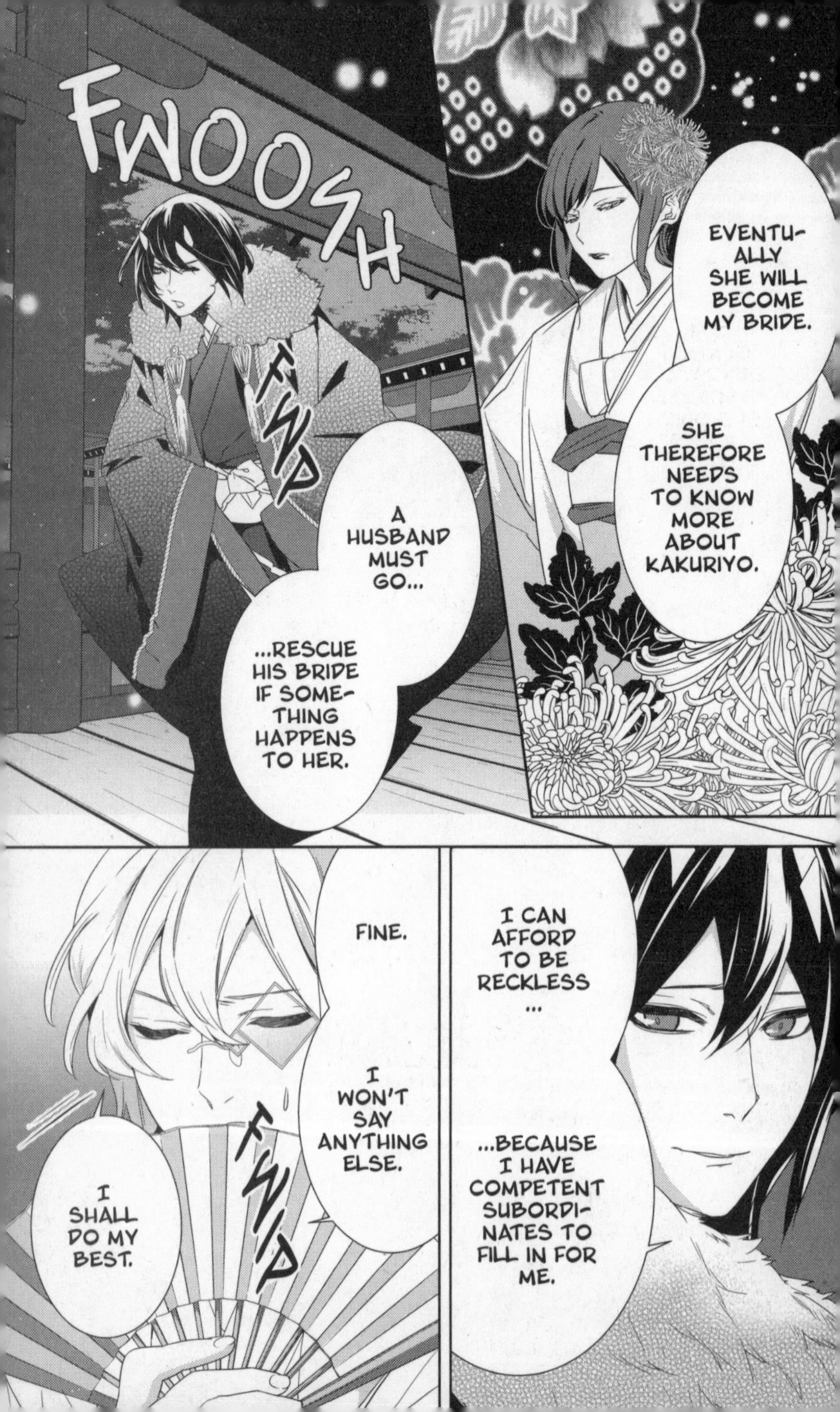
EVENTUALLY SHE WILL BECOME MY BRIDE.
SHE THEREFORE NEEDS TO KNOW MORE ABOUT KAKURIYO.
FWOOSH
FWIP
A HUSBAND MUST GO...
...RESCUE HIS BRIDE IF SOMETHING HAPPENS TO HER.
I CAN AFFORD TO BE RECKLESS ...
...BECAUSE I HAVE COMPETENT SUBORDINATES TO FILL IN FOR ME.
FINE.
I WON'T SAY ANYTHING ELSE.
FWIP
I SHALL DO MY BEST.

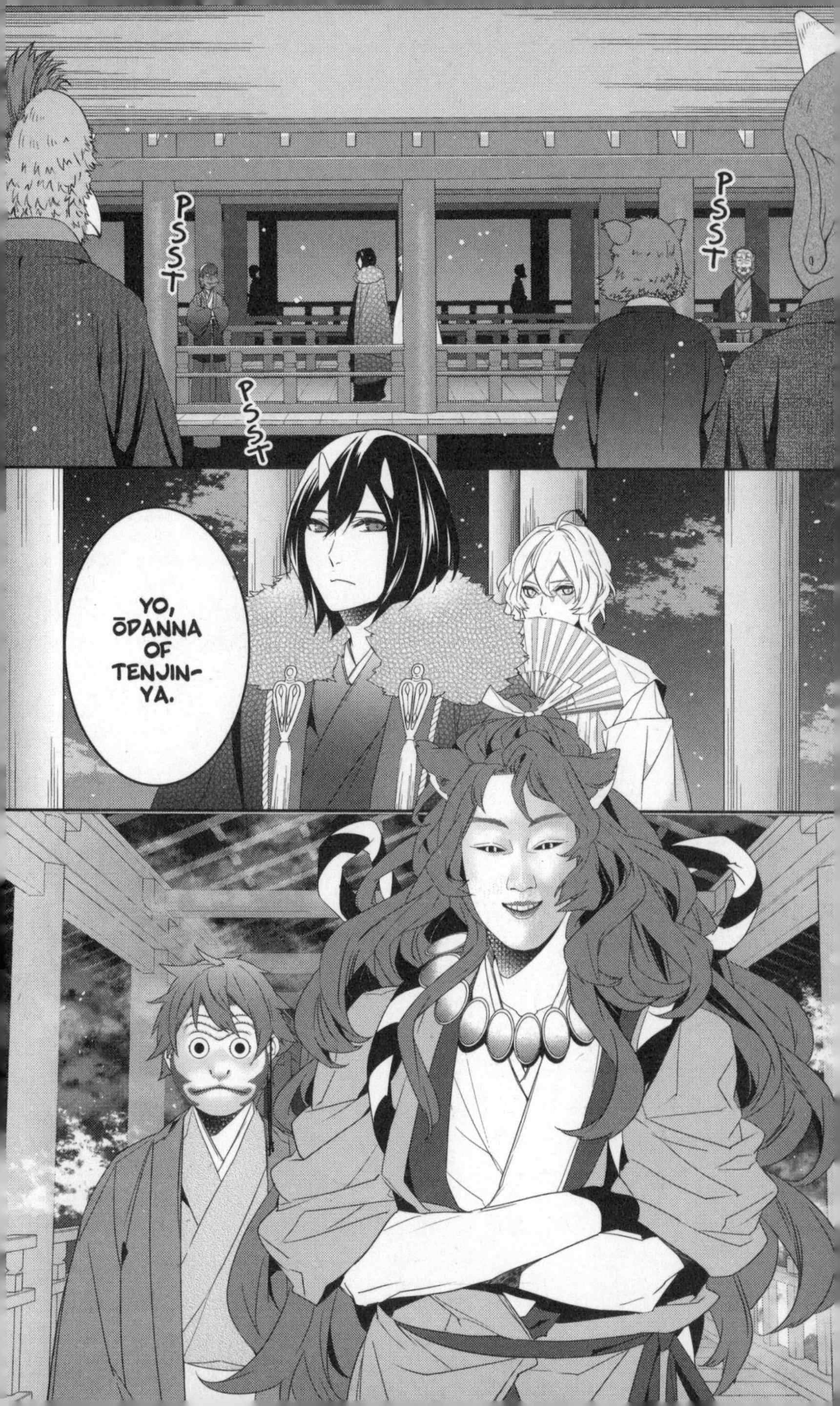
PSST
PSST
PSST
YO, ŌDANNA OF TENJIN-YA.

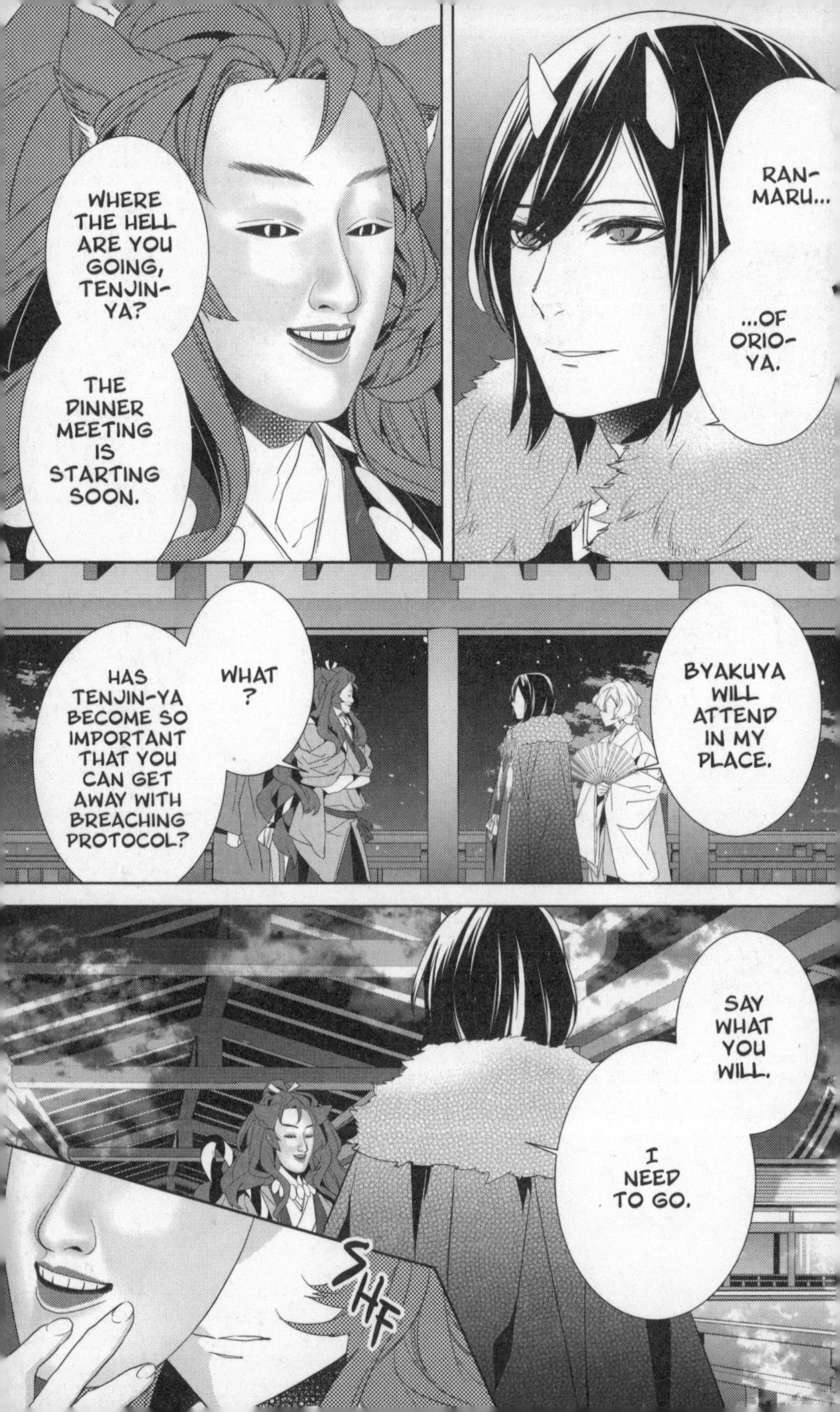
RAN-MARU...
...OF ORIO-YA.
WHERE THE HELL ARE YOU GOING, TENJIN-YA?
THE DINNER MEETING IS STARTING SOON.
BYAKUYA WILL ATTEND IN MY PLACE.
WHAT?
HAS TENJIN-YA BECOME SO IMPORTANT THAT YOU CAN GET AWAY WITH BREACHING PROTOCOL?
SAY WHAT YOU WILL.
I NEED TO GO.
SHF

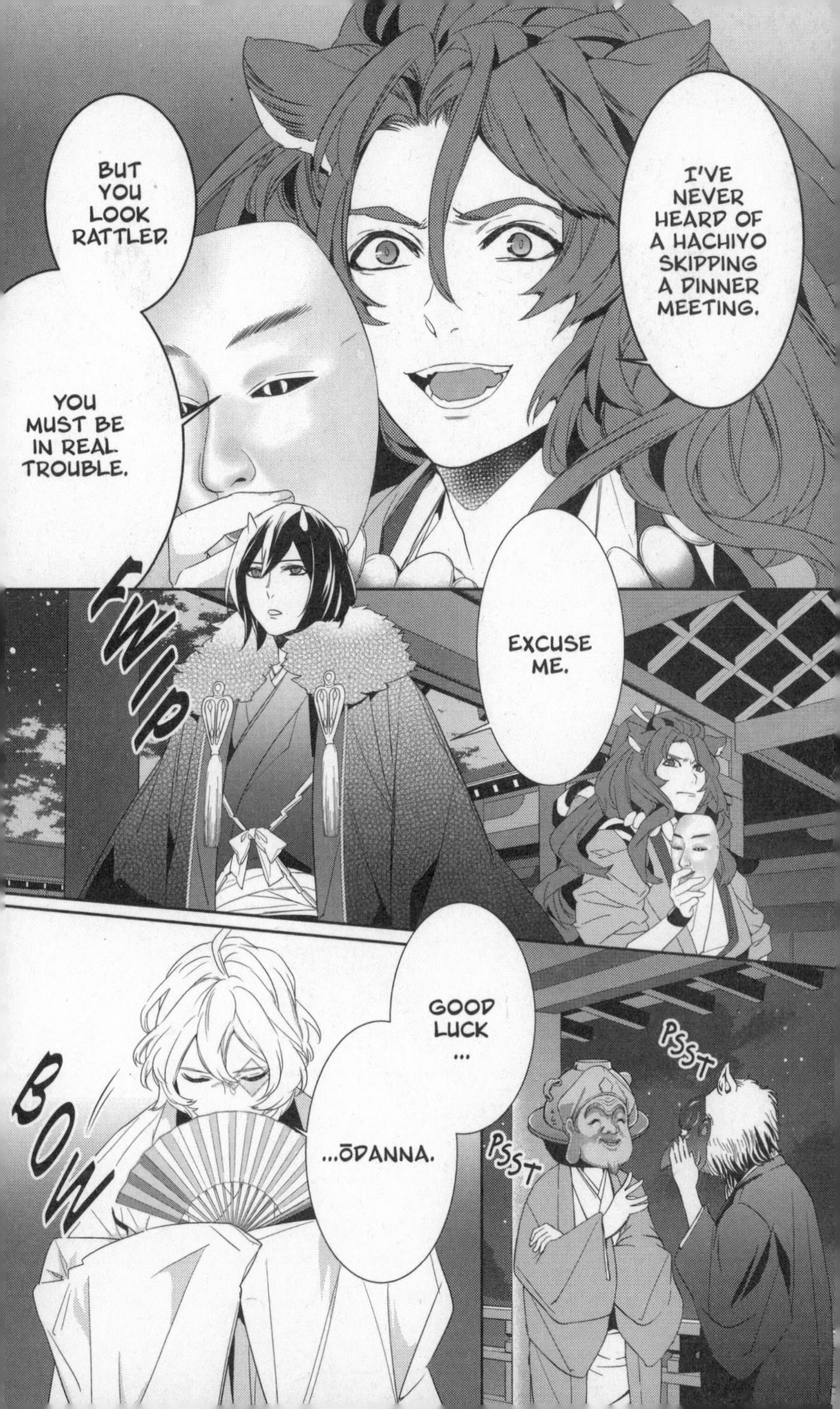
I'VE NEVER HEARD OF A HACHIYO SKIPPING A DINNER MEETING.
BUT YOU LOOK RATTLED.
YOU MUST BE IN REAL TROUBLE.
EXCUSE ME.
FWIP
PSST
PSST
GOOD LUCK ...
...ŌDANNA.
BOW

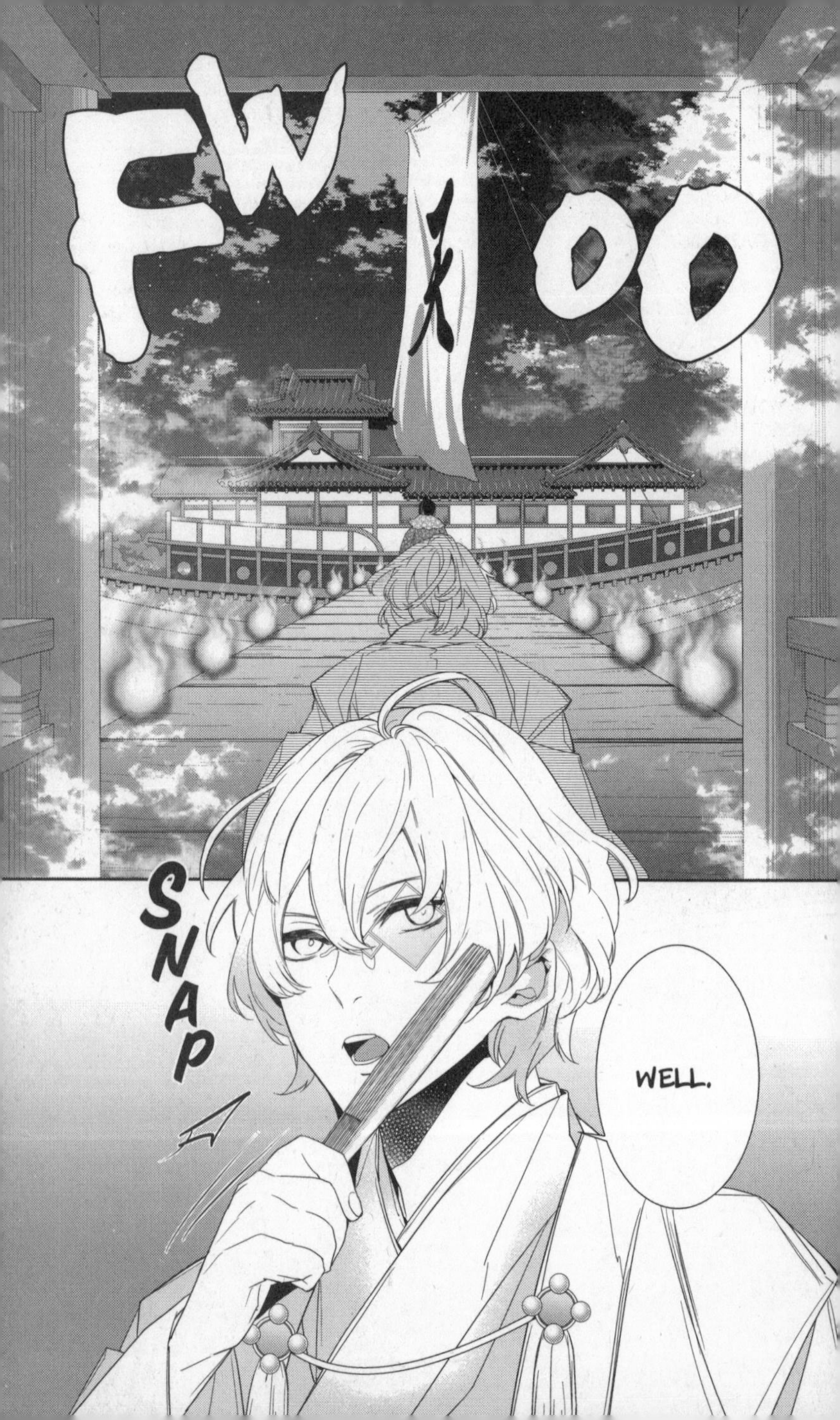
FWOOO
WELL.
SNAP

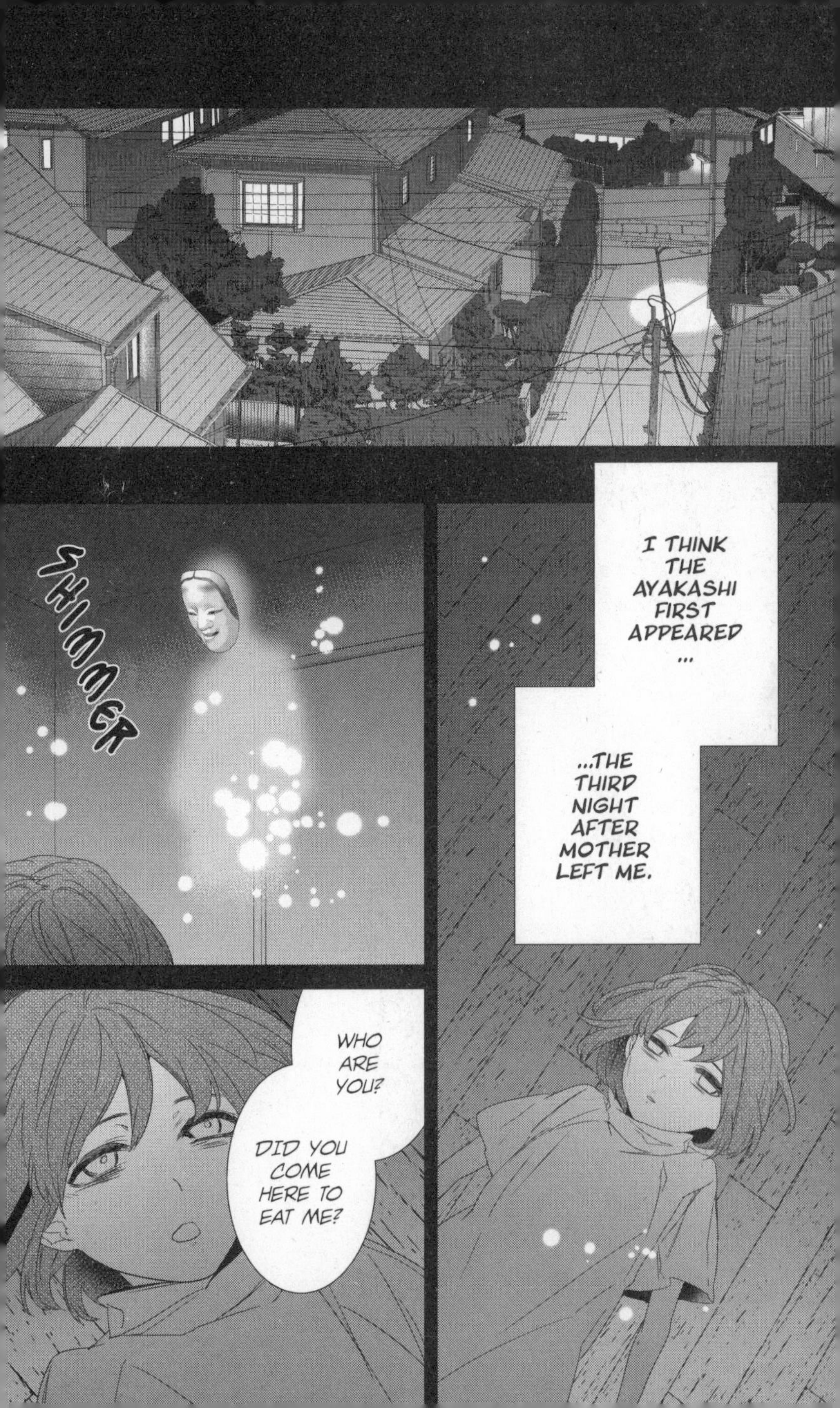
I THINK THE AYAKASHI FIRST APPEARED ...
...THE THIRD NIGHT AFTER MOTHER LEFT ME.
SHIMMER
WHO ARE YOU?
DID YOU COME HERE TO EAT ME?

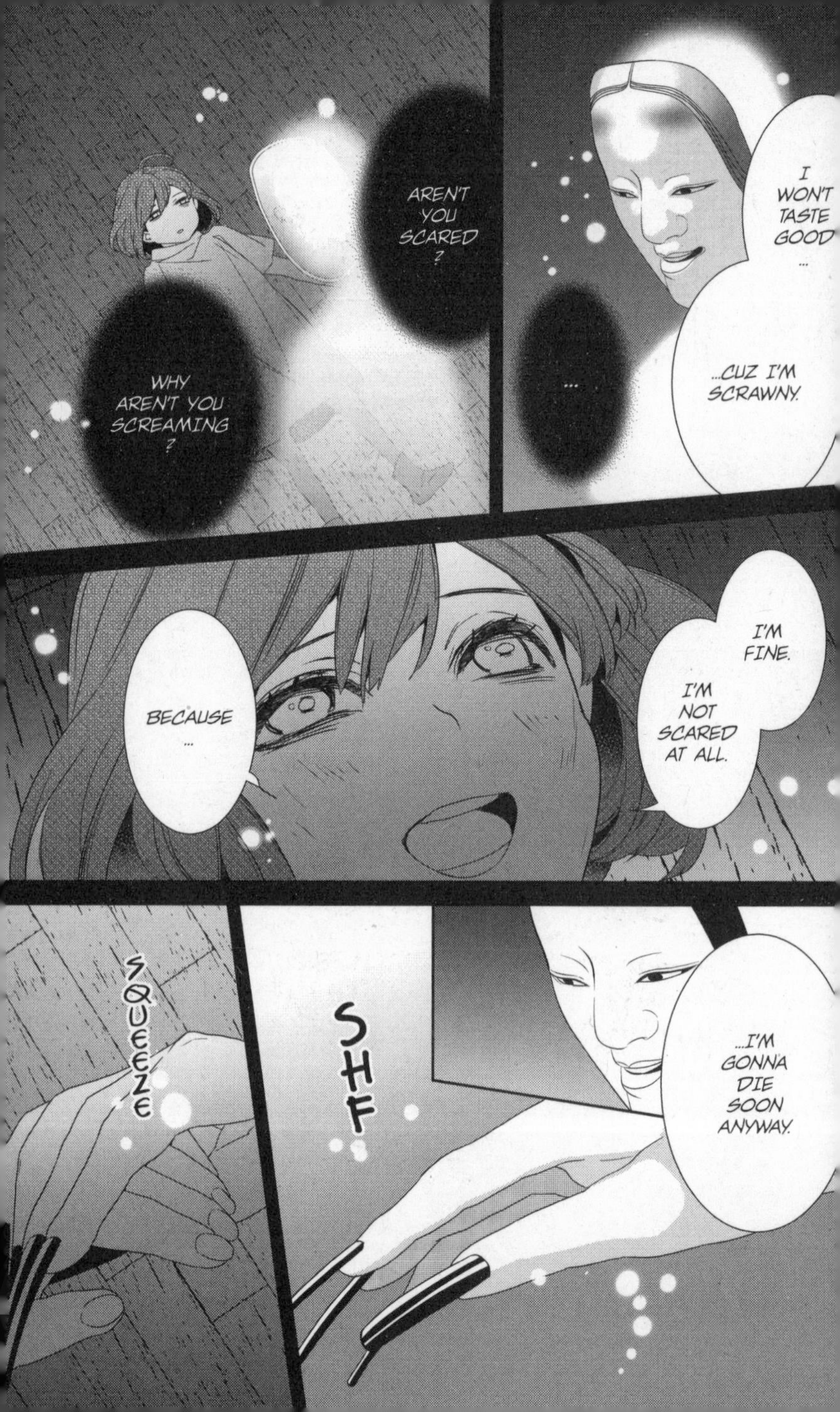
I WON'T TASTE GOOD ...
...CUZ I'M SCRAWNY.
...
AREN'T YOU SCARED ?
WHY AREN'T YOU SCREAMING ?
I'M FINE.
I'M NOT SCARED AT ALL.
BECAUSE ...
...I'M GONNA DIE SOON ANYWAY.
SHF
SQUEEZE

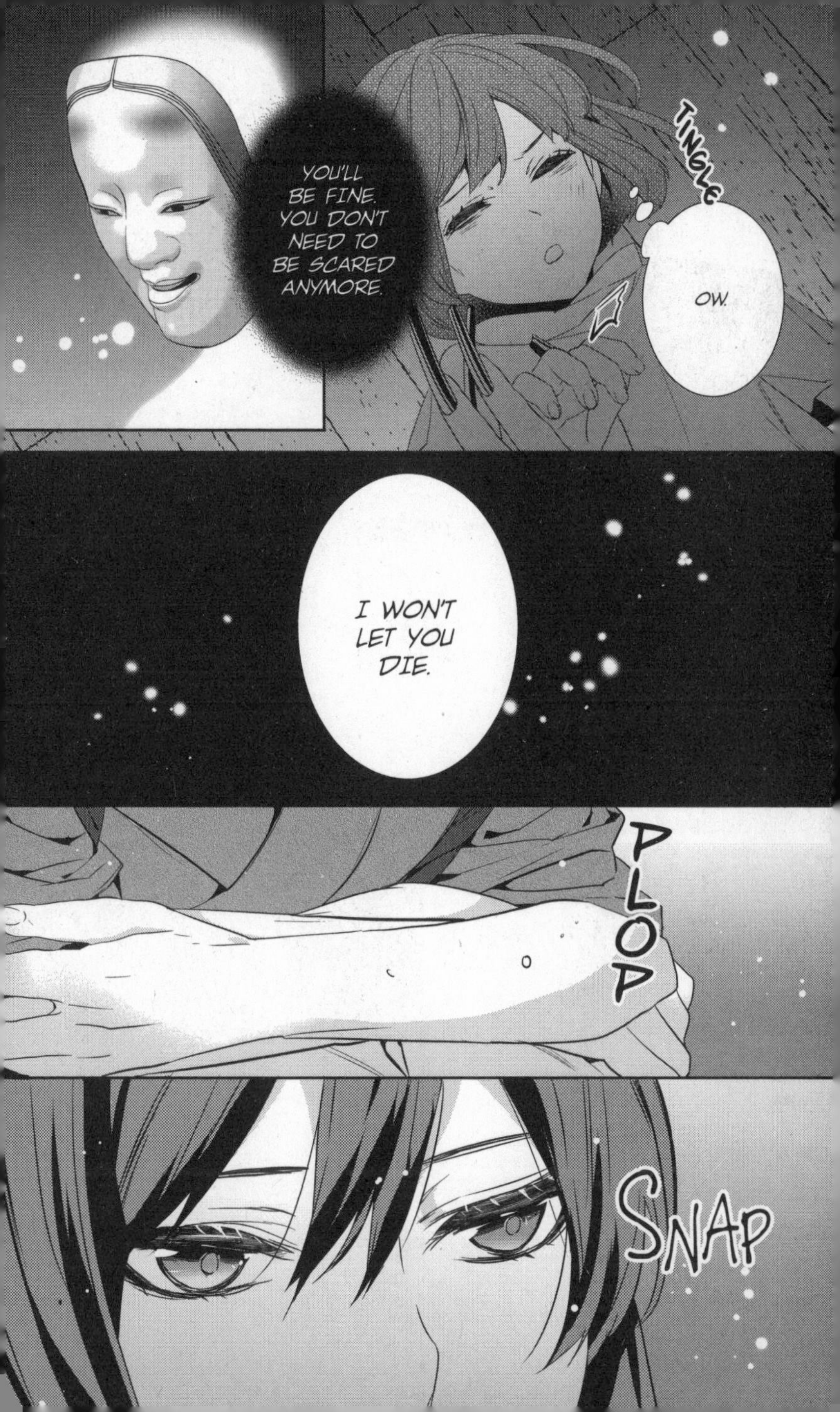
TINGLE
OW.
YOU'LL BE FINE. YOU DON'T NEED TO BE SCARED ANYMORE.
I WON'T LET YOU DIE.
PLOP
SNAP

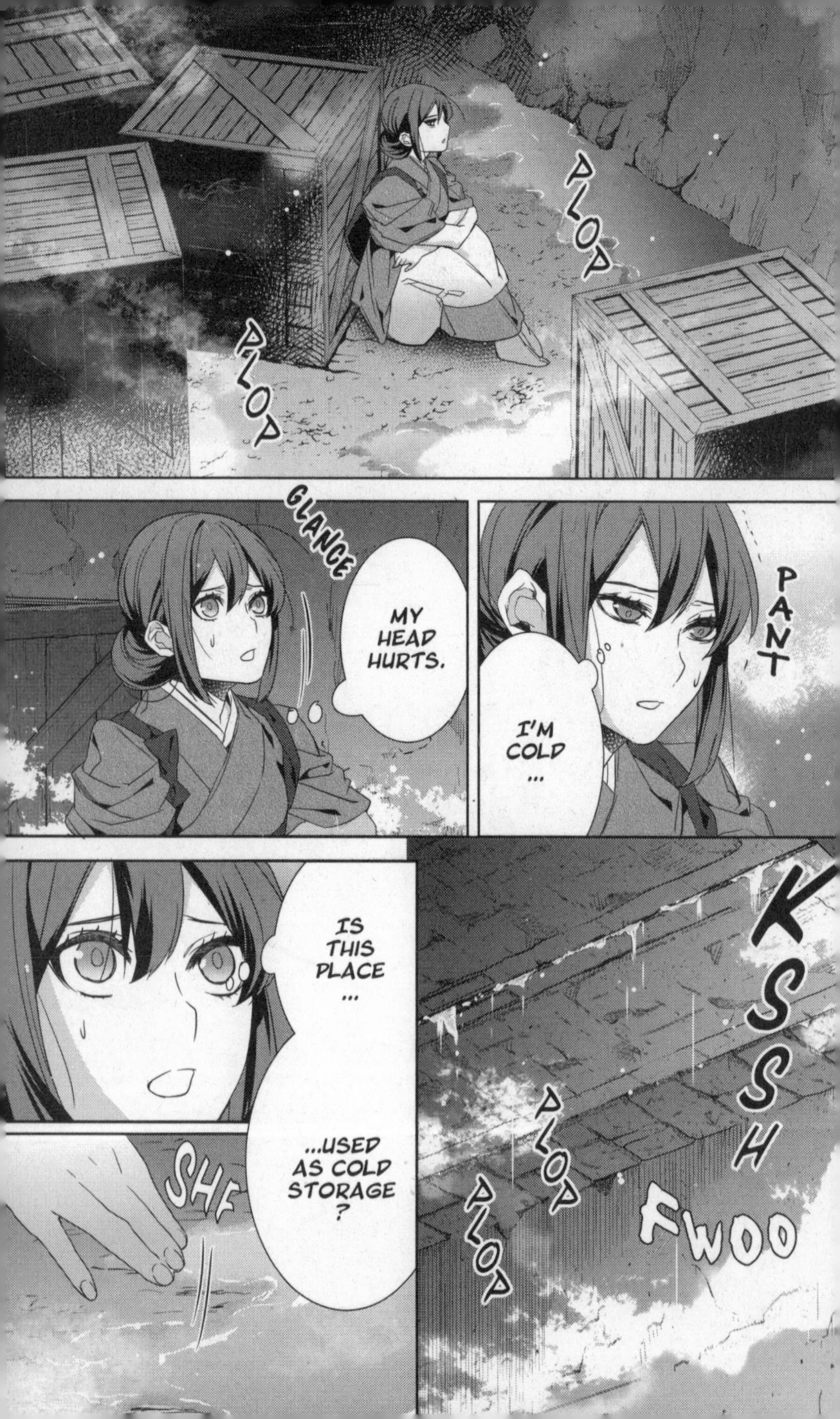
PLOP
PLOP
PANT
I'M COLD ...
GLANCE
MY HEAD HURTS.
KSSH
PLOP
PLOP
FWOO
IS THIS PLACE ...
...USED AS COLD STORAGE ?
SHF

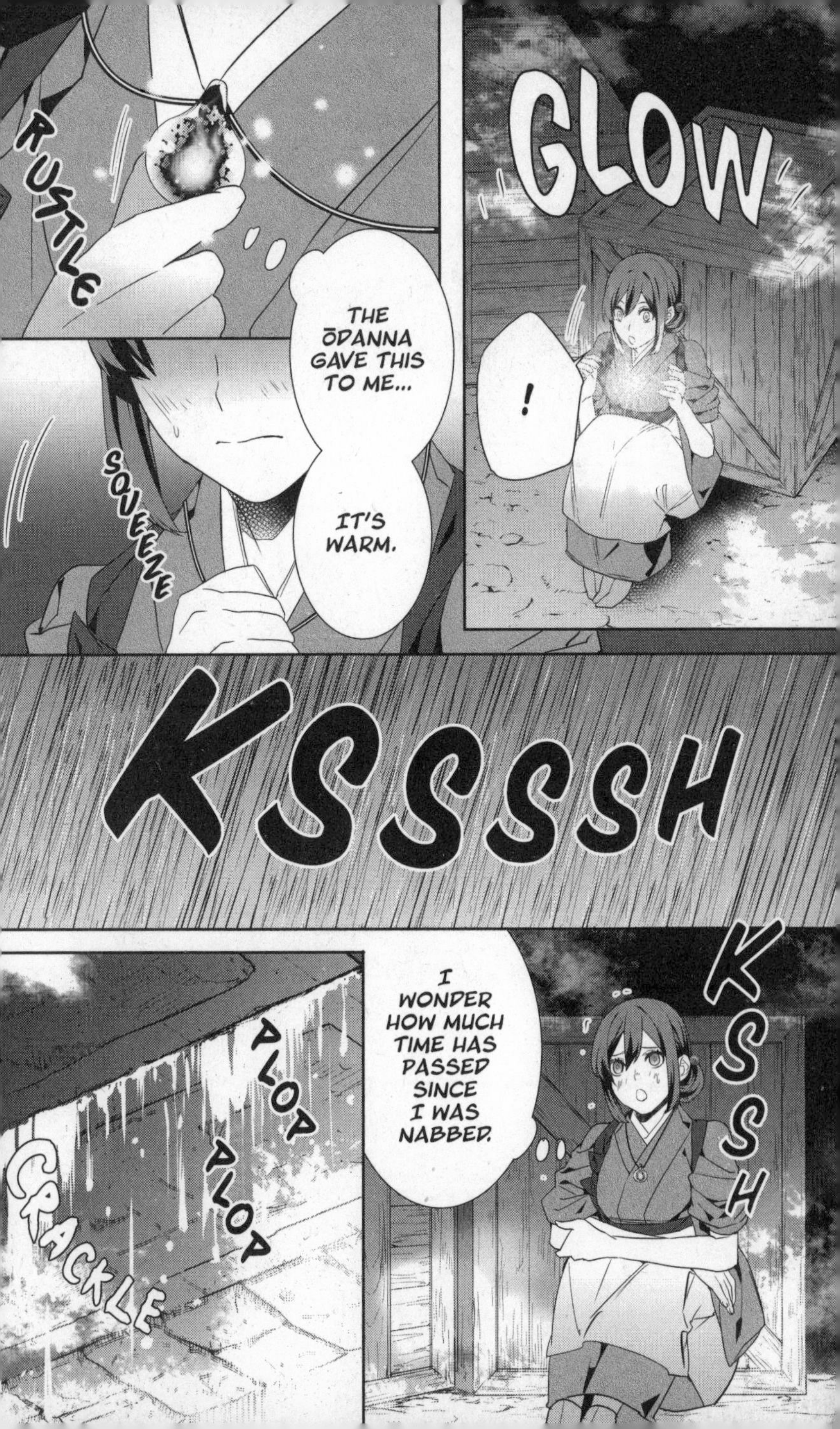
GLOW
!
RUSTLE
THE ŌDANNA GAVE THIS TO ME...
IT'S WARM.
SQUEEZE
KSSSSH
KSSSH
I WONDER HOW MUCH TIME HAS PASSED SINCE I WAS NABBED.
PLOP
PLOP
CRACKLE

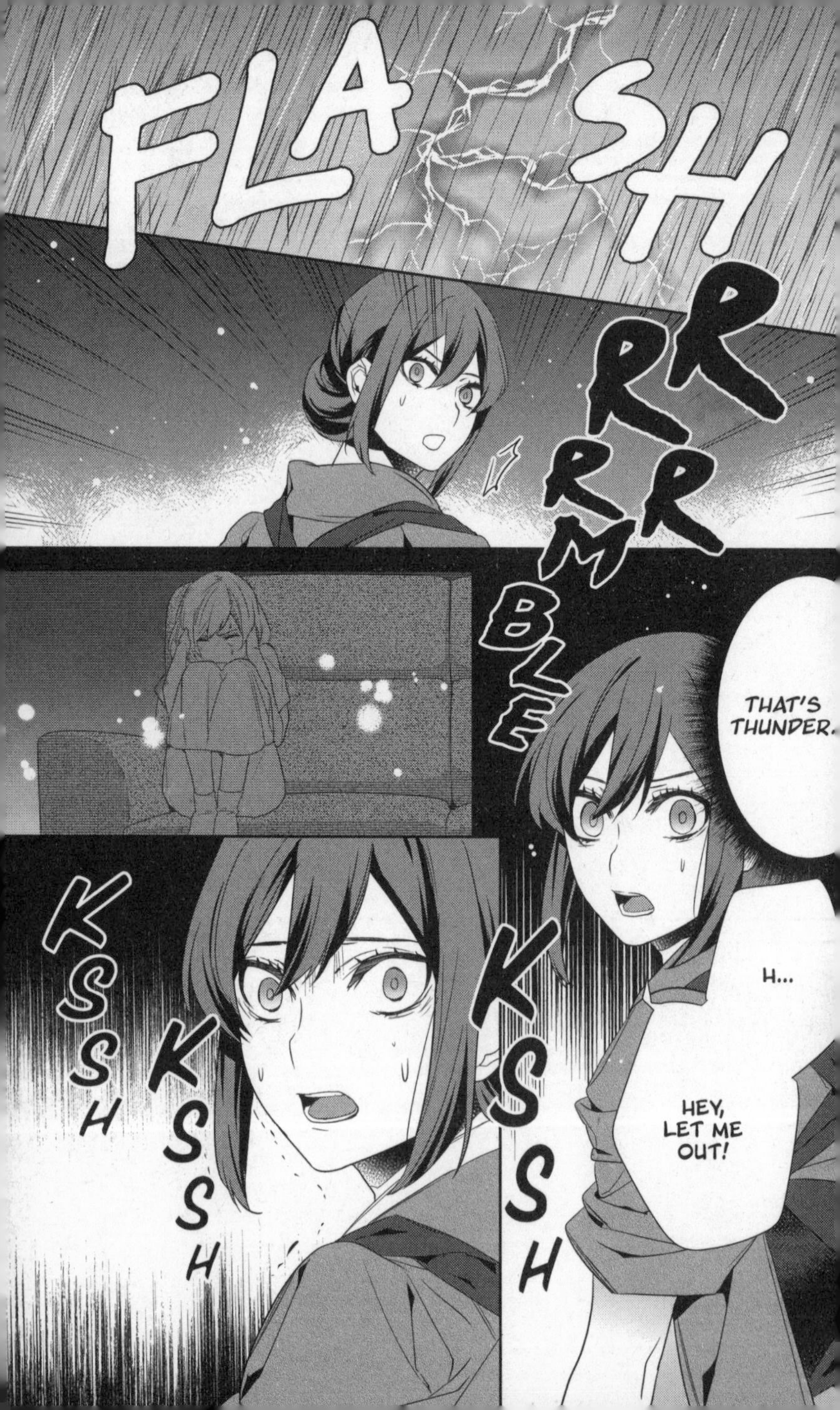
FLASH
RRRRMBLE
THAT'S THUNDER.
H...
HEY, LET ME OUT!
KSSH
KSSH
KSSH

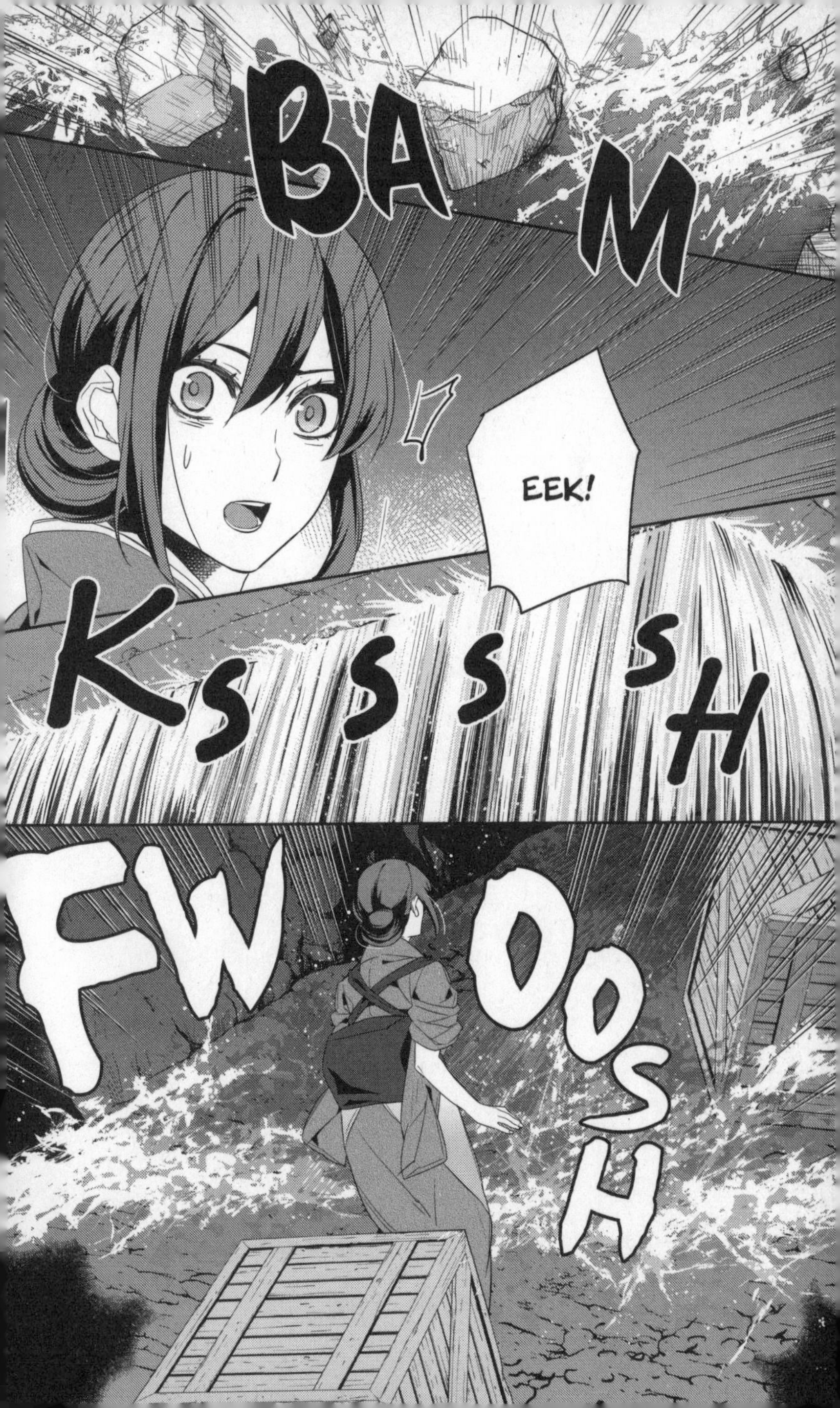
BAM
EEK!
KSSSSH
FWOOSH

Kakuriyo
Bed & Breakfast
for Spirits

Kakuriyo
Bed & Breakfast
for Spirits

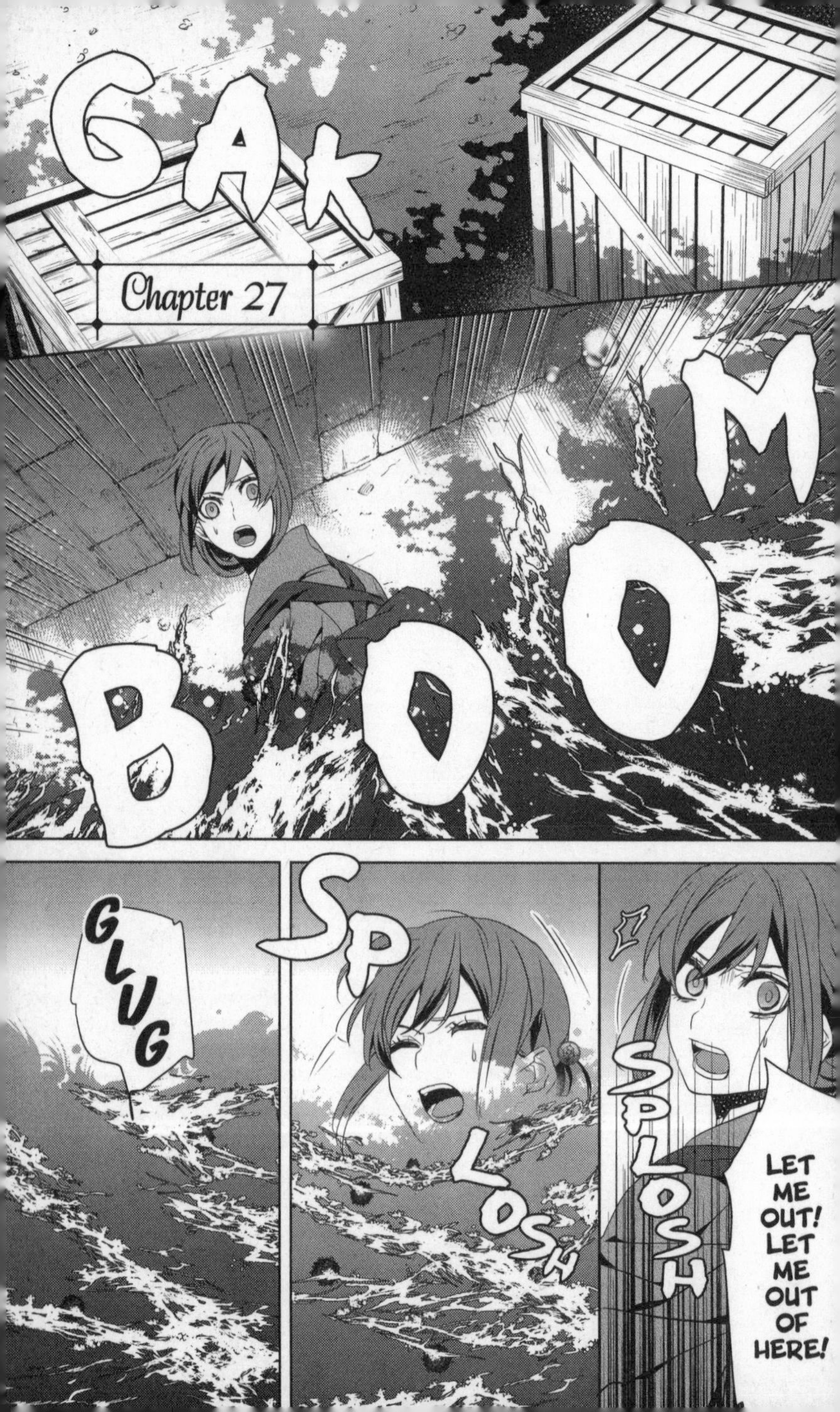
GAK
Chapter 27
BOOM
LET ME OUT! LET ME OUT OF HERE!
SPLOSH
SP
LOSH
GLUG

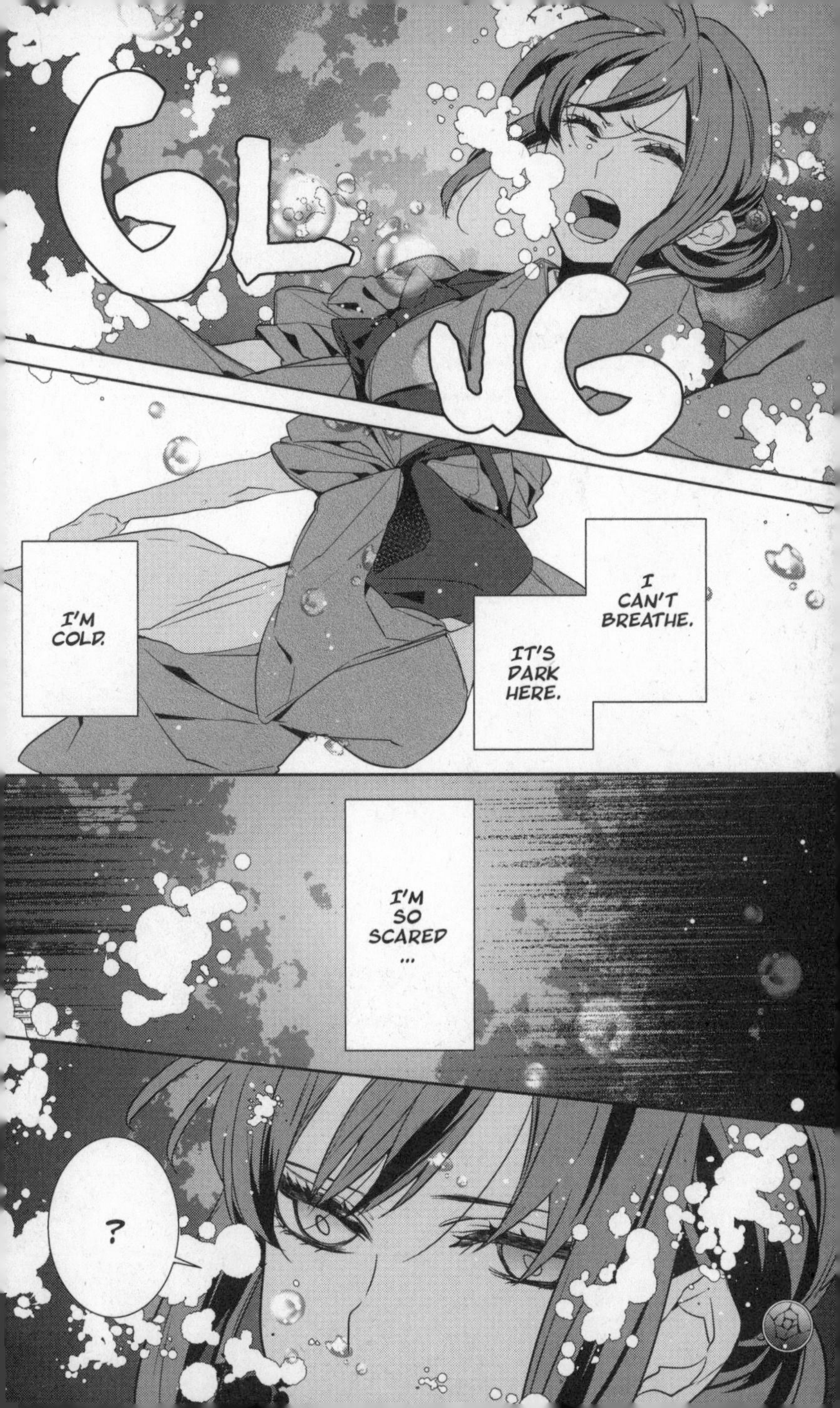
GLUG
I CAN'T BREATHE.
IT'S DARK HERE.
I'M COLD.
I'M SO SCARED ...
?

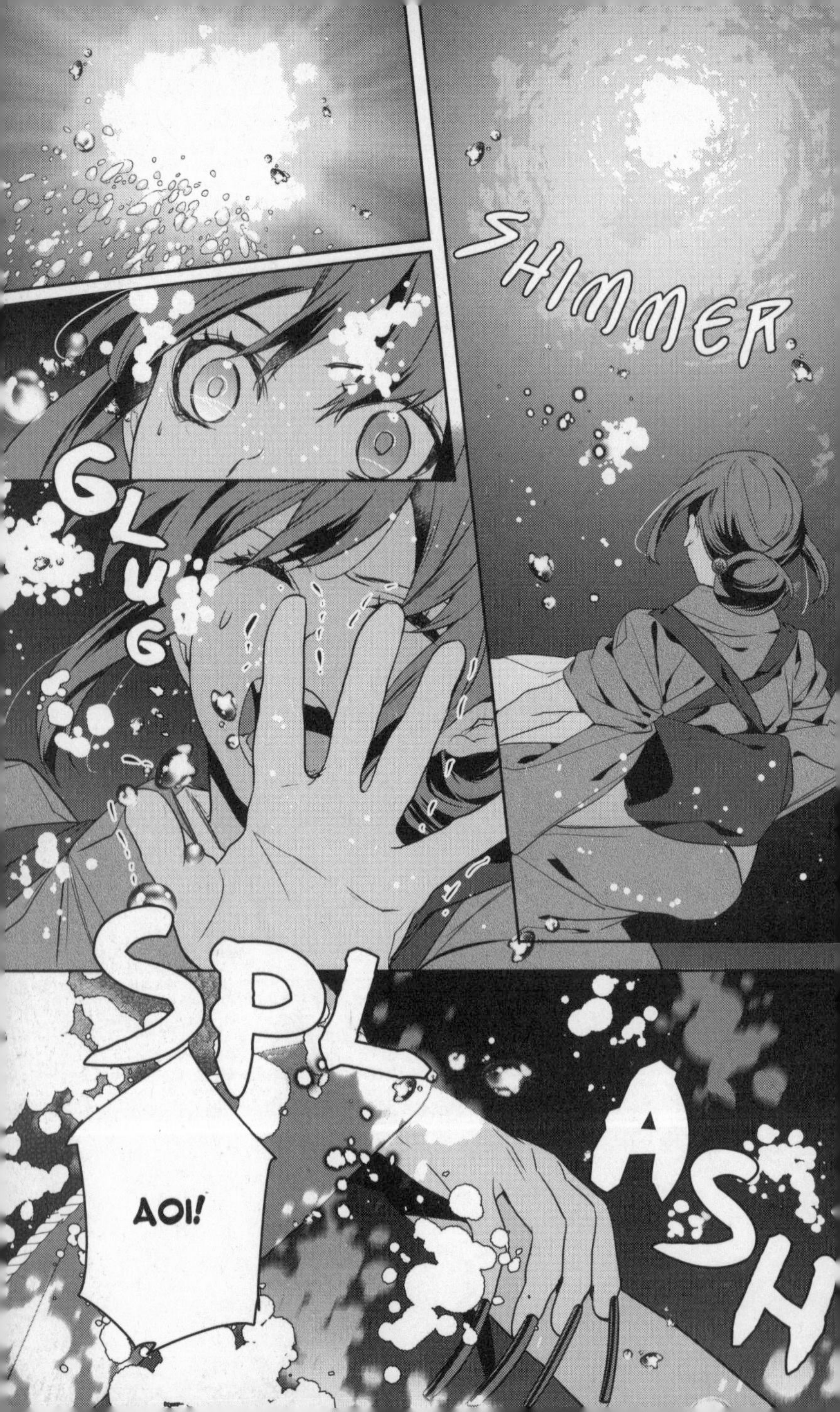
SHIMMER
GLUG
SPLASH
AOI!

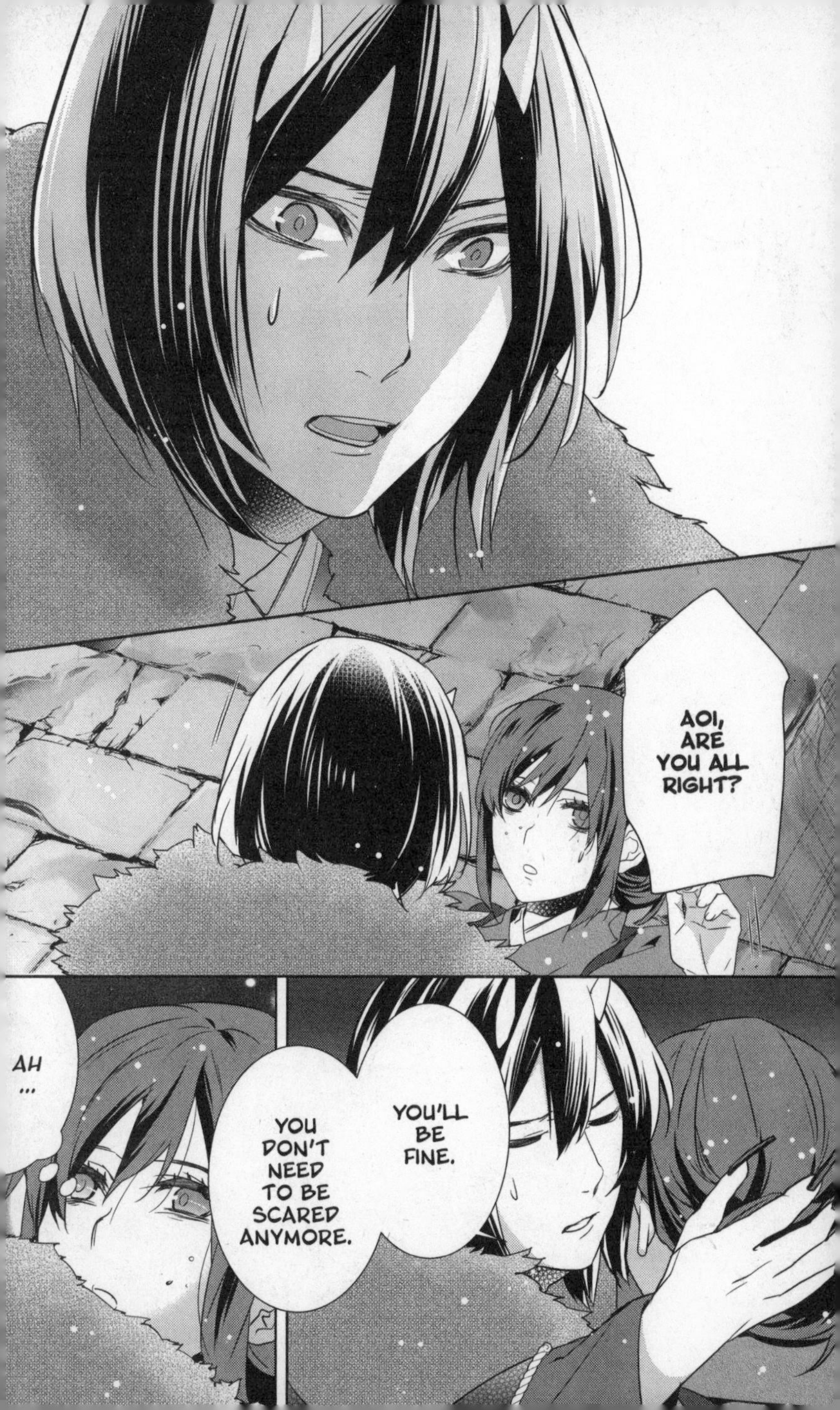
AOI, ARE YOU ALL RIGHT?
YOU'LL BE FINE.
YOU DON'T NEED TO BE SCARED ANYMORE.
AH ...

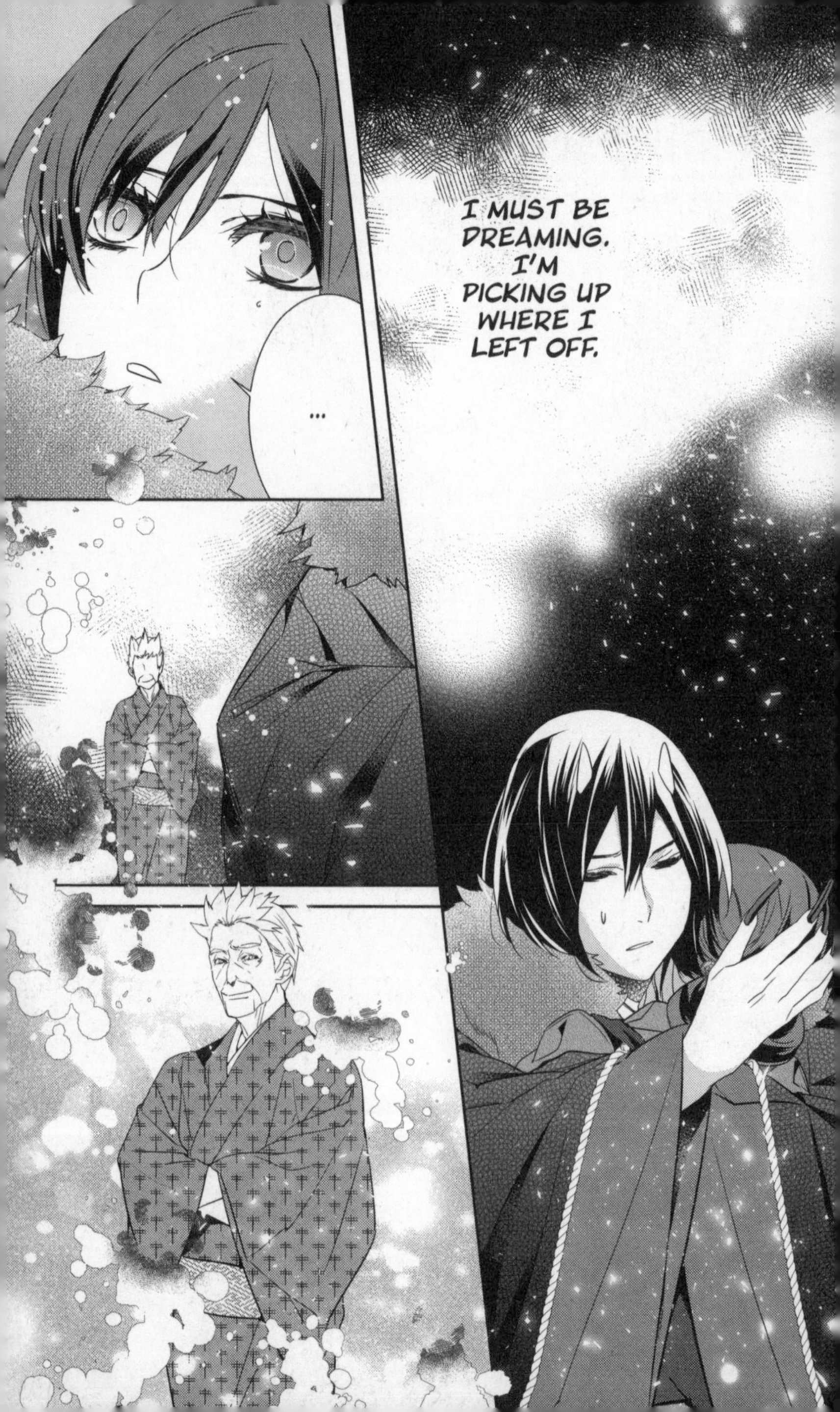
I MUST BE DREAMING. I'M PICKING UP WHERE I LEFT OFF.
...

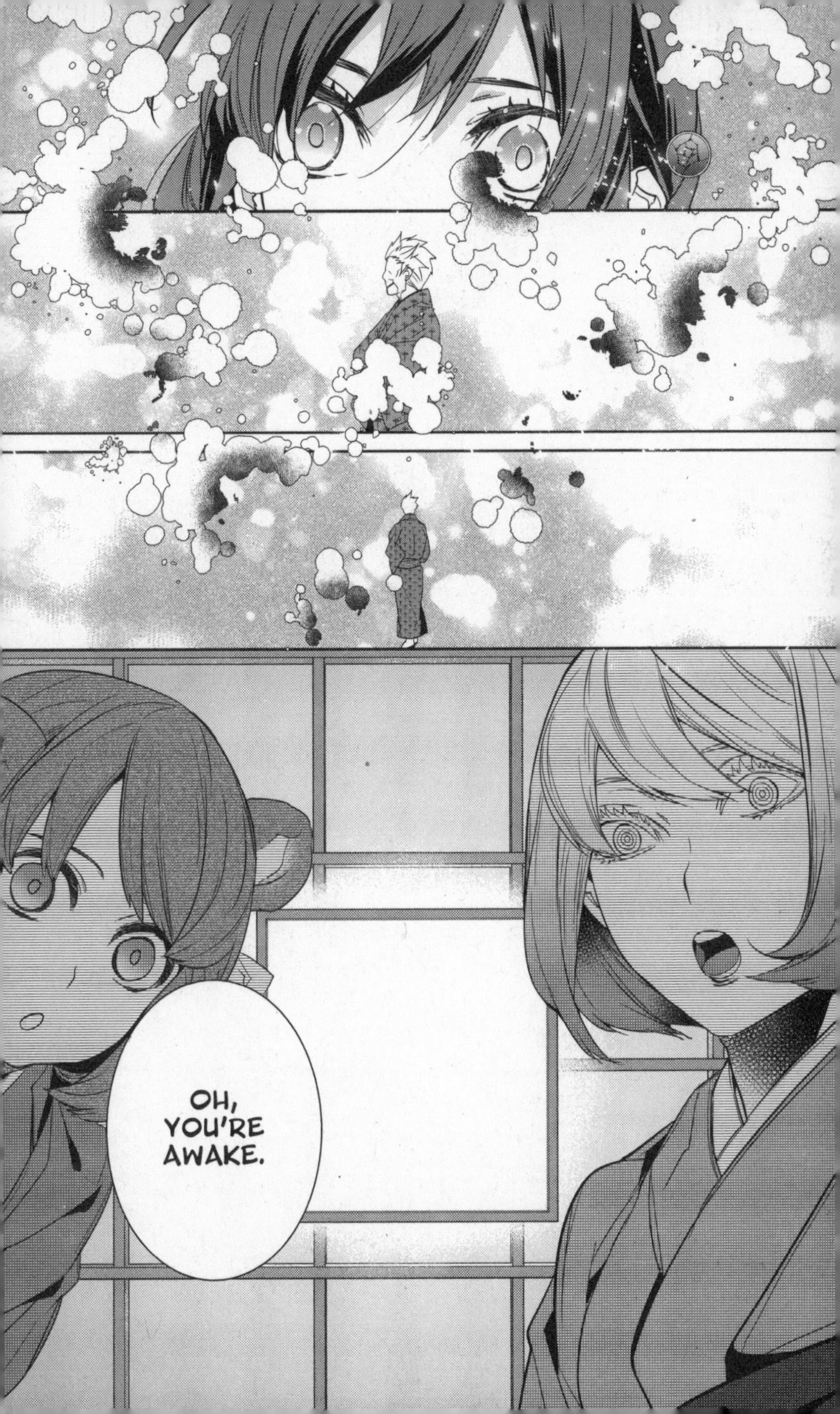
OH, YOU'RE AWAKE.

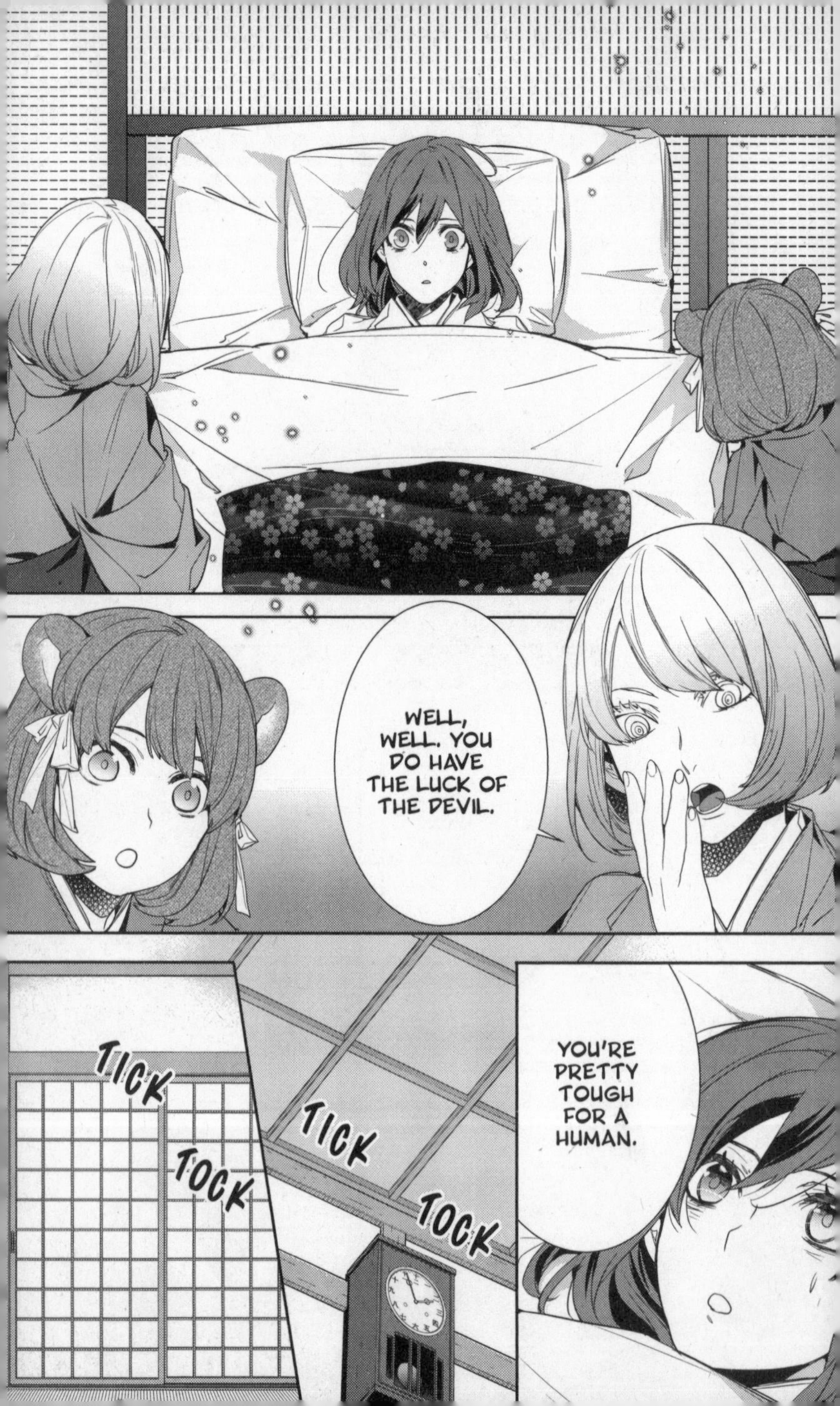
WELL, WELL. YOU DO HAVE THE LUCK OF THE DEVIL.
YOU'RE PRETTY TOUGH FOR A HUMAN.
TICK
TOCK
TICK
TOCK

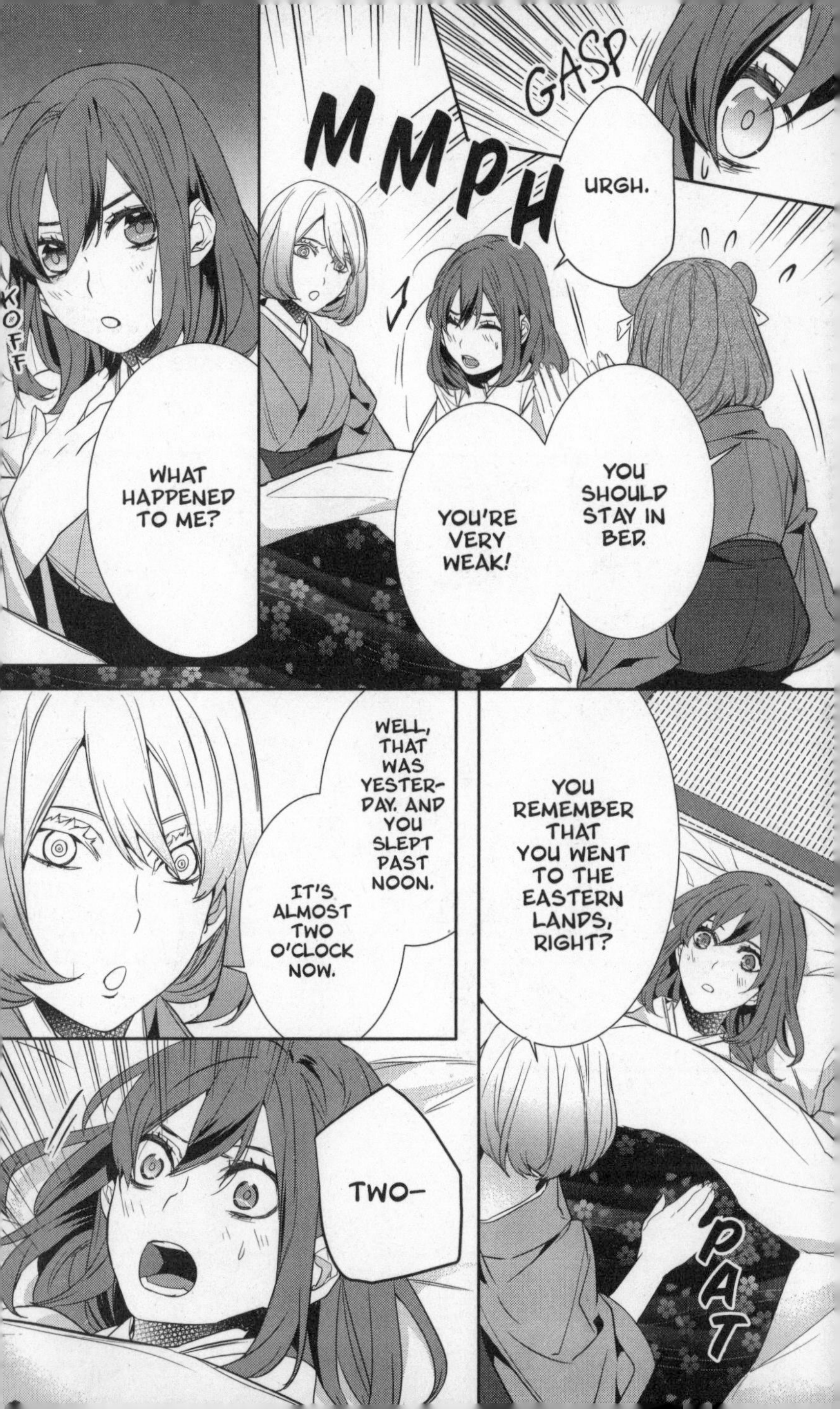
GASP
MMPH
URGH.
YOU SHOULD STAY IN BED.
YOU'RE VERY WEAK!
KOFF
WHAT HAPPENED TO ME?
YOU REMEMBER THAT YOU WENT TO THE EASTERN LANDS, RIGHT?
WELL, THAT WAS YESTER-DAY. AND YOU SLEPT PAST NOON.
IT'S ALMOST TWO O'CLOCK NOW.
PAT
TWO-

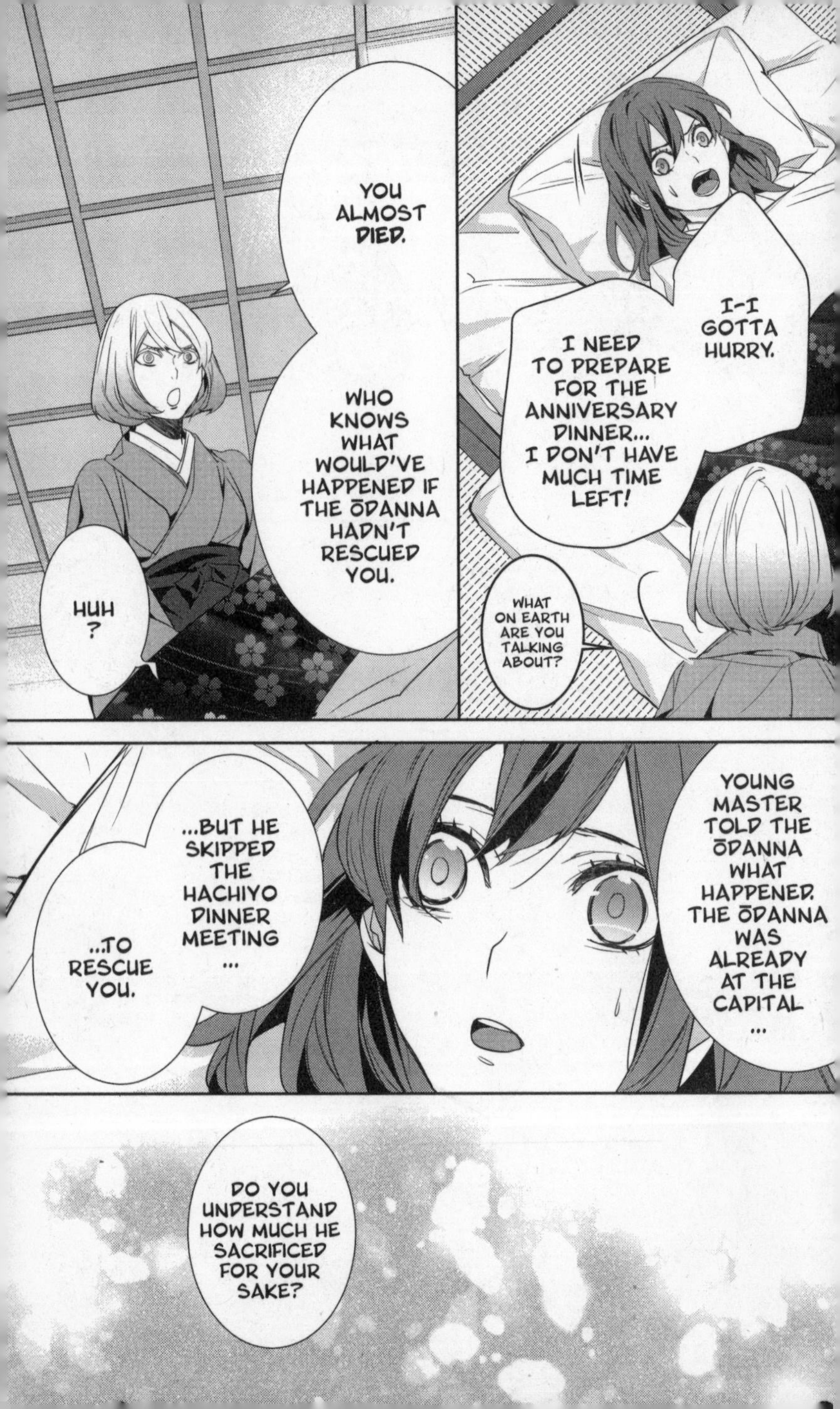
I-I GOTTA HURRY.
I NEED TO PREPARE FOR THE ANNIVERSARY DINNER... I DON'T HAVE MUCH TIME LEFT!
WHAT ON EARTH ARE YOU TALKING ABOUT?
YOU ALMOST DIED.
WHO KNOWS WHAT WOULD'VE HAPPENED IF THE ŌDANNA HADN'T RESCUED YOU.
HUH?
YOUNG MASTER TOLD THE ŌDANNA WHAT HAPPENED. THE ŌDANNA WAS ALREADY AT THE CAPITAL...
...BUT HE SKIPPED THE HACHIYO DINNER MEETING...
...TO RESCUE YOU.
DO YOU UNDERSTAND HOW MUCH HE SACRIFICED FOR YOUR SAKE?

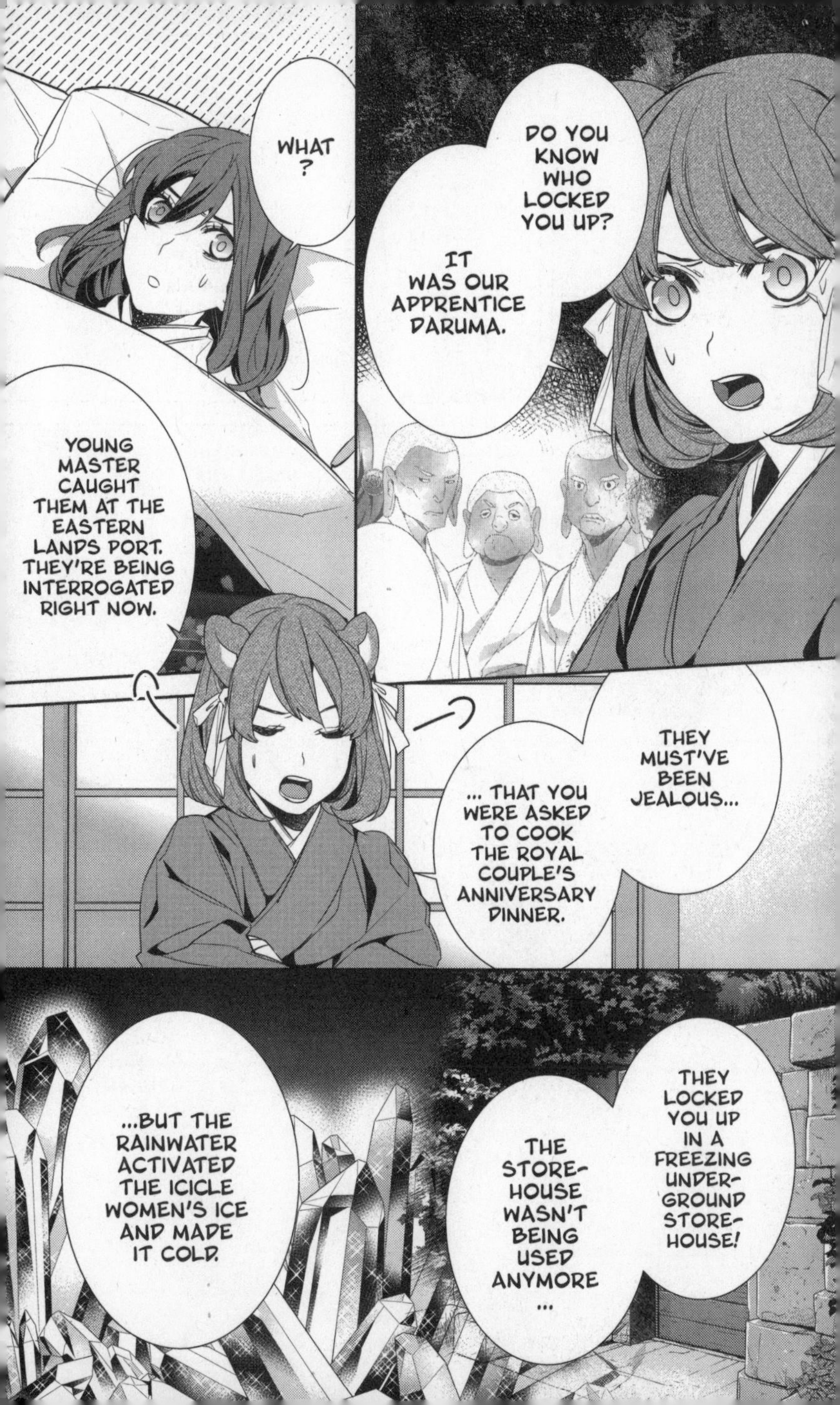
DO YOU KNOW WHO LOCKED YOU UP?
IT WAS OUR APPRENTICE DARUMA.
WHAT?
YOUNG MASTER CAUGHT THEM AT THE EASTERN LANDS PORT. THEY'RE BEING INTERROGATED RIGHT NOW.
THEY MUST'VE BEEN JEALOUS...
... THAT YOU WERE ASKED TO COOK THE ROYAL COUPLE'S ANNIVERSARY DINNER.
THEY LOCKED YOU UP IN A FREEZING UNDER-GROUND STORE-HOUSE!
THE STORE-HOUSE WASN'T BEING USED ANYMORE ...
...BUT THE RAINWATER ACTIVATED THE ICICLE WOMEN'S ICE AND MADE IT COLD.

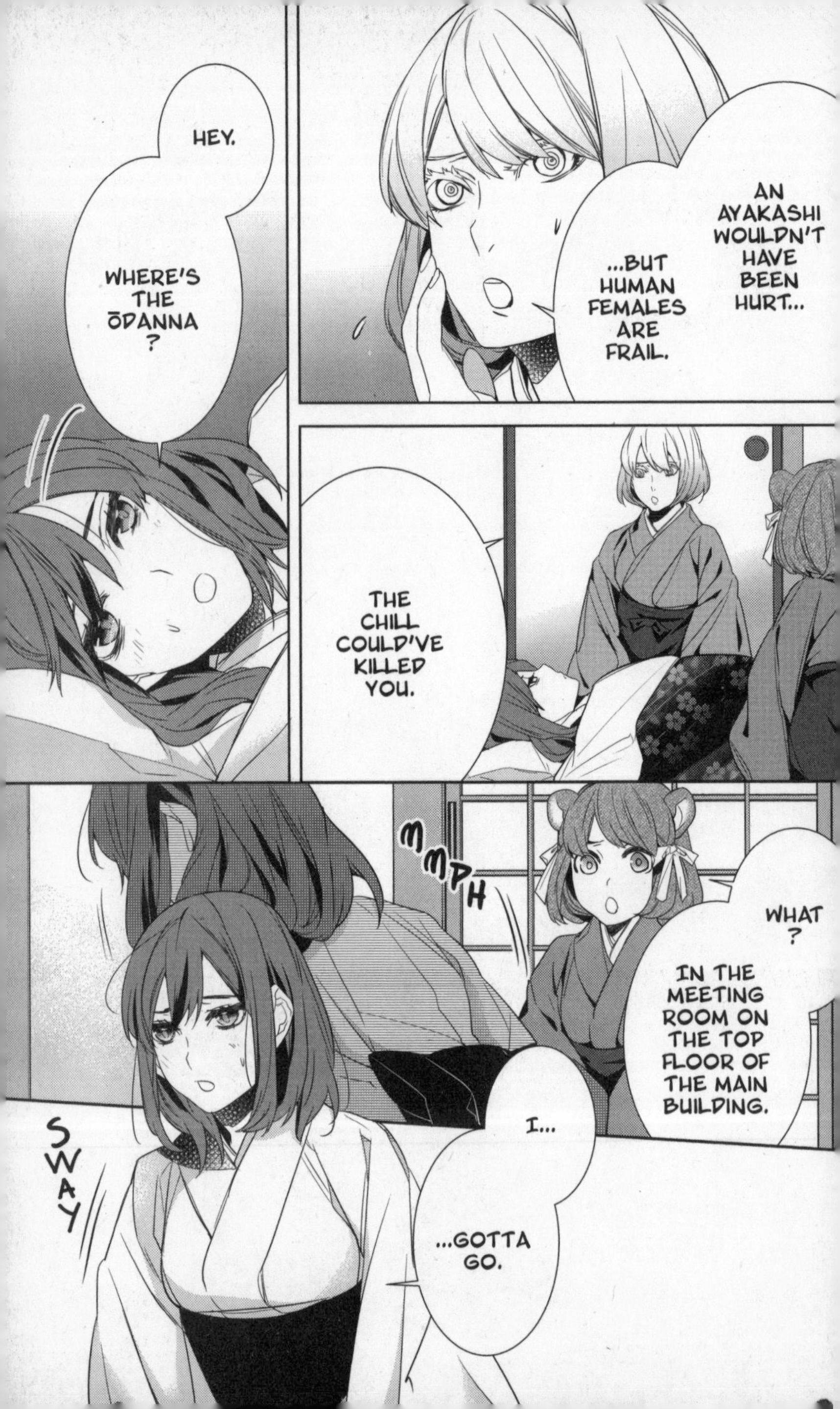
AN AYAKASHI WOULDN'T HAVE BEEN HURT...
...BUT HUMAN FEMALES ARE FRAIL.
THE CHILL COULD'VE KILLED YOU.
HEY.
WHERE'S THE ŌDANNA?
WHAT?
MMMPH
IN THE MEETING ROOM ON THE TOP FLOOR OF THE MAIN BUILDING.
I...
SWAY
...GOTTA GO.

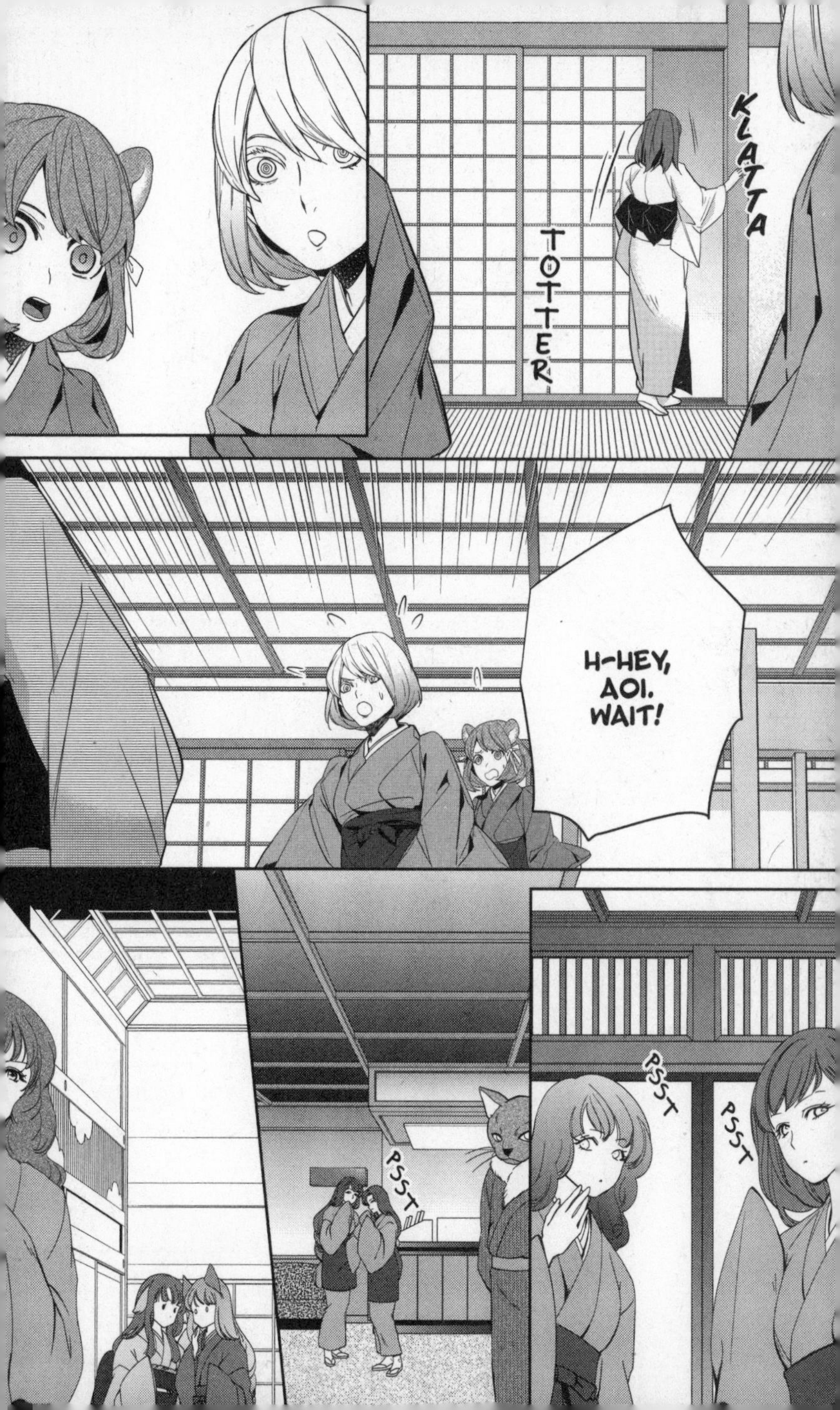
KLATTA
TOTTER
H-HEY, AOI. WAIT!
PSST
PSST
PSST

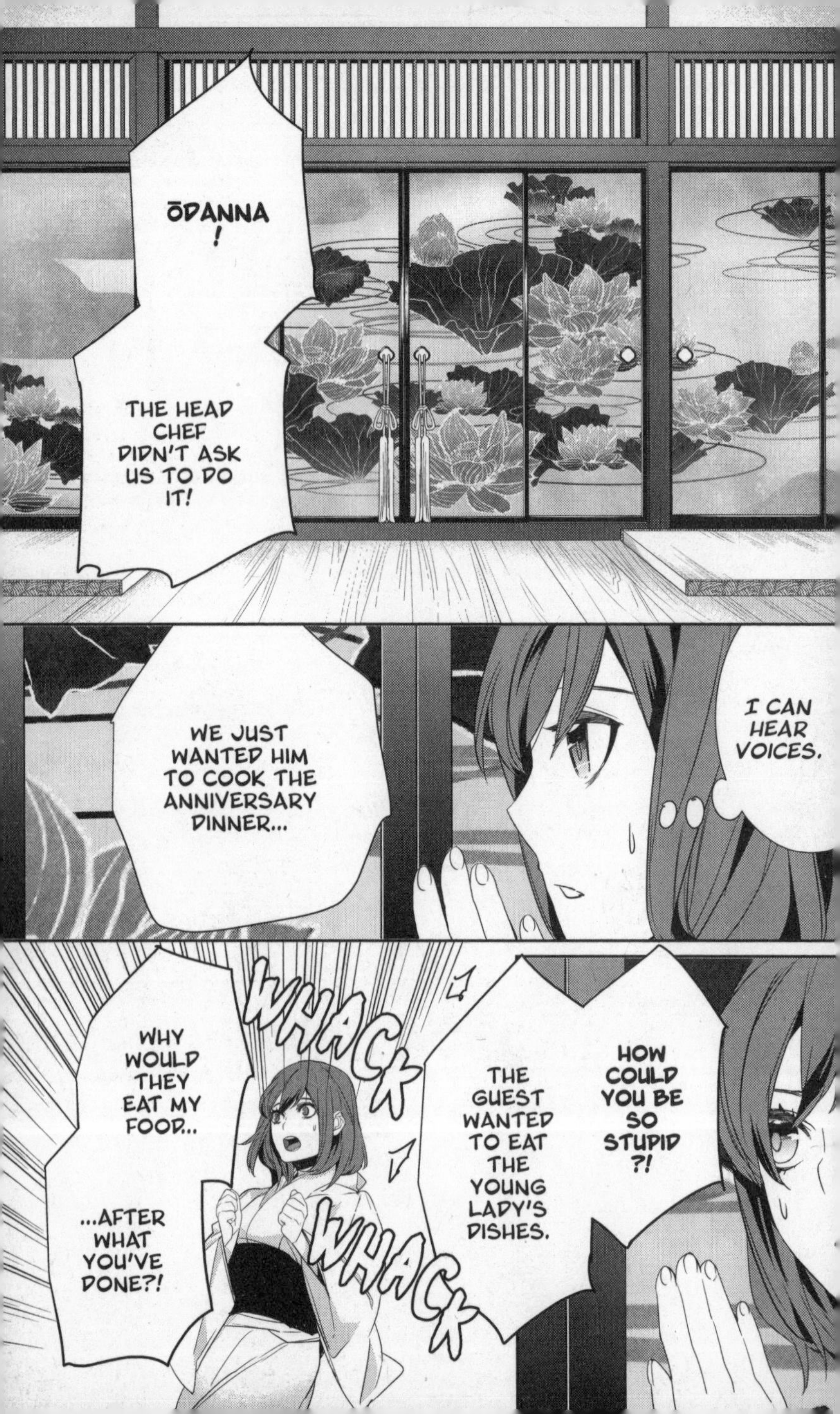
ŌDANNA!
THE HEAD CHEF DIDN'T ASK US TO DO IT!
I CAN HEAR VOICES.
WE JUST WANTED HIM TO COOK THE ANNIVERSARY DINNER...
HOW COULD YOU BE SO STUPID?!
THE GUEST WANTED TO EAT THE YOUNG LADY'S DISHES.
WHACK
WHACK
WHY WOULD THEY EAT MY FOOD...
...AFTER WHAT YOU'VE DONE?!

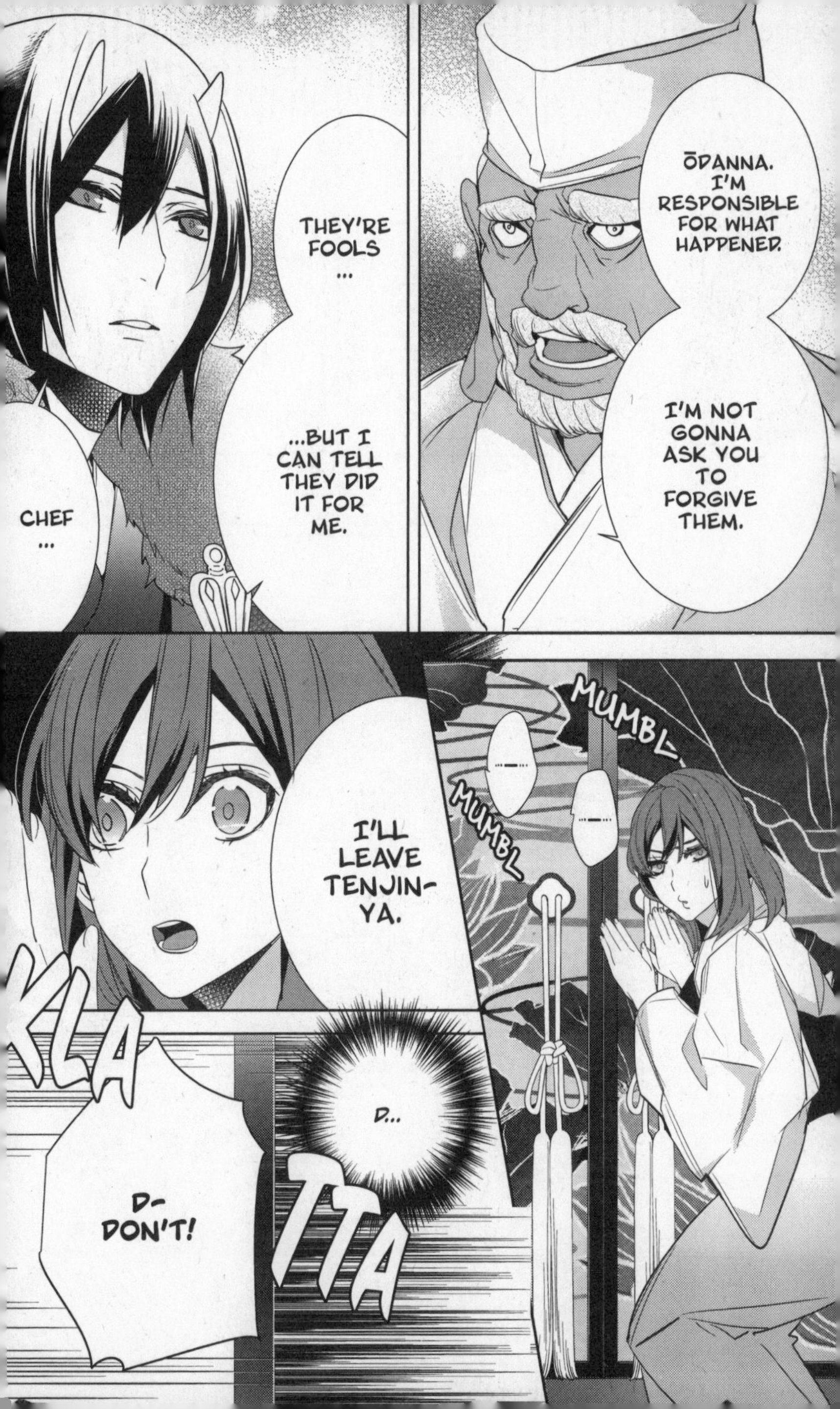
ŌDANNA. I'M RESPONSIBLE FOR WHAT HAPPENED.
I'M NOT GONNA ASK YOU TO FORGIVE THEM.
THEY'RE FOOLS ...
...BUT I CAN TELL THEY DID IT FOR ME.
CHEF ...
MUMBL
MUMBL
...—...
...—...
I'LL LEAVE TENJIN-YA.
KLA
TTA
D...
D- DON'T!

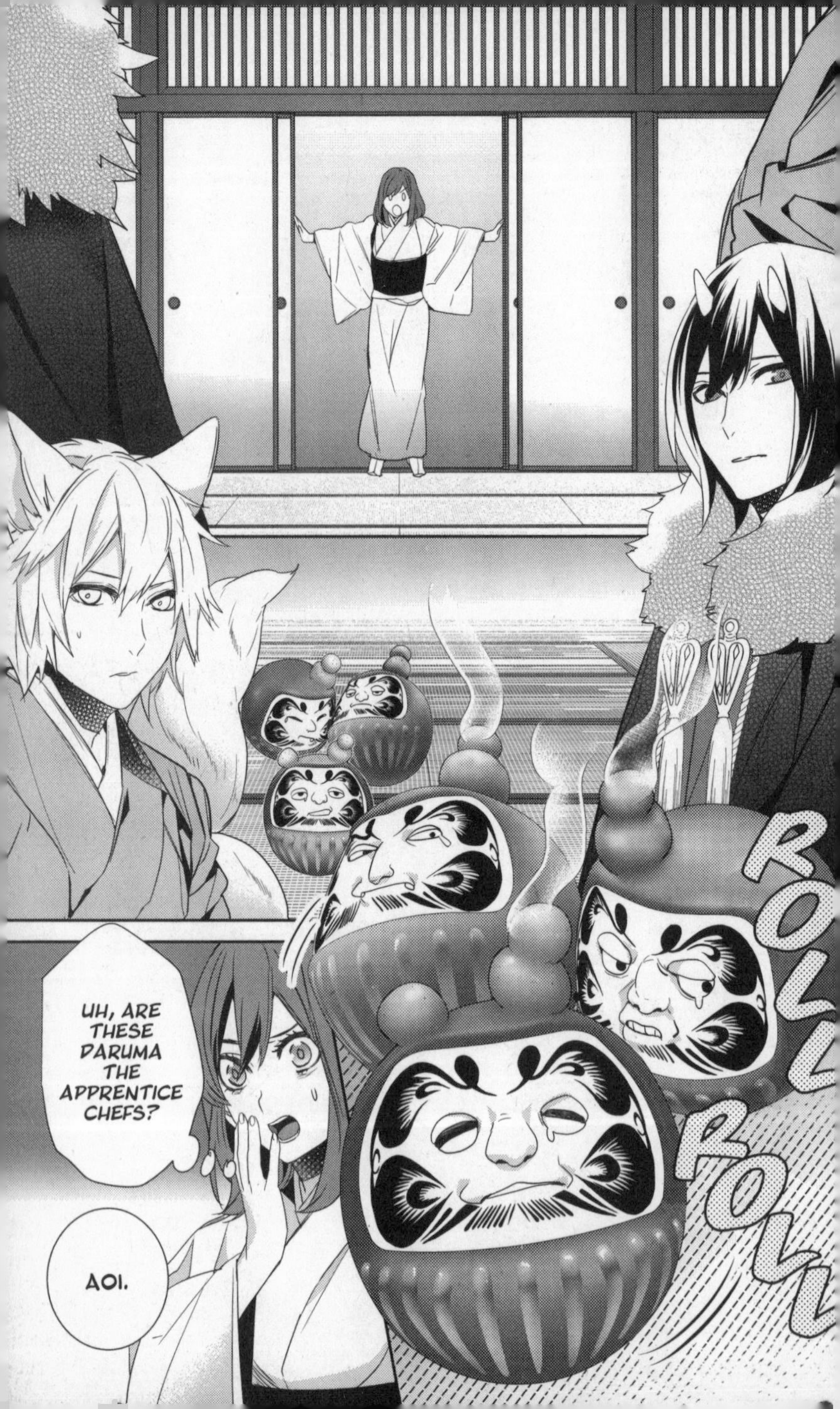
ROLL ROLL
UH, ARE THESE DARUMA THE APPRENTICE CHEFS?
AOI.

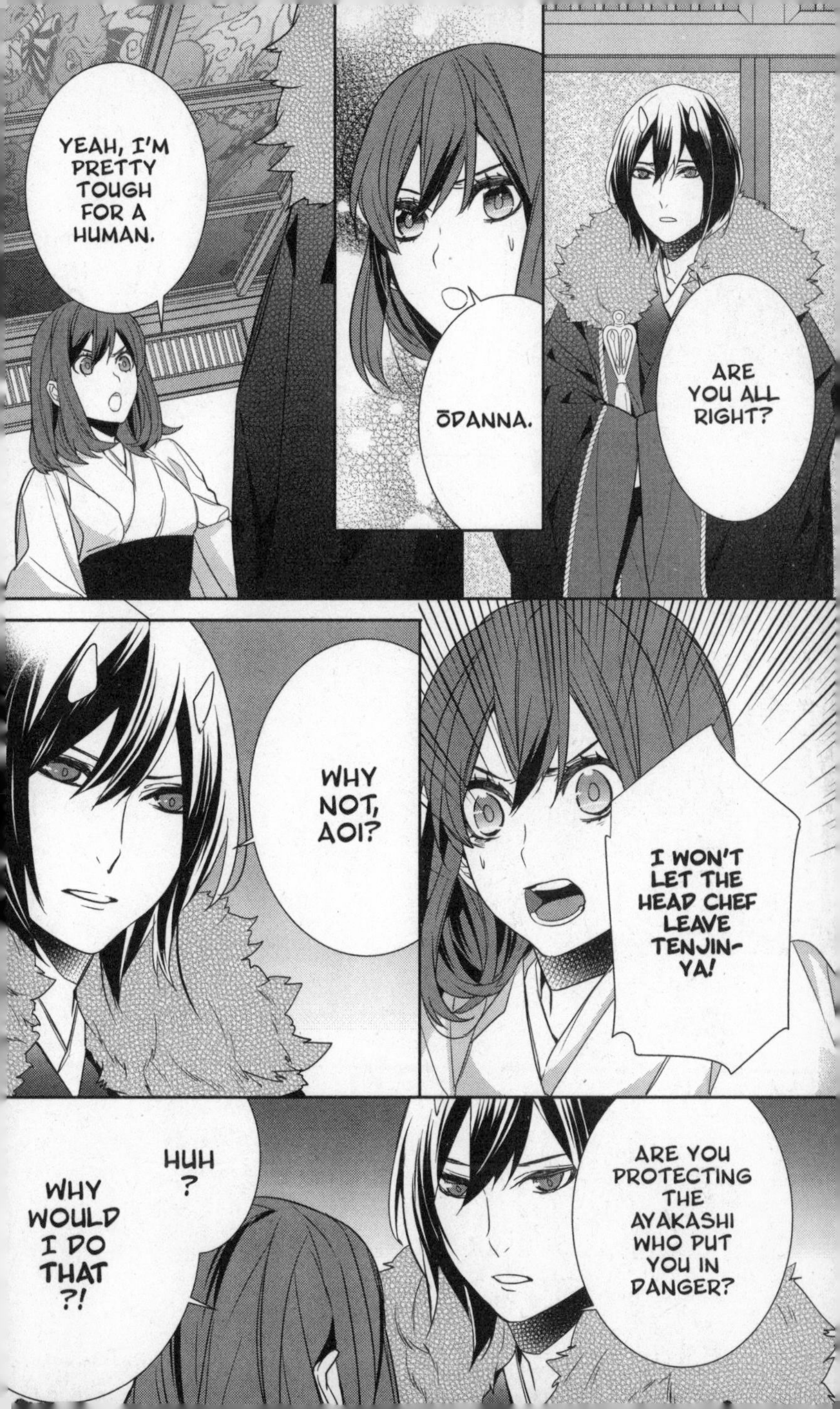
ARE YOU ALL RIGHT?
ŌDANNA.
YEAH, I'M PRETTY TOUGH FOR A HUMAN.
I WON'T LET THE HEAD CHEF LEAVE TENJIN-YA!
WHY NOT, AOI?
ARE YOU PROTECTING THE AYAKASHI WHO PUT YOU IN DANGER?
HUH?
WHY WOULD I DO THAT?!

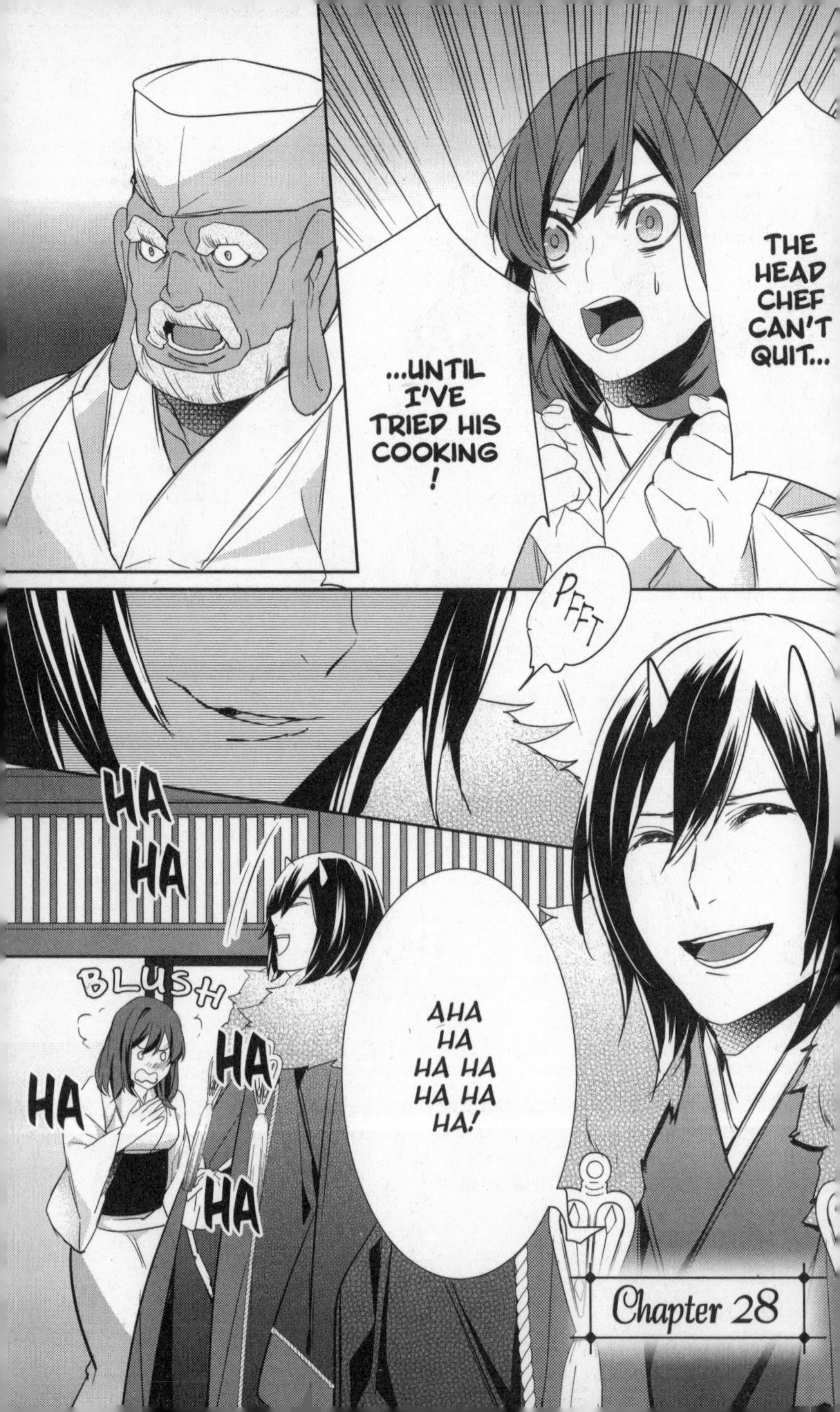
THE HEAD CHEF CAN'T QUIT...
...UNTIL I'VE TRIED HIS COOKING!
PFFT
AHA HA HA HA HA HA HA!
HA HA
BLUSH
HA
HA
HA
Chapter 28

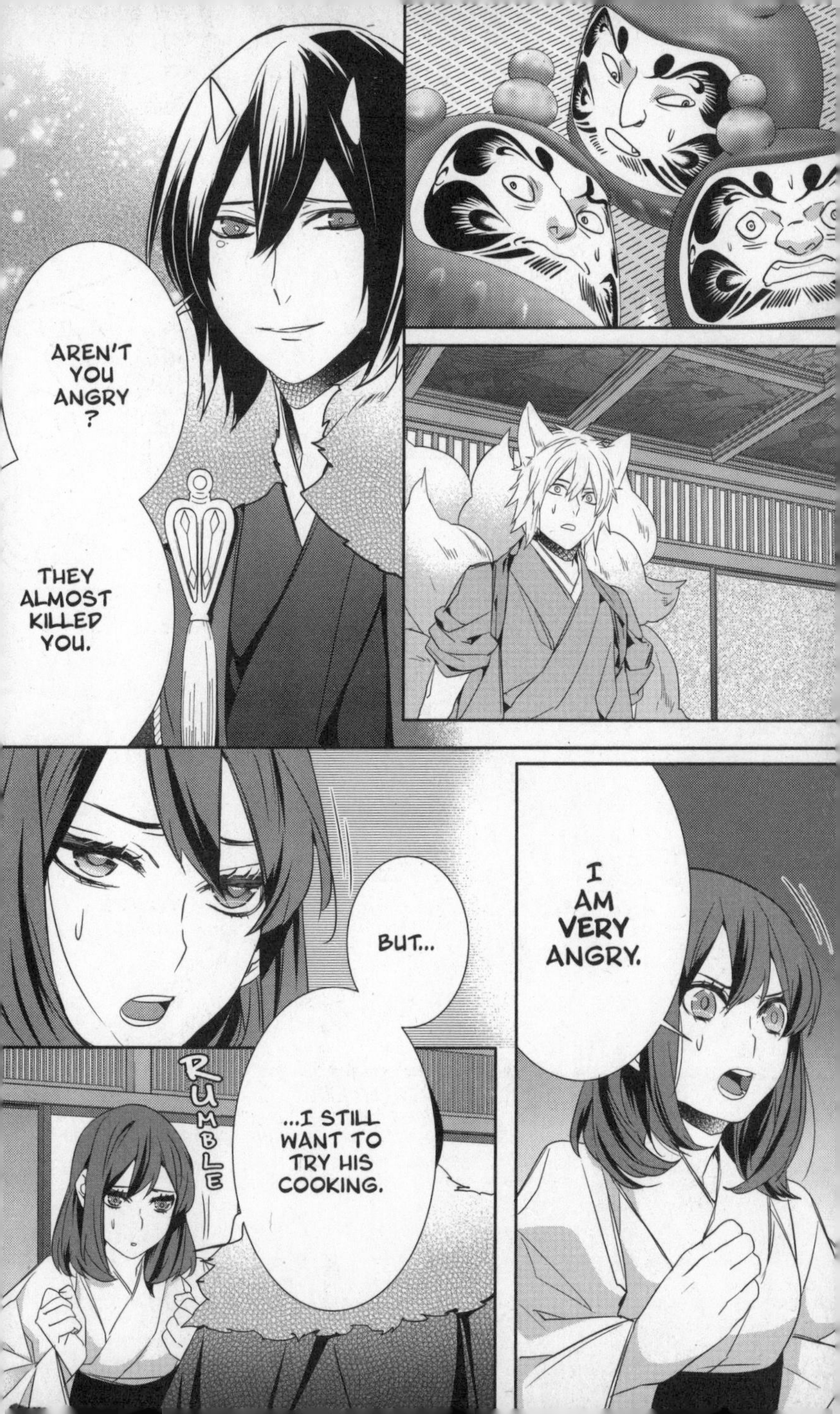
AREN'T YOU ANGRY?
THEY ALMOST KILLED YOU.
I AM VERY ANGRY.
BUT...
RUMBLE
...I STILL WANT TO TRY HIS COOKING.

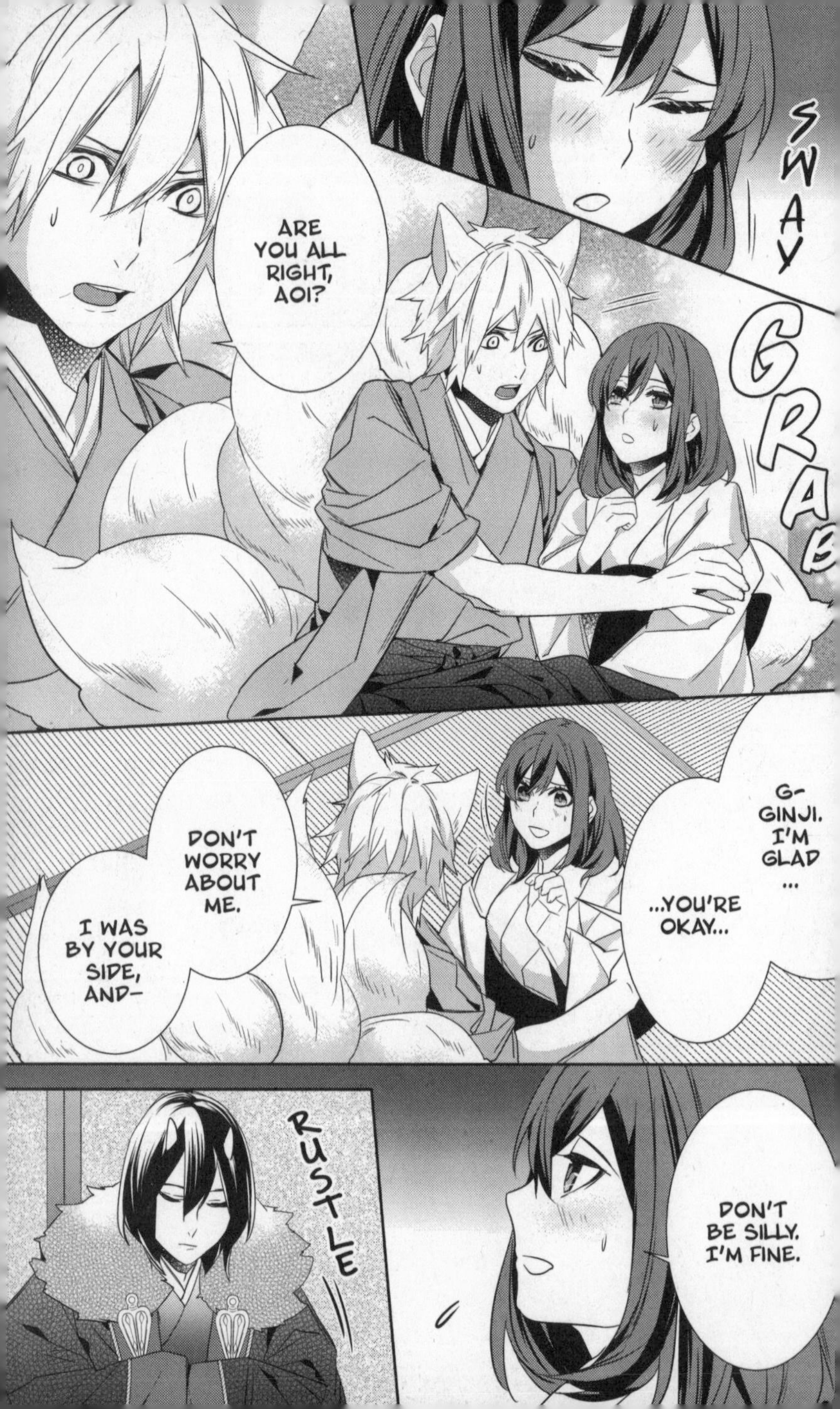
SWAY
GRAB
ARE YOU ALL RIGHT, AOI?
G-GINJI. I'M GLAD ...
...YOU'RE OKAY...
DON'T WORRY ABOUT ME.
I WAS BY YOUR SIDE, AND–
DON'T BE SILLY. I'M FINE.
RUSTLE

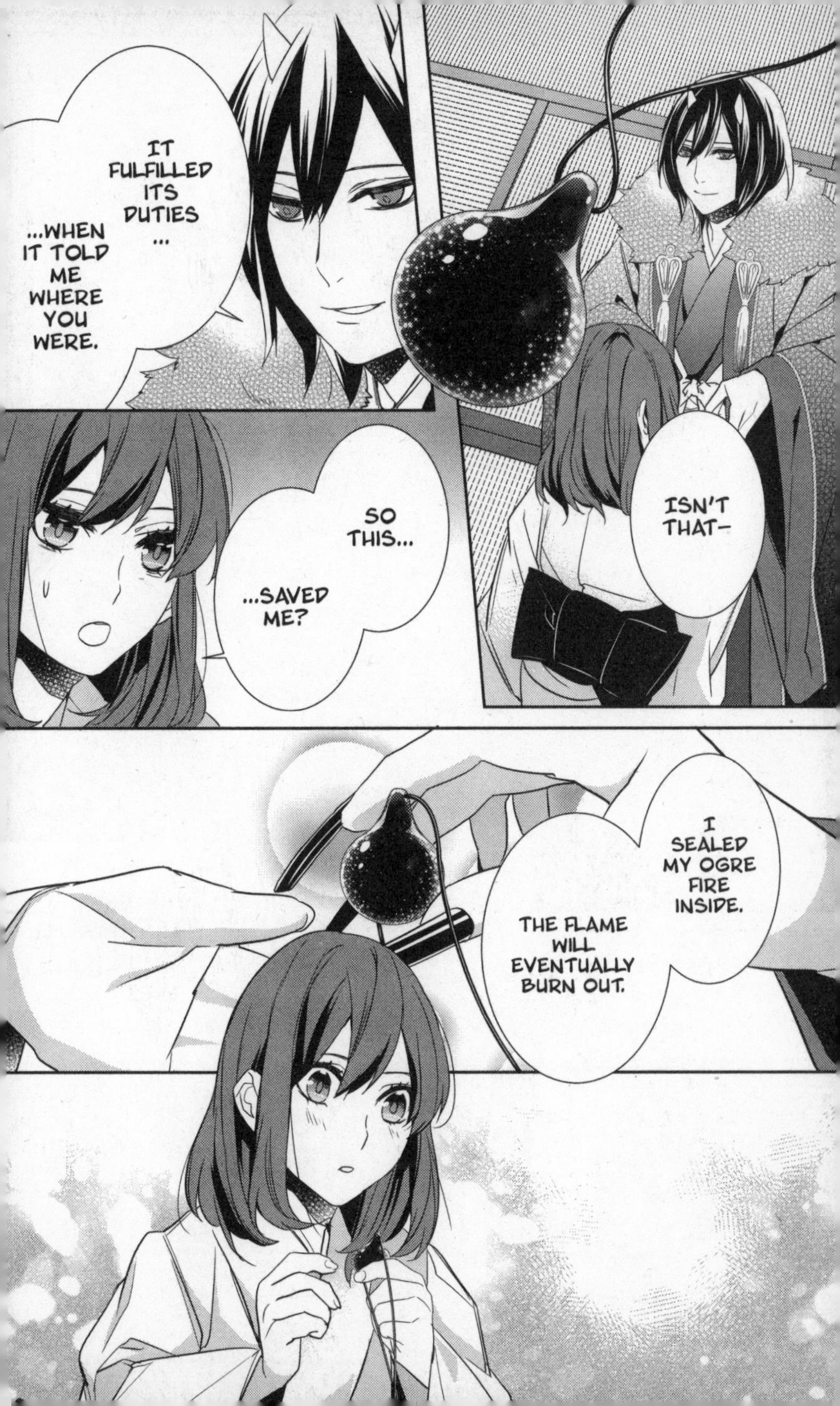
ISN'T THAT–
IT FULFILLED ITS DUTIES...
...WHEN IT TOLD ME WHERE YOU WERE.
SO THIS...
...SAVED ME?
I SEALED MY OGRE FIRE INSIDE.
THE FLAME WILL EVENTUALLY BURN OUT.

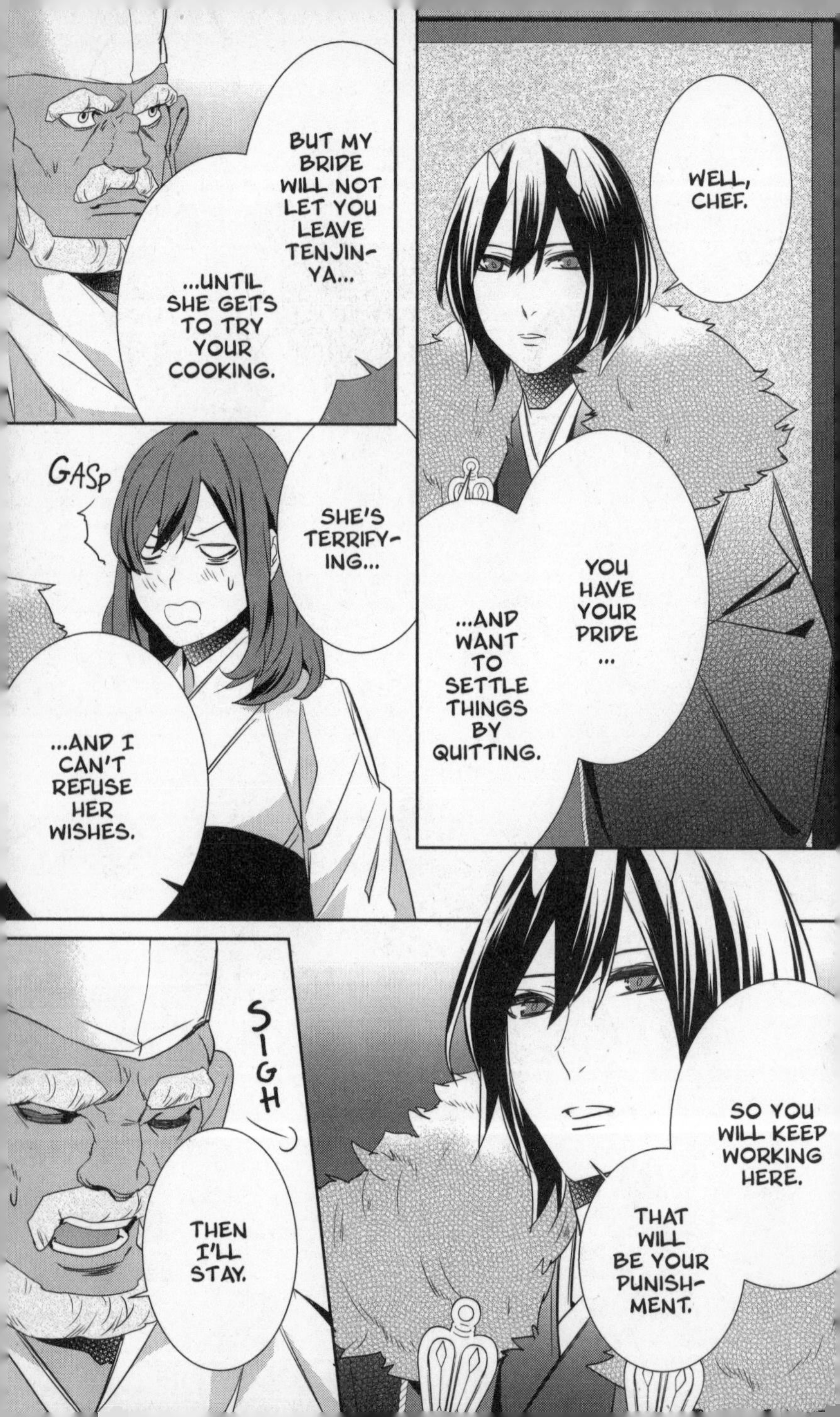
WELL, CHEF.
YOU HAVE YOUR PRIDE...
...AND WANT TO SETTLE THINGS BY QUITTING.
BUT MY BRIDE WILL NOT LET YOU LEAVE TENJIN-YA...
...UNTIL SHE GETS TO TRY YOUR COOKING.
GASP
SHE'S TERRIFY-ING...
...AND I CAN'T REFUSE HER WISHES.
SO YOU WILL KEEP WORKING HERE.
THAT WILL BE YOUR PUNISH-MENT.
SIGH
THEN I'LL STAY.

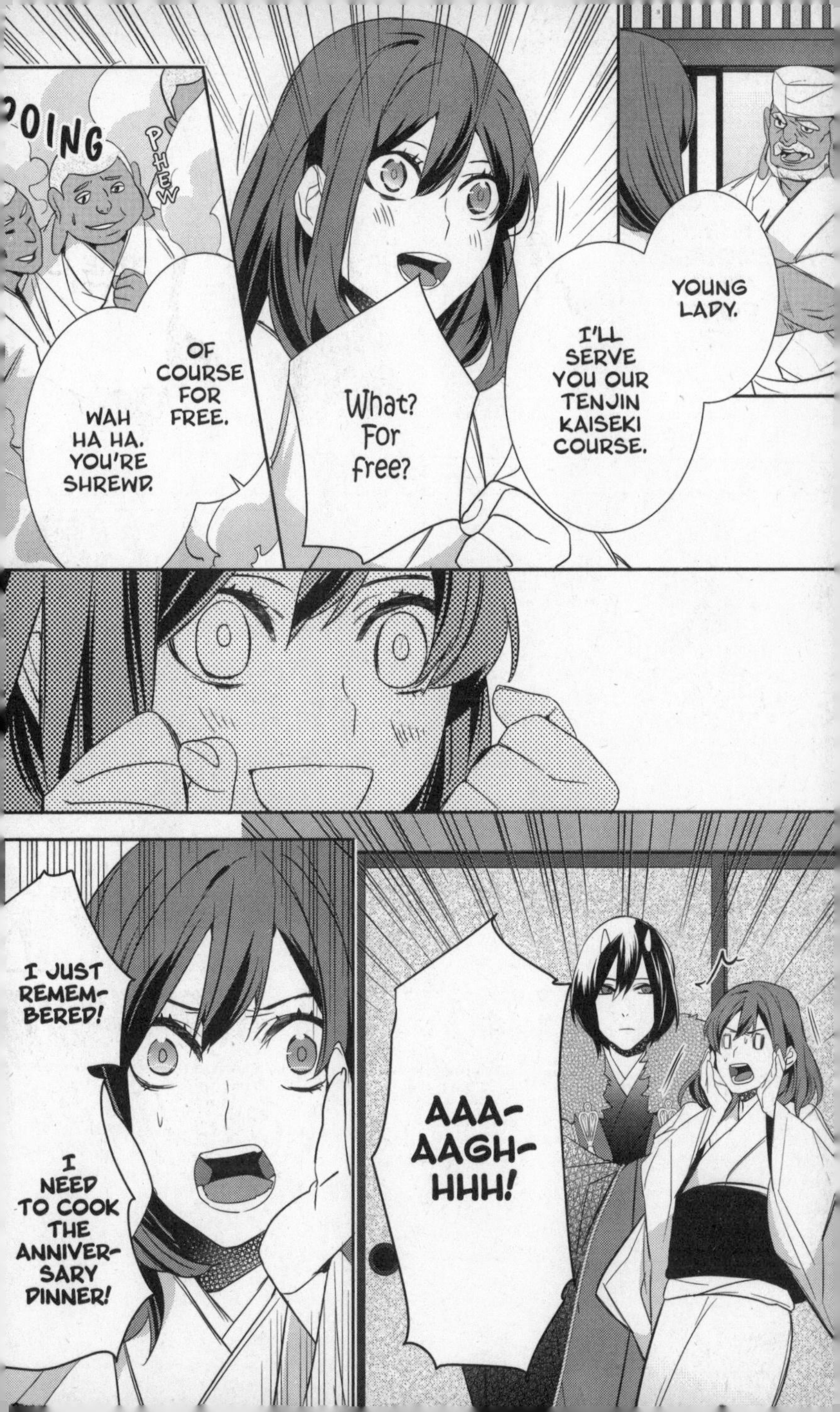
YOUNG LADY.
I'LL SERVE YOU OUR TENJIN KAISEKI COURSE.
What? For free?
PHEW
OING
OF COURSE FOR FREE.
WAH HA HA. YOU'RE SHREWD.
AAA-AAGH-HHH!
I JUST REMEM-BERED!
I NEED TO COOK THE ANNIVER-SARY DINNER!

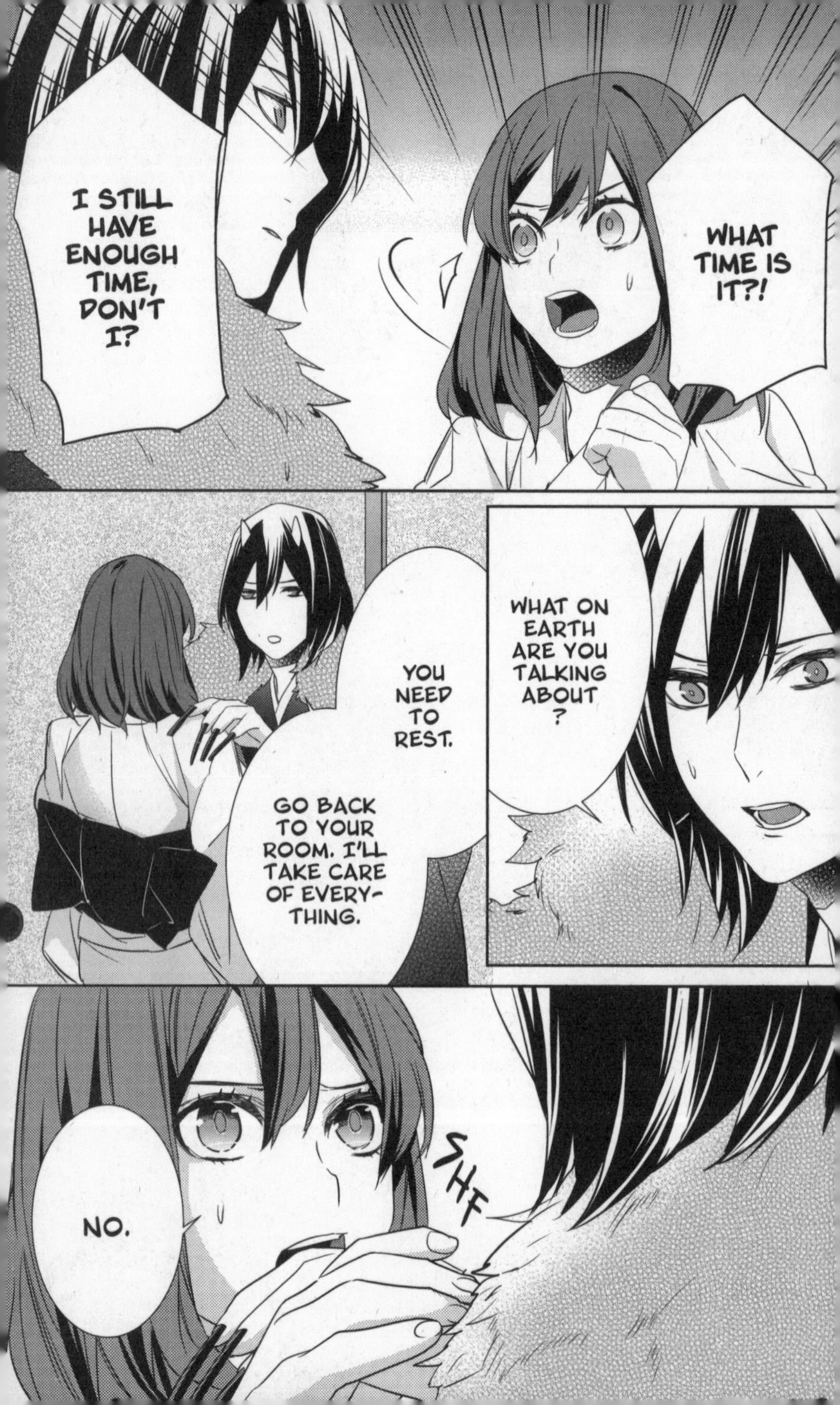
WHAT TIME IS IT?!
I STILL HAVE ENOUGH TIME, DON'T I?
WHAT ON EARTH ARE YOU TALKING ABOUT?
YOU NEED TO REST.
GO BACK TO YOUR ROOM. I'LL TAKE CARE OF EVERY-THING.
SHF
NO.

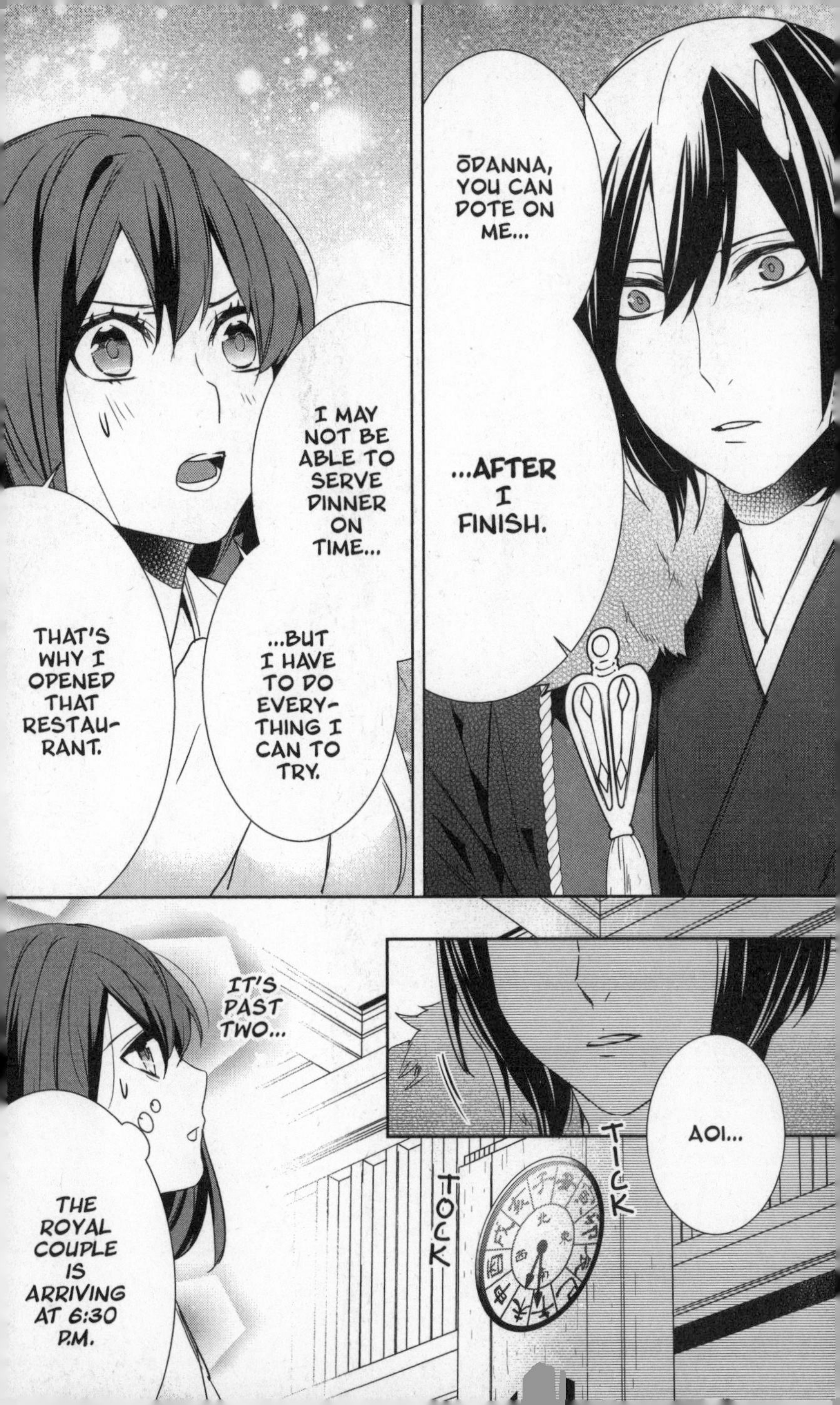
ŌDANNA, YOU CAN DOTE ON ME...
...AFTER I FINISH.
I MAY NOT BE ABLE TO SERVE DINNER ON TIME...
...BUT I HAVE TO DO EVERYTHING I CAN TO TRY.
THAT'S WHY I OPENED THAT RESTAURANT.
AOI...
TICK
TOCK
IT'S PAST TWO...
THE ROYAL COUPLE IS ARRIVING AT 6:30 P.M.

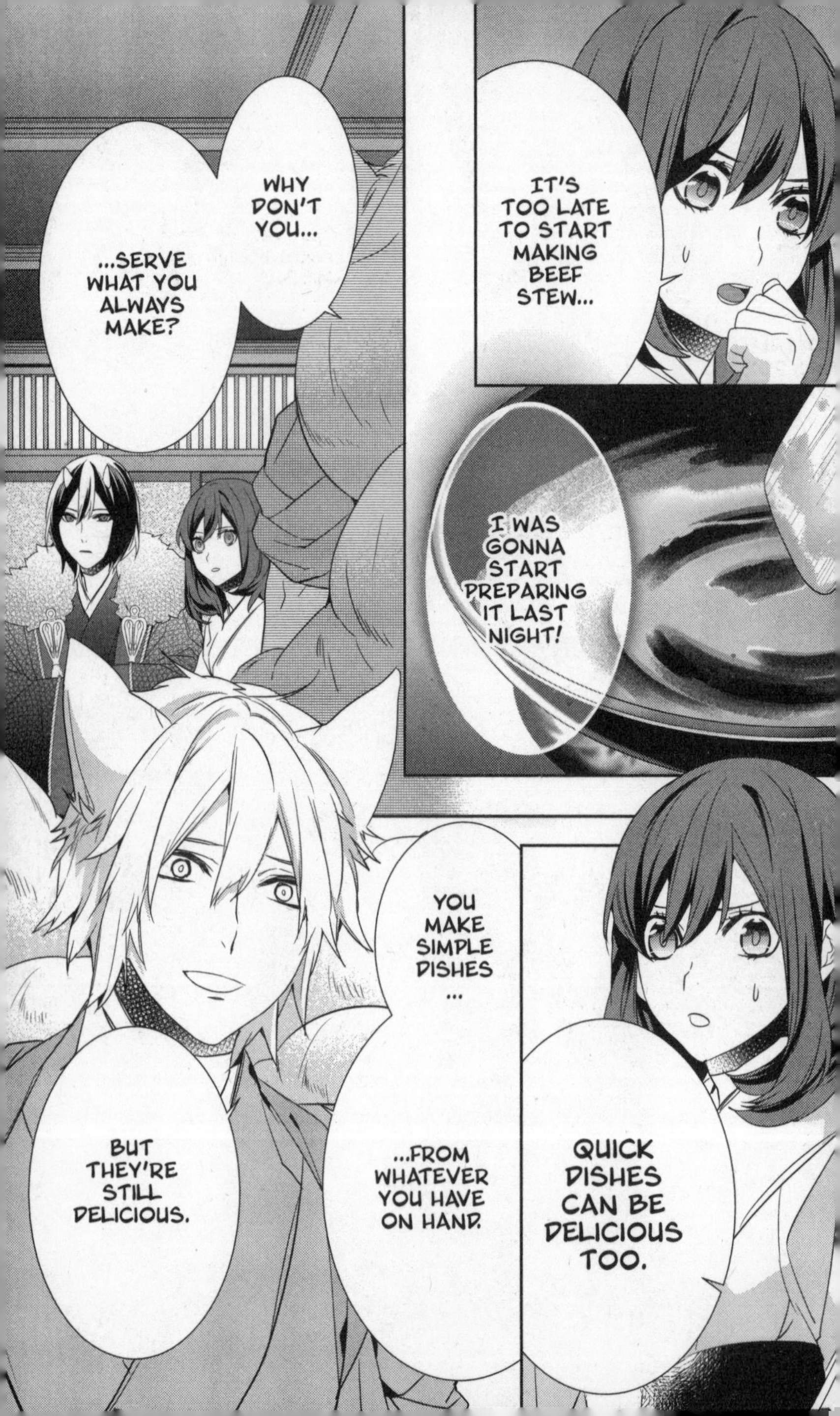
IT'S TOO LATE TO START MAKING BEEF STEW...
I WAS GONNA START PREPARING IT LAST NIGHT!
WHY DON'T YOU...
...SERVE WHAT YOU ALWAYS MAKE?
QUICK DISHES CAN BE DELICIOUS TOO.
YOU MAKE SIMPLE DISHES...
...FROM WHATEVER YOU HAVE ON HAND.
BUT THEY'RE STILL DELICIOUS.

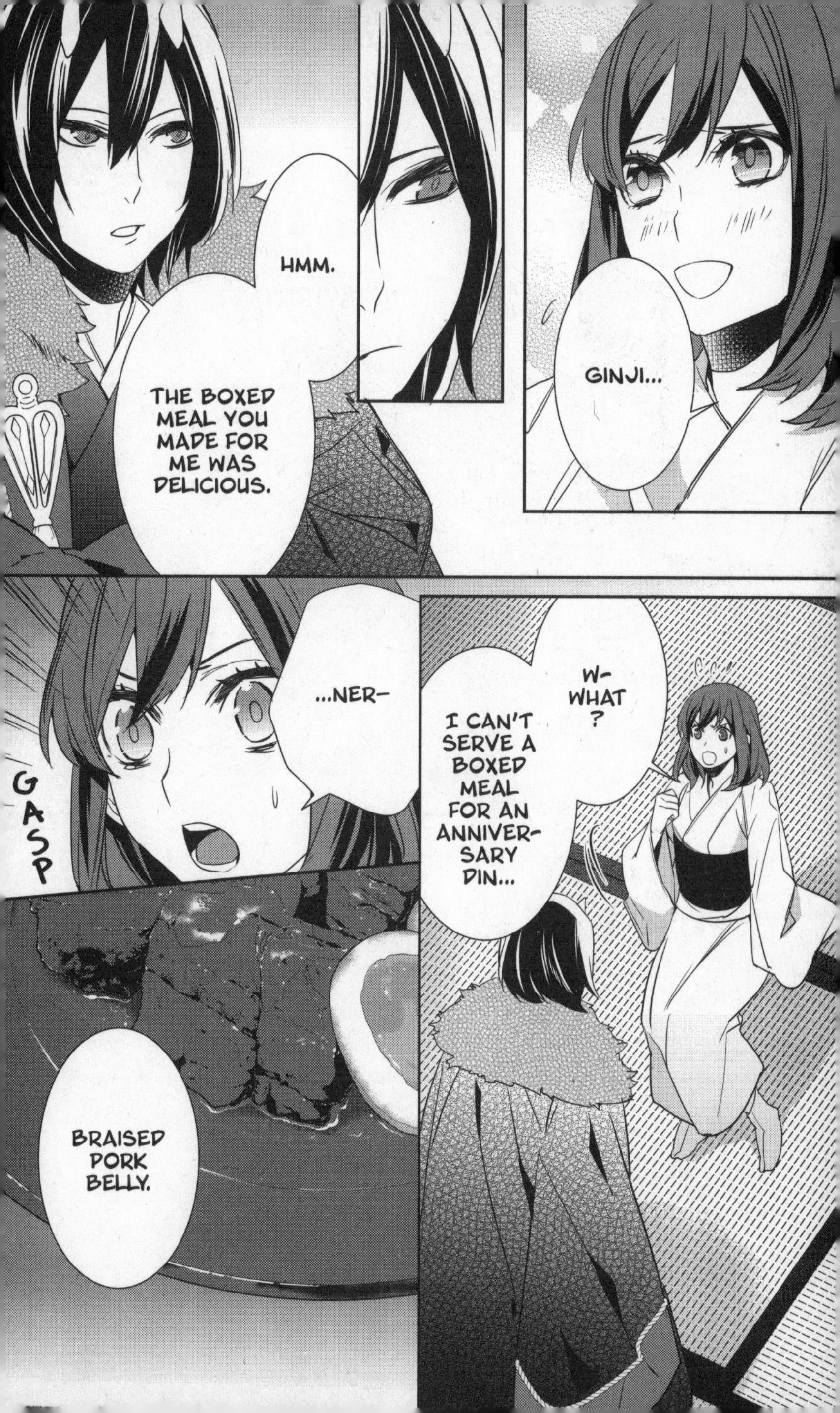
GINJI...
HMM.
THE BOXED MEAL YOU MADE FOR ME WAS DELICIOUS.
W-WHAT?
I CAN'T SERVE A BOXED MEAL FOR AN ANNIVERSARY DIN...
...NER-
GASP
BRAISED PORK BELLY.

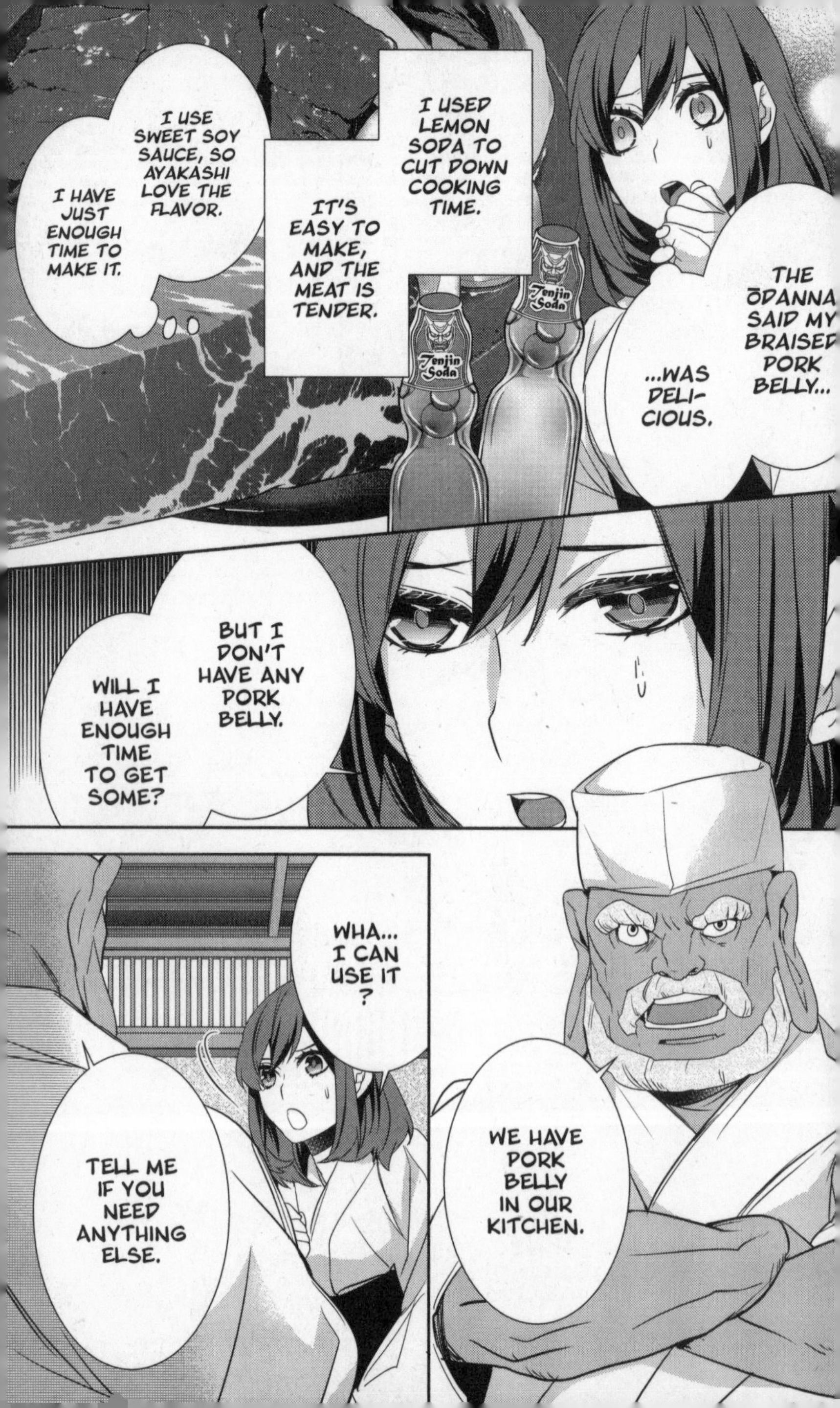
THE ŌDANNA SAID MY BRAISED PORK BELLY...
...WAS DELICIOUS.
Tenjin Soda
Tenjin Soda
I USED LEMON SODA TO CUT DOWN COOKING TIME.
IT'S EASY TO MAKE, AND THE MEAT IS TENDER.
I USE SWEET SOY SAUCE, SO AYAKASHI LOVE THE FLAVOR.
I HAVE JUST ENOUGH TIME TO MAKE IT.
BUT I DON'T HAVE ANY PORK BELLY.
WILL I HAVE ENOUGH TIME TO GET SOME?
WE HAVE PORK BELLY IN OUR KITCHEN.
WHA... I CAN USE IT?
TELL ME IF YOU NEED ANYTHING ELSE.

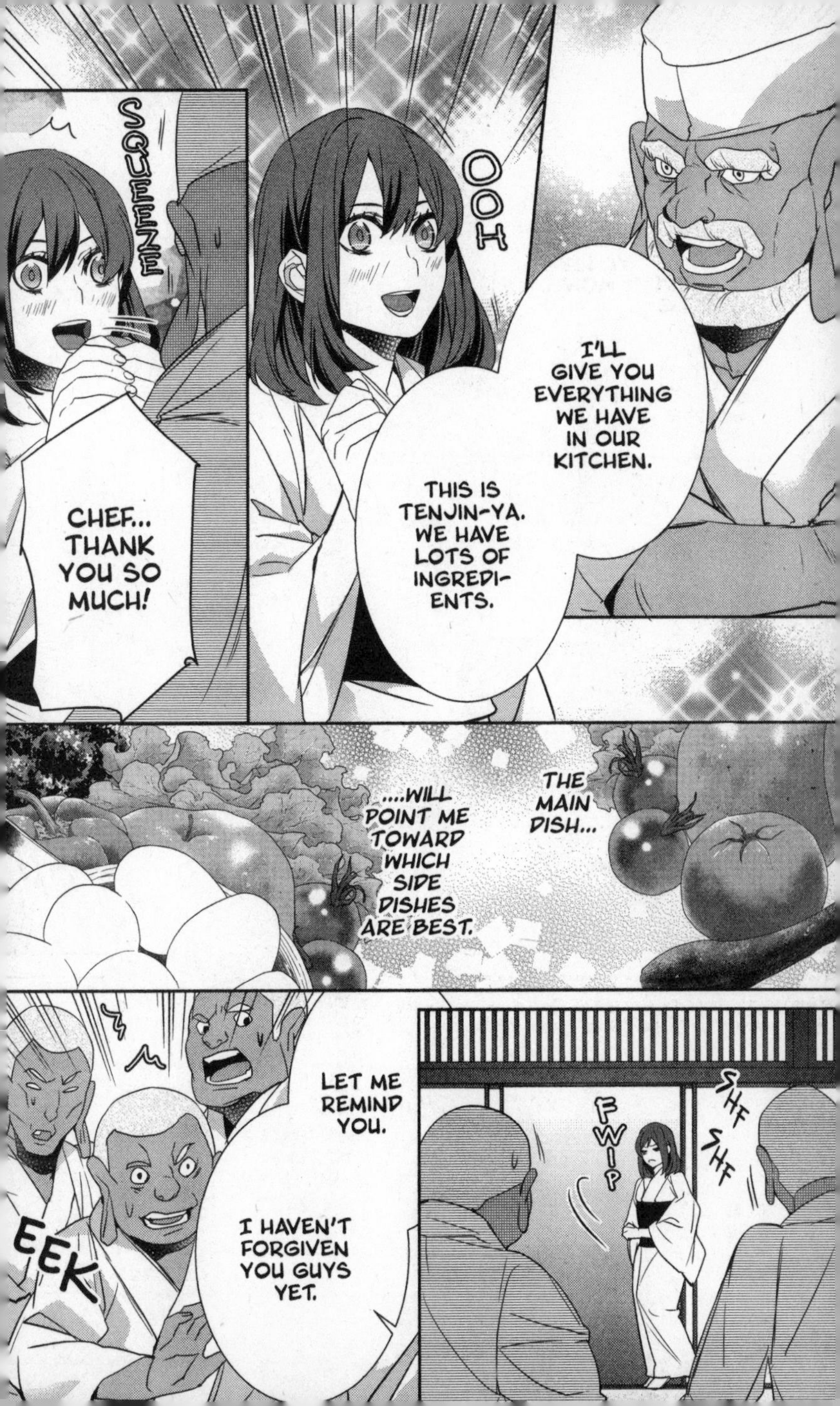
I'LL GIVE YOU EVERYTHING WE HAVE IN OUR KITCHEN.
THIS IS TENJIN-YA. WE HAVE LOTS OF INGREDI-ENTS.
OOH
SQUEEZE
CHEF... THANK YOU SO MUCH!
THE MAIN DISH...
....WILL POINT ME TOWARD WHICH SIDE DISHES ARE BEST.
SHF SHF
FWIP
LET ME REMIND YOU.
I HAVEN'T FORGIVEN YOU GUYS YET.
EEK

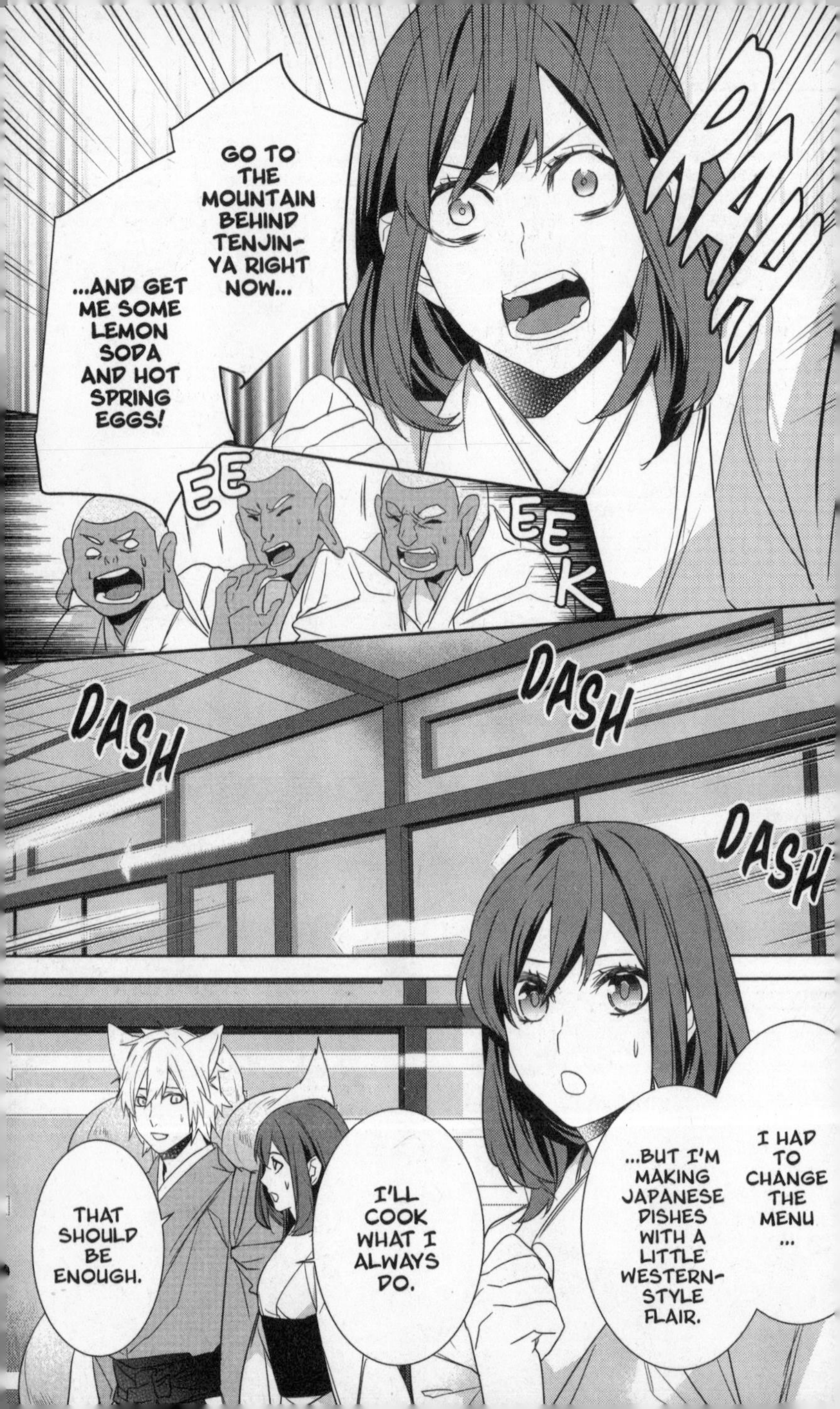
RAAH
GO TO THE MOUNTAIN BEHIND TENJIN-YA RIGHT NOW...
...AND GET ME SOME LEMON SODA AND HOT SPRING EGGS!
EEEK
EE
DASH
DASH
DASH
I HAD TO CHANGE THE MENU...
...BUT I'M MAKING JAPANESE DISHES WITH A LITTLE WESTERN-STYLE FLAIR.
I'LL COOK WHAT I ALWAYS DO.
THAT SHOULD BE ENOUGH.

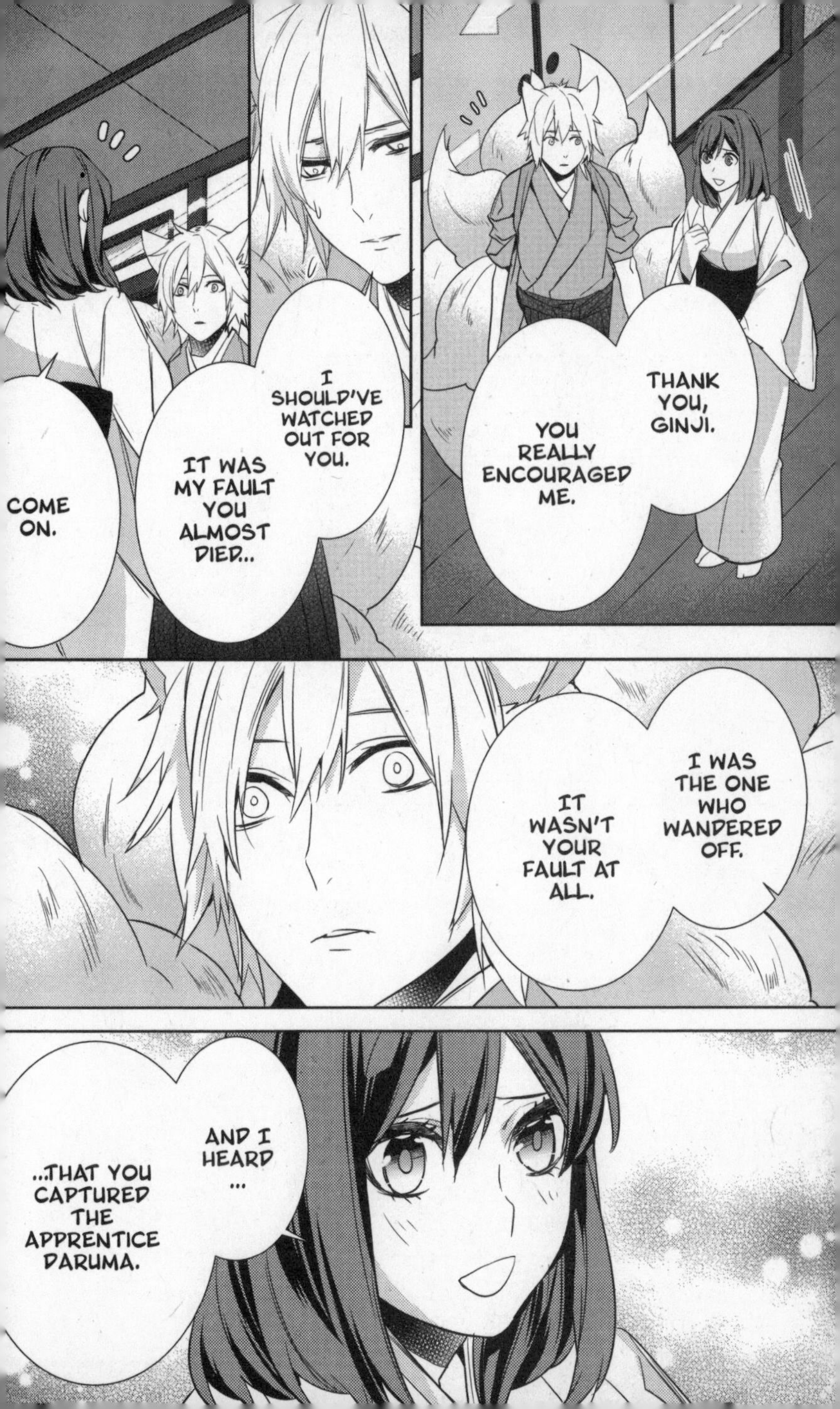
THANK YOU, GINJI.
YOU REALLY ENCOURAGED ME.
I SHOULD'VE WATCHED OUT FOR YOU.
IT WAS MY FAULT YOU ALMOST DIED...
COME ON.
I WAS THE ONE WHO WANDERED OFF.
IT WASN'T YOUR FAULT AT ALL.
AND I HEARD ...
...THAT YOU CAPTURED THE APPRENTICE DARUMA.

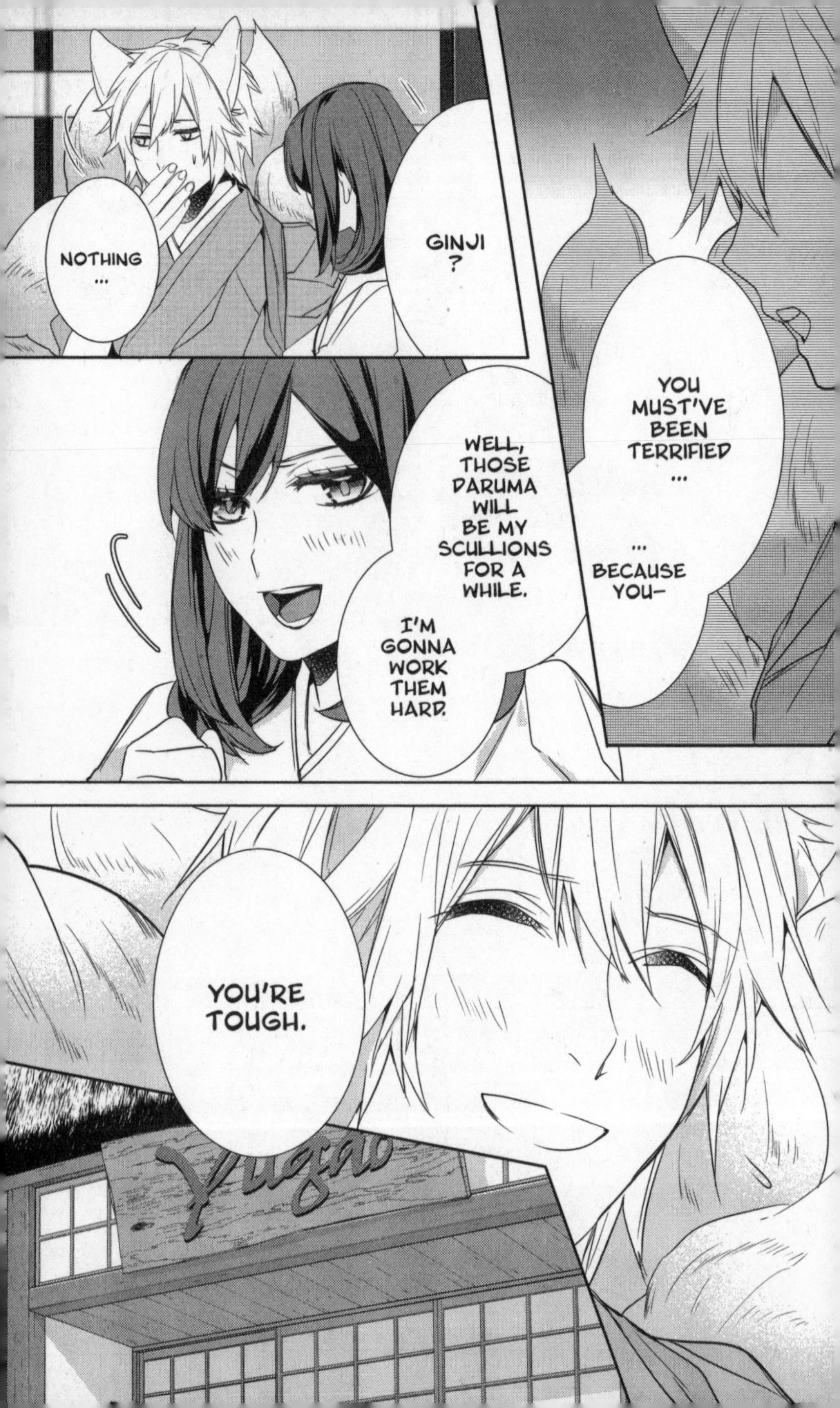
YOU MUST'VE BEEN TERRIFIED ...
... BECAUSE YOU–
GINJI ?
NOTHING ...
WELL, THOSE DARUMA WILL BE MY SCULLIONS FOR A WHILE.
I'M GONNA WORK THEM HARD.
YOU'RE TOUGH.
Yugao

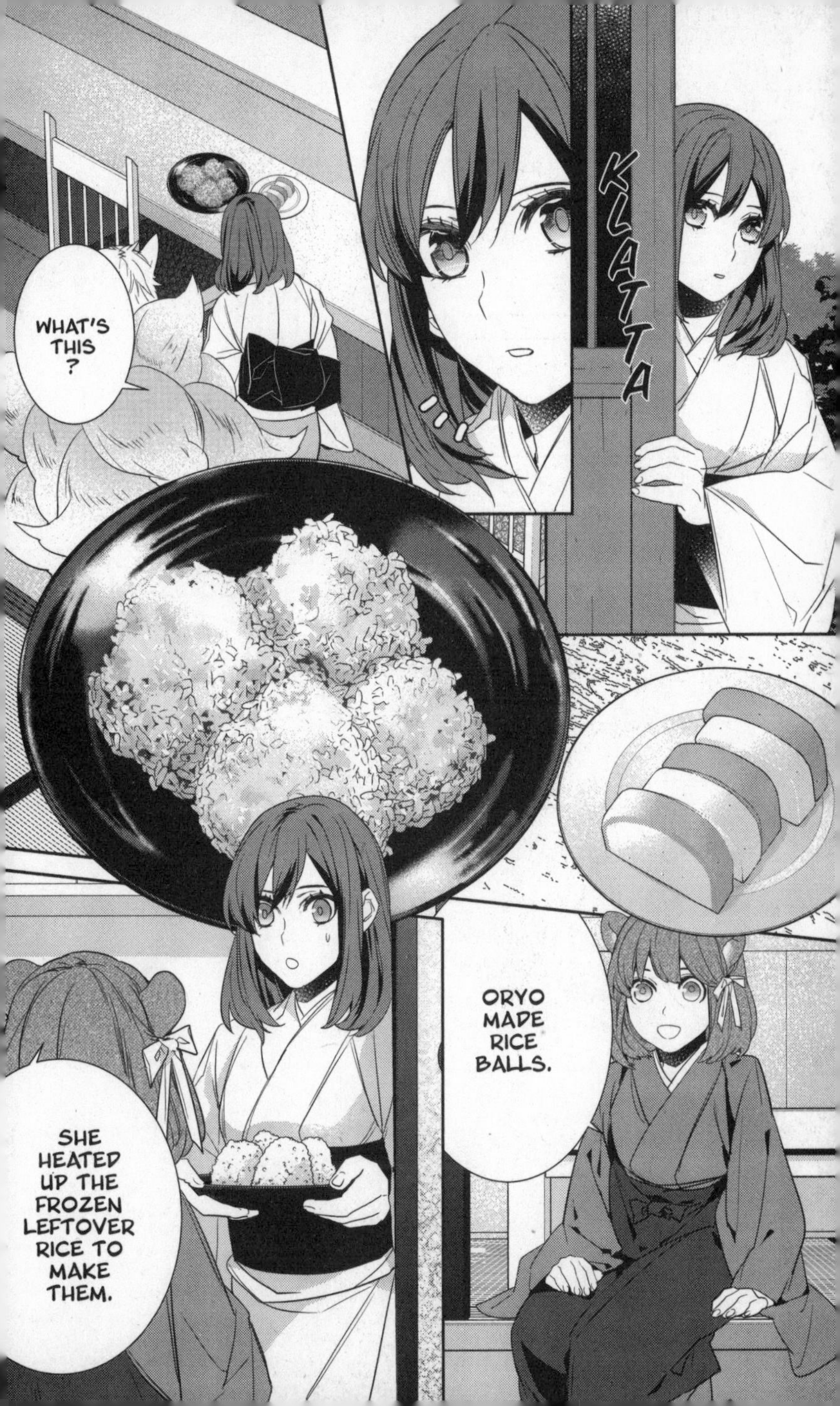
KLATTA
WHAT'S THIS?
ORYO MADE RICE BALLS.
SHE HEATED UP THE FROZEN LEFTOVER RICE TO MAKE THEM.

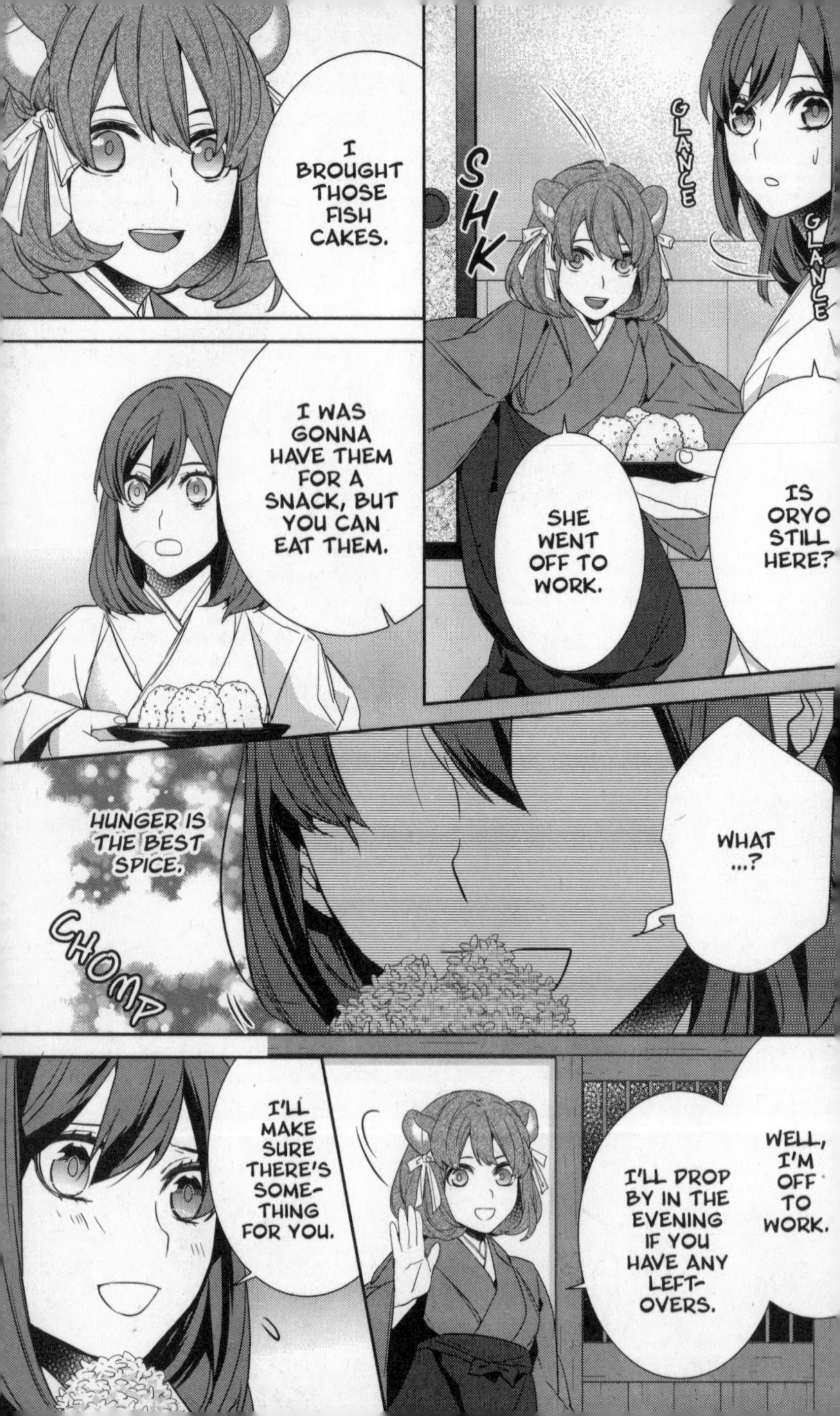
GLANCE
GLANCE
SHK
IS ORYO STILL HERE?
SHE WENT OFF TO WORK.
I BROUGHT THOSE FISH CAKES.
I WAS GONNA HAVE THEM FOR A SNACK, BUT YOU CAN EAT THEM.
WHAT ...?
HUNGER IS THE BEST SPICE.
CHOMP
WELL, I'M OFF TO WORK.
I'LL DROP BY IN THE EVENING IF YOU HAVE ANY LEFT-OVERS.
I'LL MAKE SURE THERE'S SOME-THING FOR YOU.

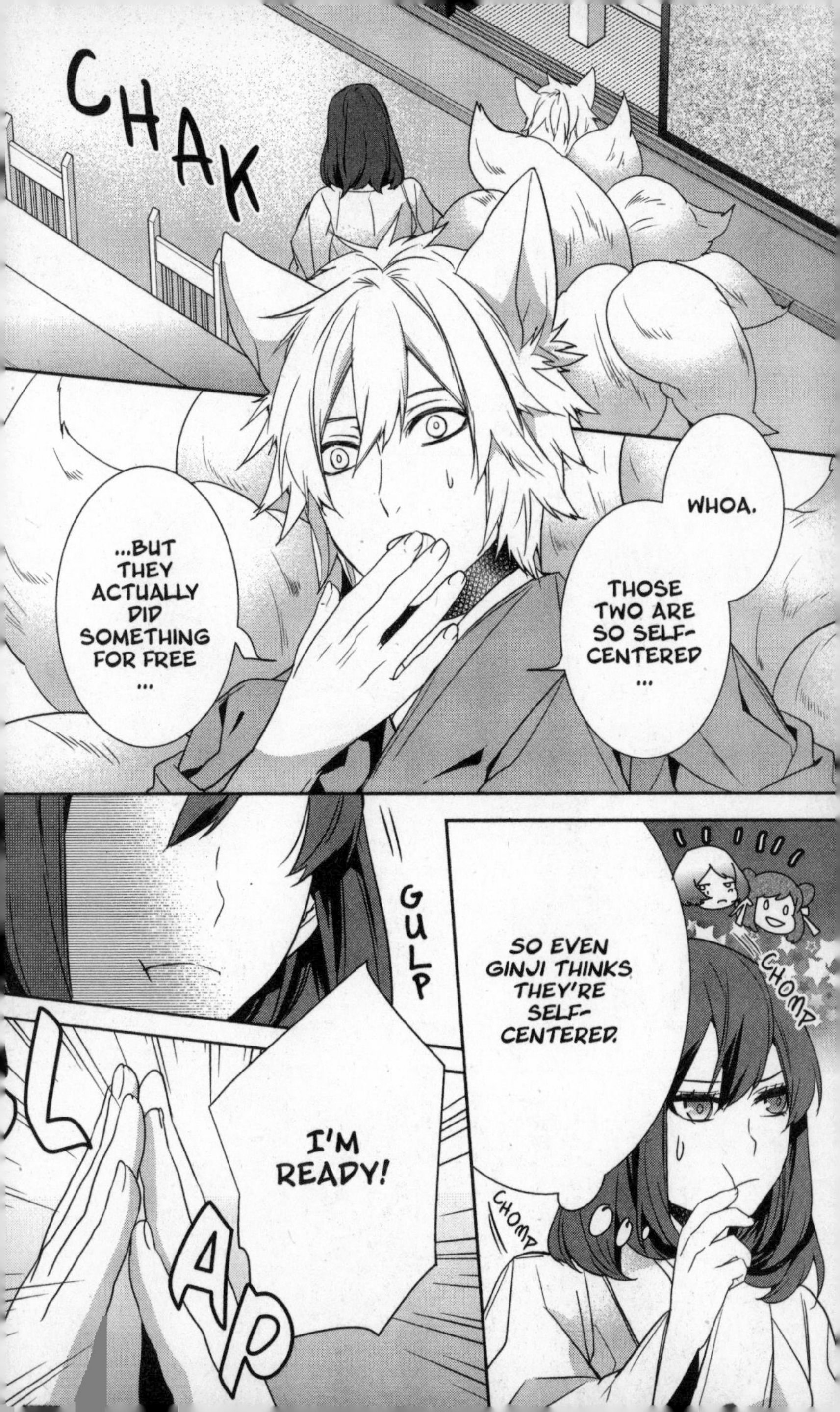
CHAK
WHOA.
THOSE TWO ARE SO SELF-CENTERED...
...BUT THEY ACTUALLY DID SOMETHING FOR FREE...
SO EVEN GINJI THINKS THEY'RE SELF-CENTERED.
CHOMP
CHOMP
GULP
I'M READY!

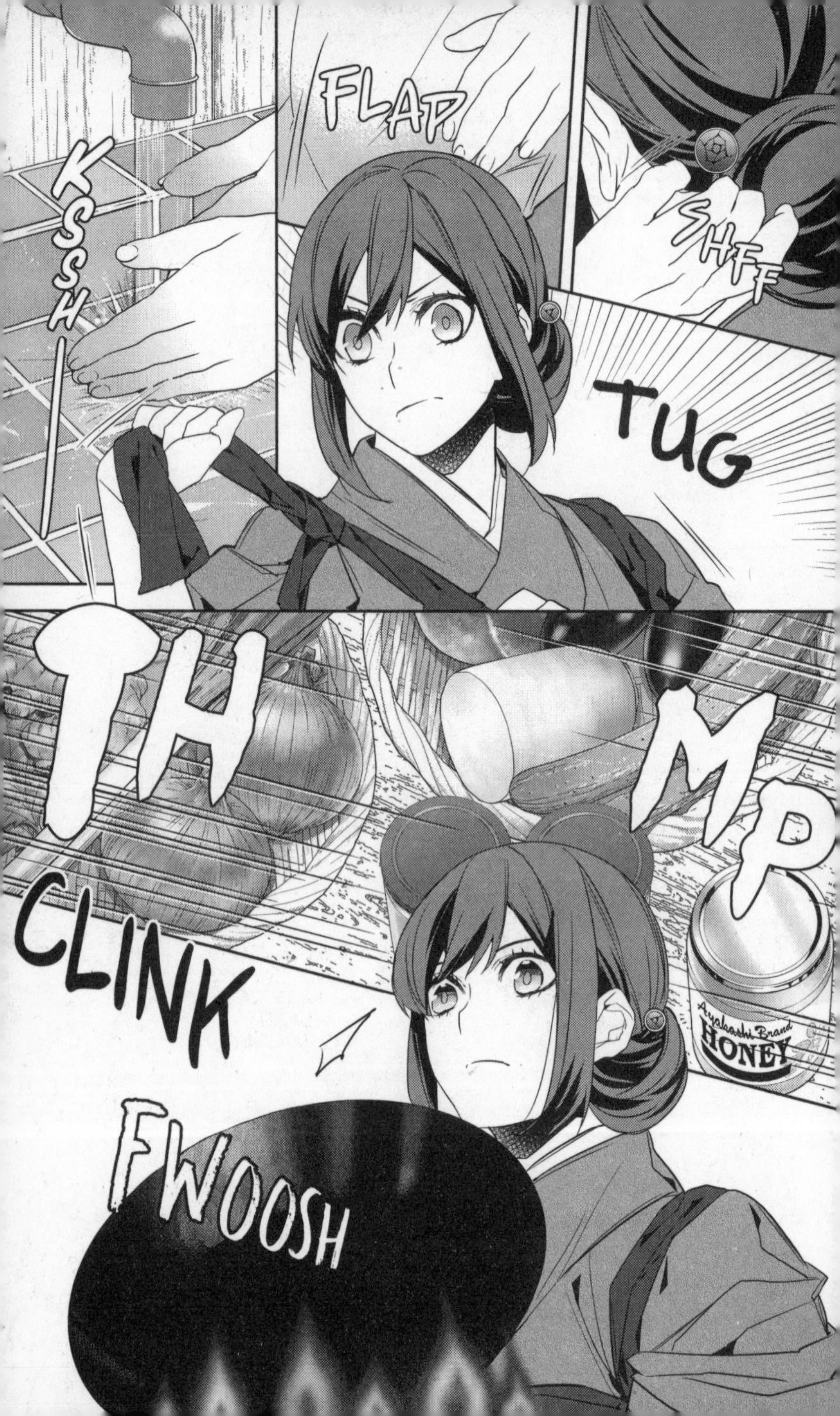
SHFF
FLAP
TUG
KSSH
THMP
Ayakashi Brand
HONEY
CLINK
FWOOSH

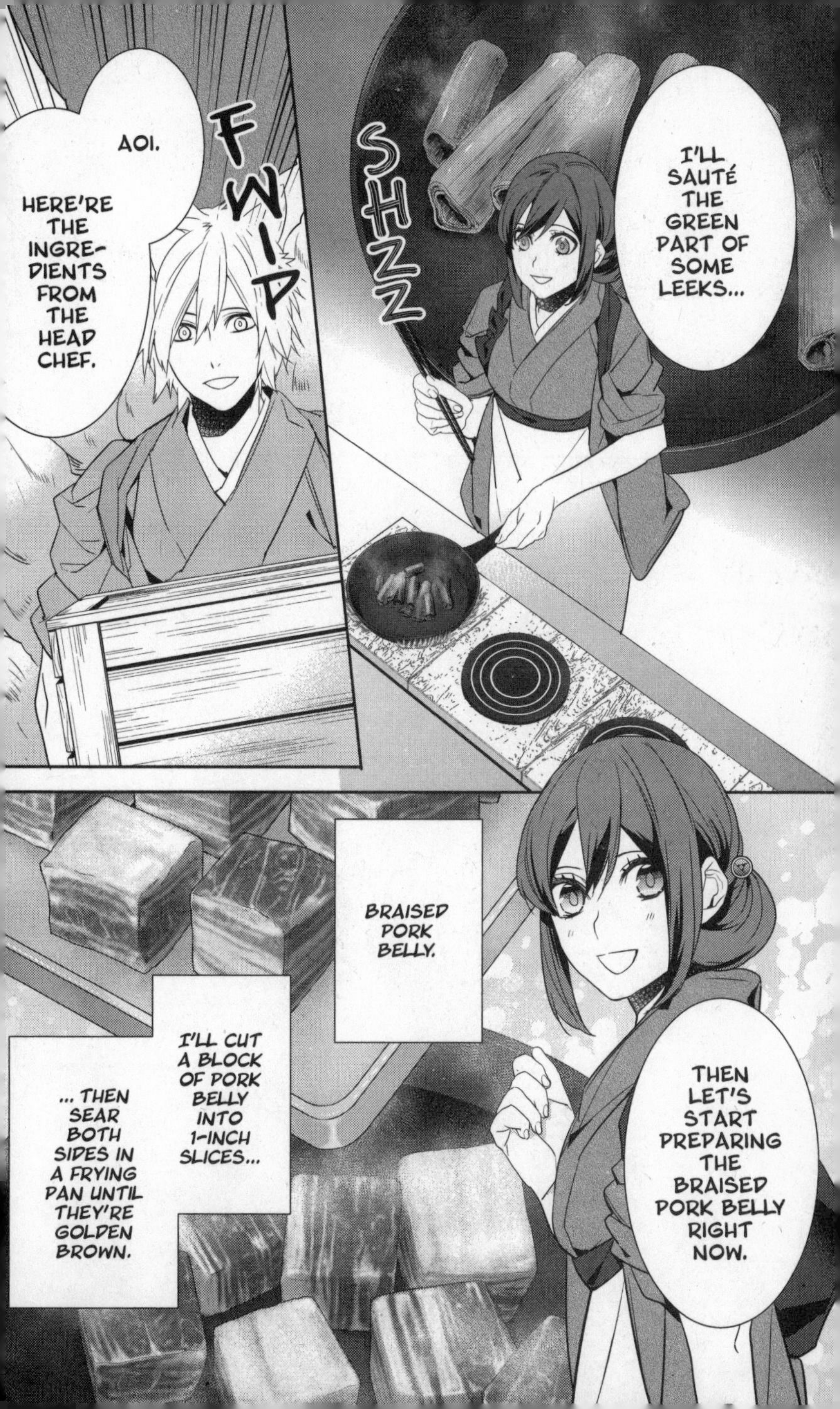
SHZZ
I'LL SAUTÉ THE GREEN PART OF SOME LEEKS...
FWIP
AOI.
HERE'RE THE INGRE-DIENTS FROM THE HEAD CHEF.
THEN LET'S START PREPARING THE BRAISED PORK BELLY RIGHT NOW.
BRAISED PORK BELLY.
I'LL CUT A BLOCK OF PORK BELLY INTO 1-INCH SLICES...
... THEN SEAR BOTH SIDES IN A FRYING PAN UNTIL THEY'RE GOLDEN BROWN.

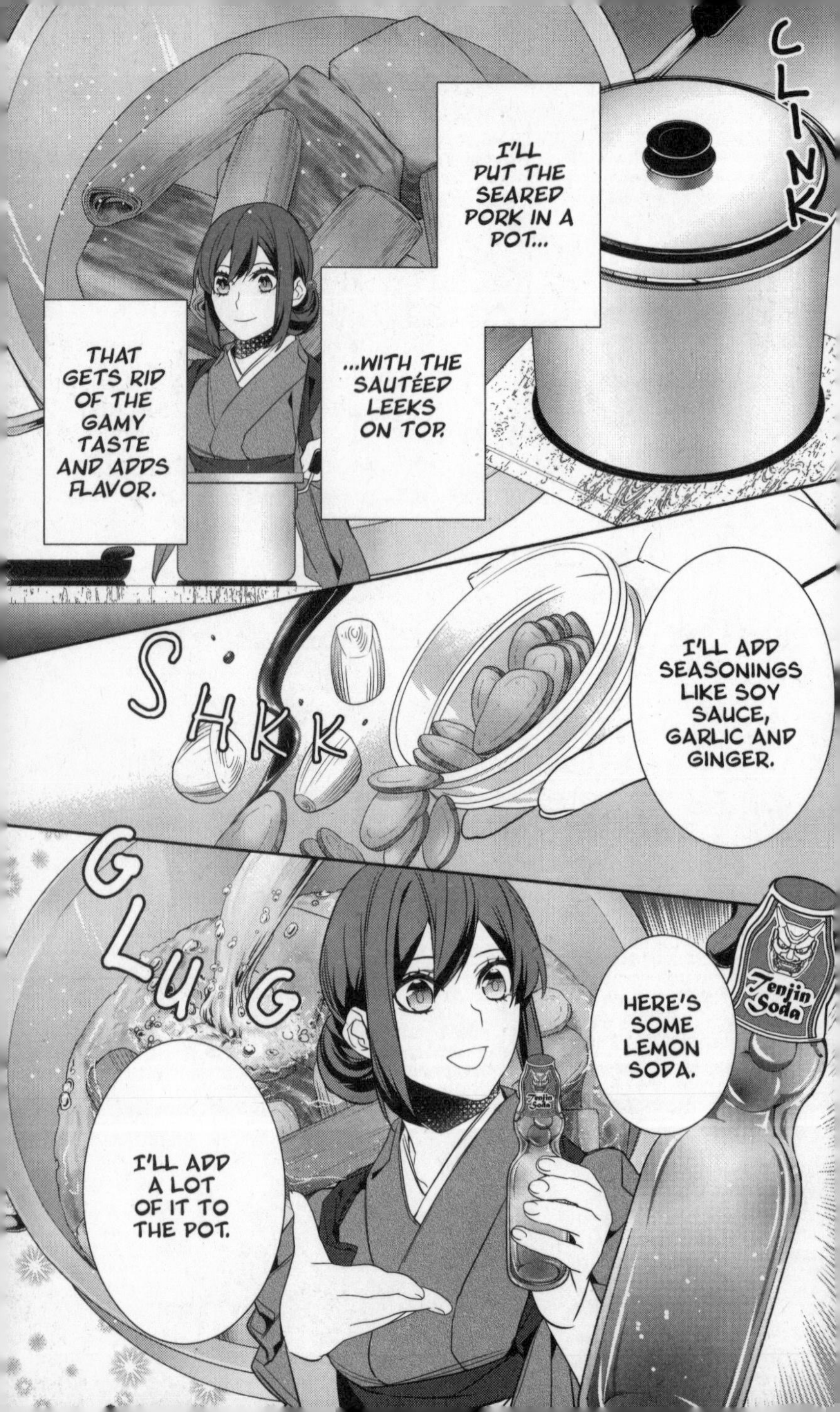
CLINK
I'LL PUT THE SEARED PORK IN A POT...
...WITH THE SAUTÉED LEEKS ON TOP.
THAT GETS RID OF THE GAMY TASTE AND ADDS FLAVOR.
I'LL ADD SEASONINGS LIKE SOY SAUCE, GARLIC AND GINGER.
SHKK
Tenjin Soda
HERE'S SOME LEMON SODA.
GLUG
I'LL ADD A LOT OF IT TO THE POT.
Tenjin Soda

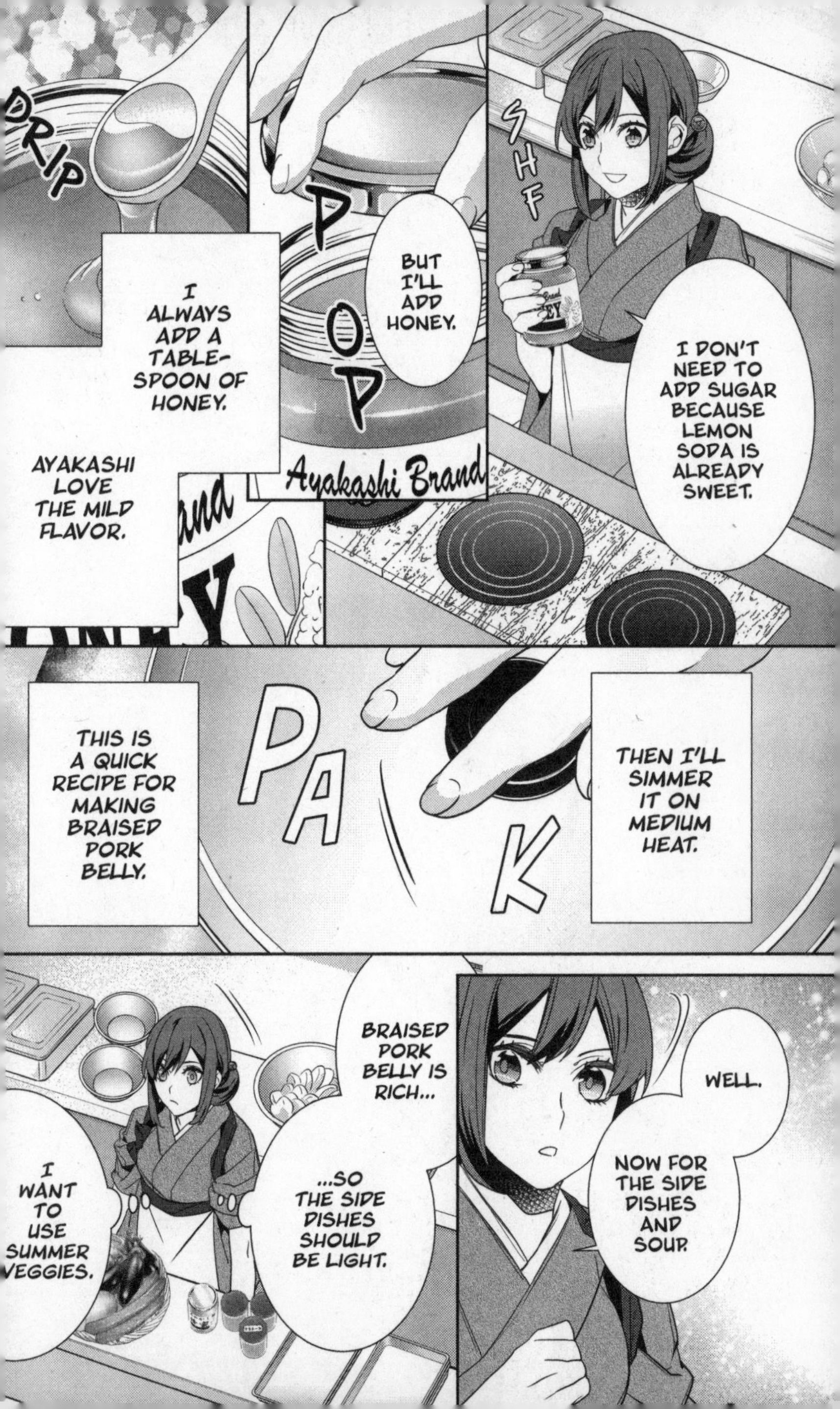
SHF
I DON'T NEED TO ADD SUGAR BECAUSE LEMON SODA IS ALREADY SWEET.
BUT I'LL ADD HONEY.
POP
Ayakashi Brand
DRIP
I ALWAYS ADD A TABLE-SPOON OF HONEY.
AYAKASHI LOVE THE MILD FLAVOR.
THEN I'LL SIMMER IT ON MEDIUM HEAT.
PAK
THIS IS A QUICK RECIPE FOR MAKING BRAISED PORK BELLY.
WELL.
NOW FOR THE SIDE DISHES AND SOUP.
BRAISED PORK BELLY IS RICH...
...SO THE SIDE DISHES SHOULD BE LIGHT.
I WANT TO USE SUMMER VEGGIES.

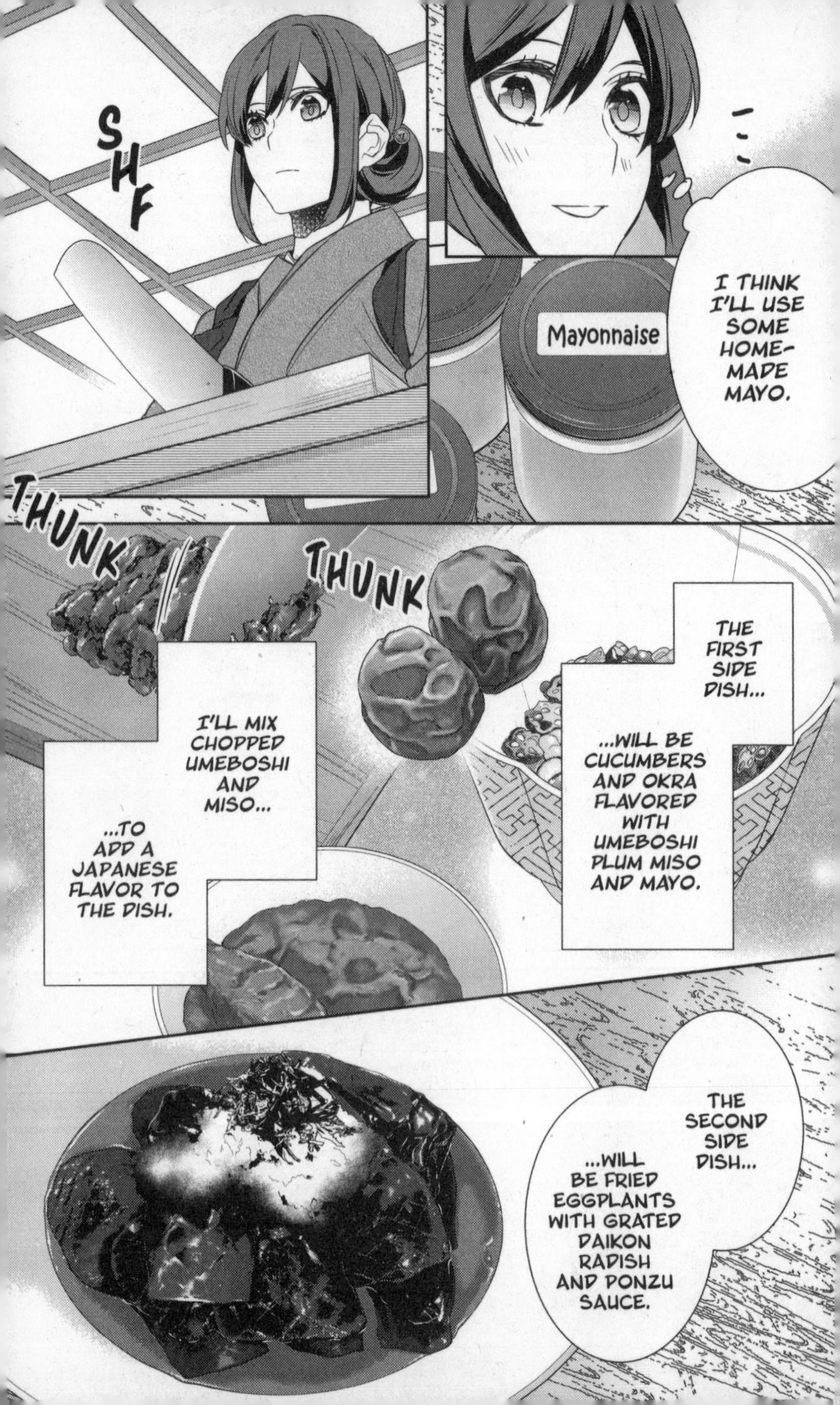
...
I THINK I'LL USE SOME HOME-MADE MAYO.
Mayonnaise
SHF
THUNK
THUNK
THE FIRST SIDE DISH...
...WILL BE CUCUMBERS AND OKRA FLAVORED WITH UMEBOSHI PLUM MISO AND MAYO.
I'LL MIX CHOPPED UMEBOSHI AND MISO...
...TO ADD A JAPANESE FLAVOR TO THE DISH.
THE SECOND SIDE DISH...
...WILL BE FRIED EGGPLANTS WITH GRATED DAIKON RADISH AND PONZU SAUCE.

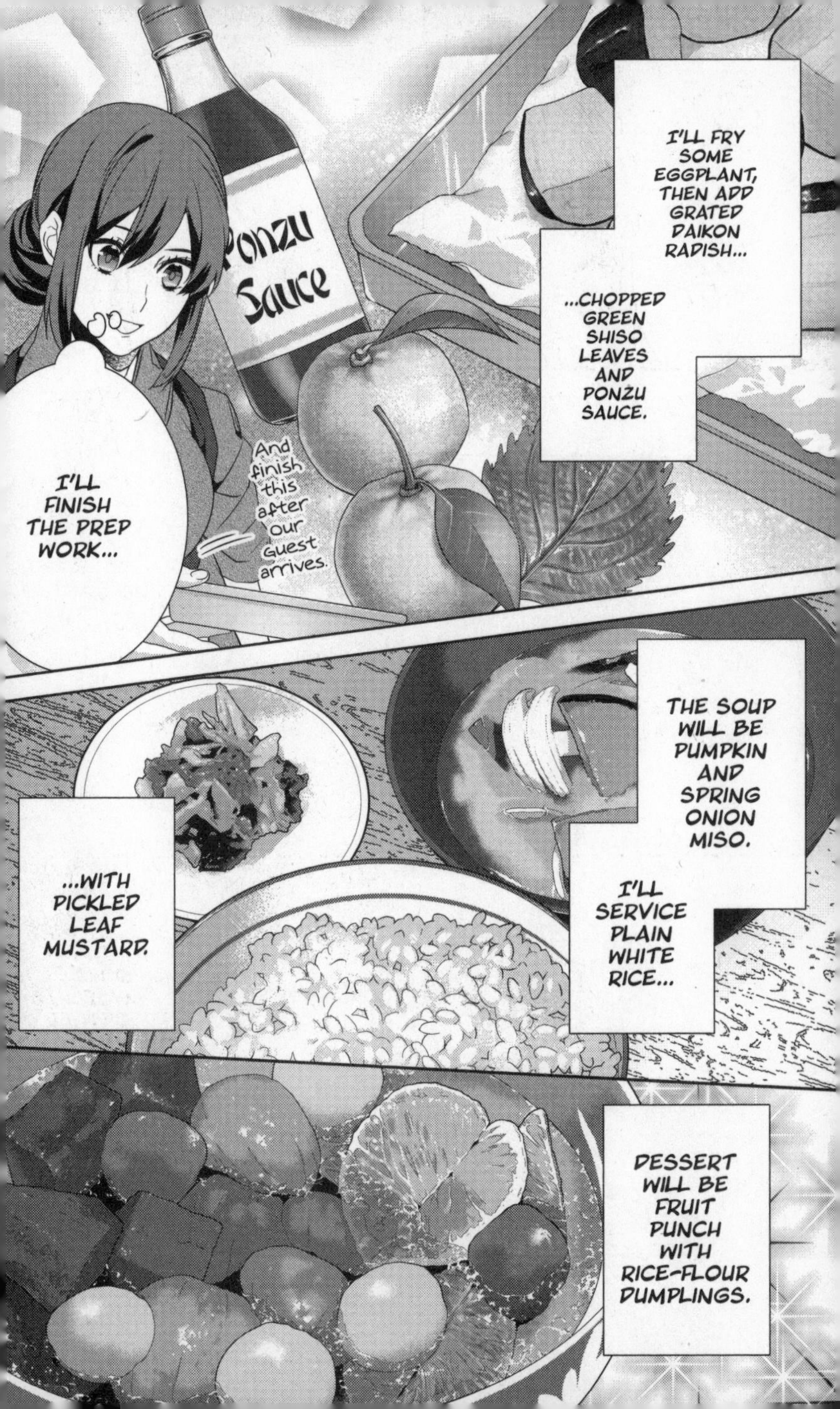
Ponzu Sauce
I'LL FRY SOME EGGPLANT, THEN ADD GRATED DAIKON RADISH...
...CHOPPED GREEN SHISO LEAVES AND PONZU SAUCE.
I'LL FINISH THE PREP WORK...
And finish this after our guest arrives.
THE SOUP WILL BE PUMPKIN AND SPRING ONION MISO.
I'LL SERVICE PLAIN WHITE RICE...
...WITH PICKLED LEAF MUSTARD.
DESSERT WILL BE FRUIT PUNCH WITH RICE-FLOUR DUMPLINGS.

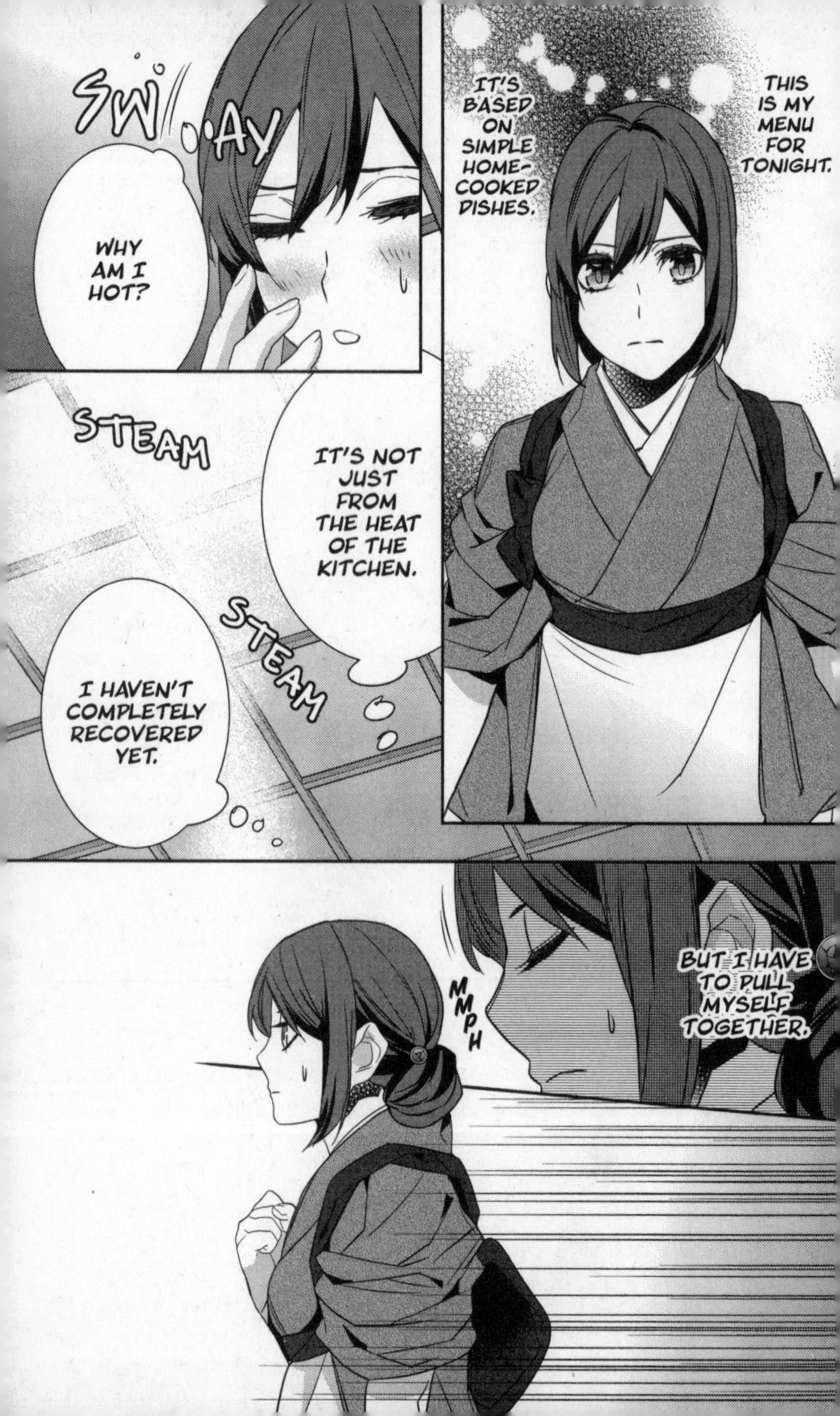
THIS IS MY MENU FOR TONIGHT.
IT'S BASED ON SIMPLE HOME-COOKED DISHES.
SWAY
WHY AM I HOT?
IT'S NOT JUST FROM THE HEAT OF THE KITCHEN.
STEAM
STEAM
I HAVEN'T COMPLETELY RECOVERED YET.
BUT I HAVE TO PULL MYSELF TOGETHER.
MMPH

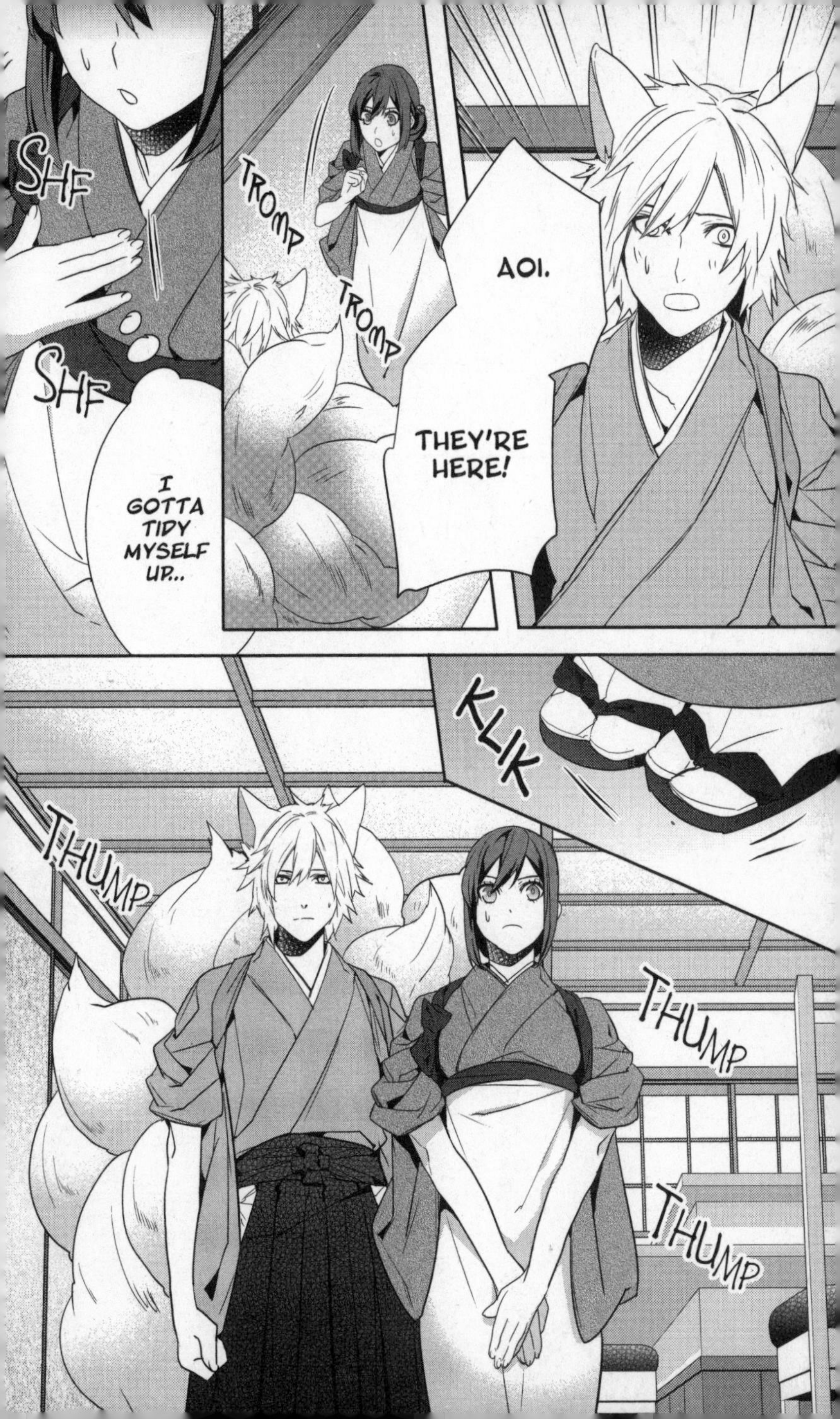
AOI.
THEY'RE HERE!
TROMP
TROMP
SHF
SHF
I GOTTA TIDY MYSELF UP...
KLIK
THUMP
THUMP
THUMP

Kakuriyo
Bed & Breakfast
for Spirits

Kakuriyo
Bed & Breakfast
for Spirits

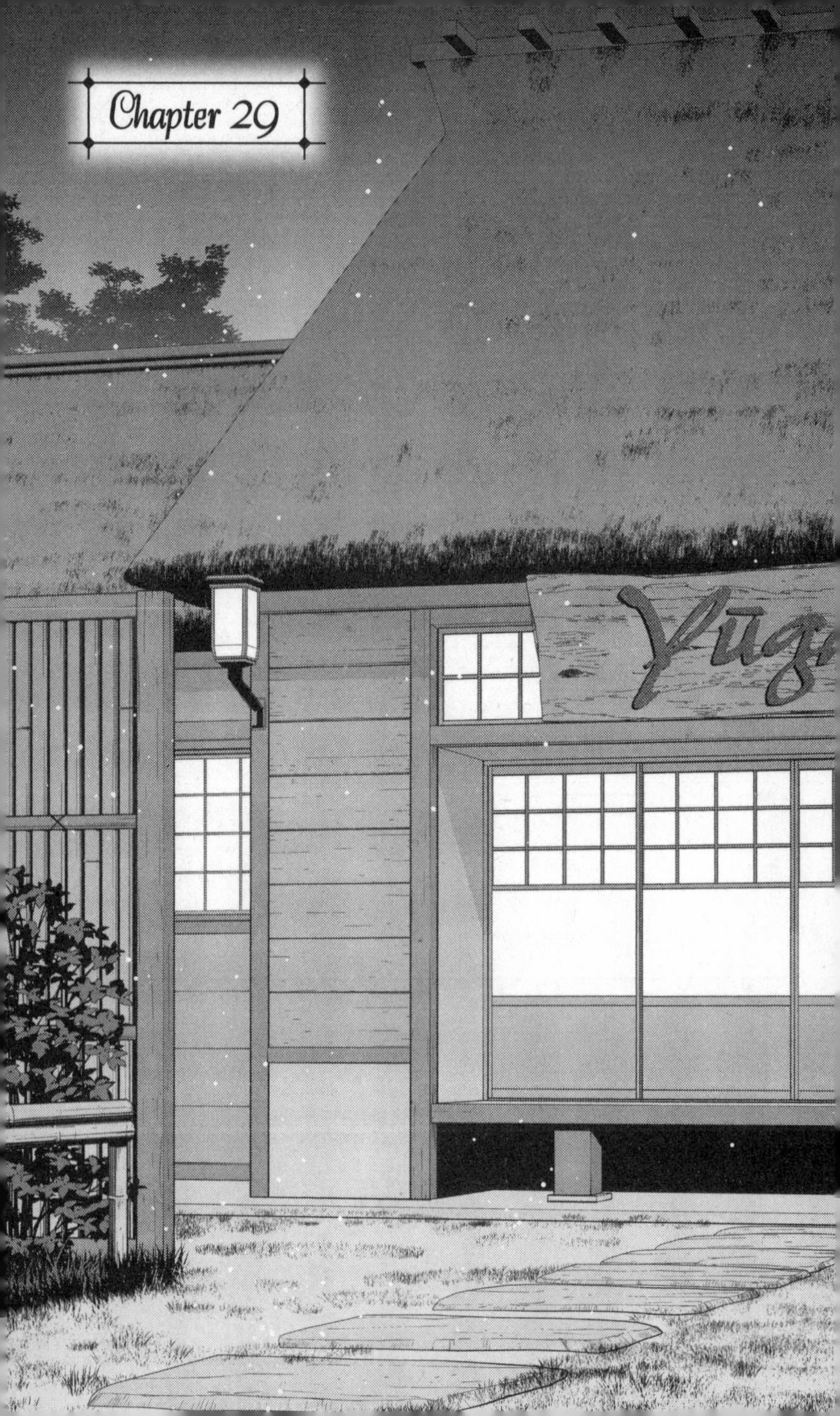
Chapter 29

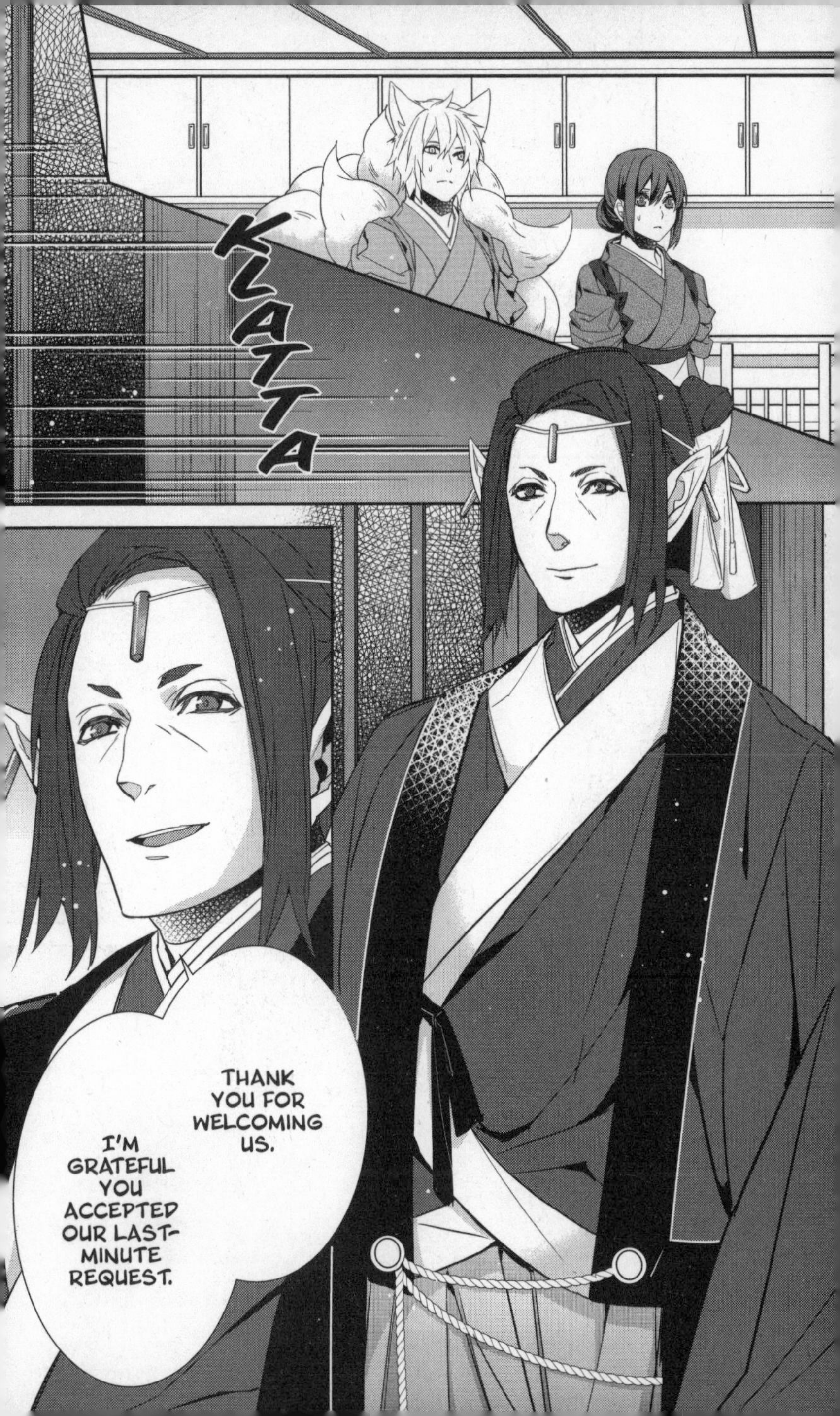
KLATTA
THANK YOU FOR WELCOMING US.
I'M GRATEFUL YOU ACCEPTED OUR LAST-MINUTE REQUEST.

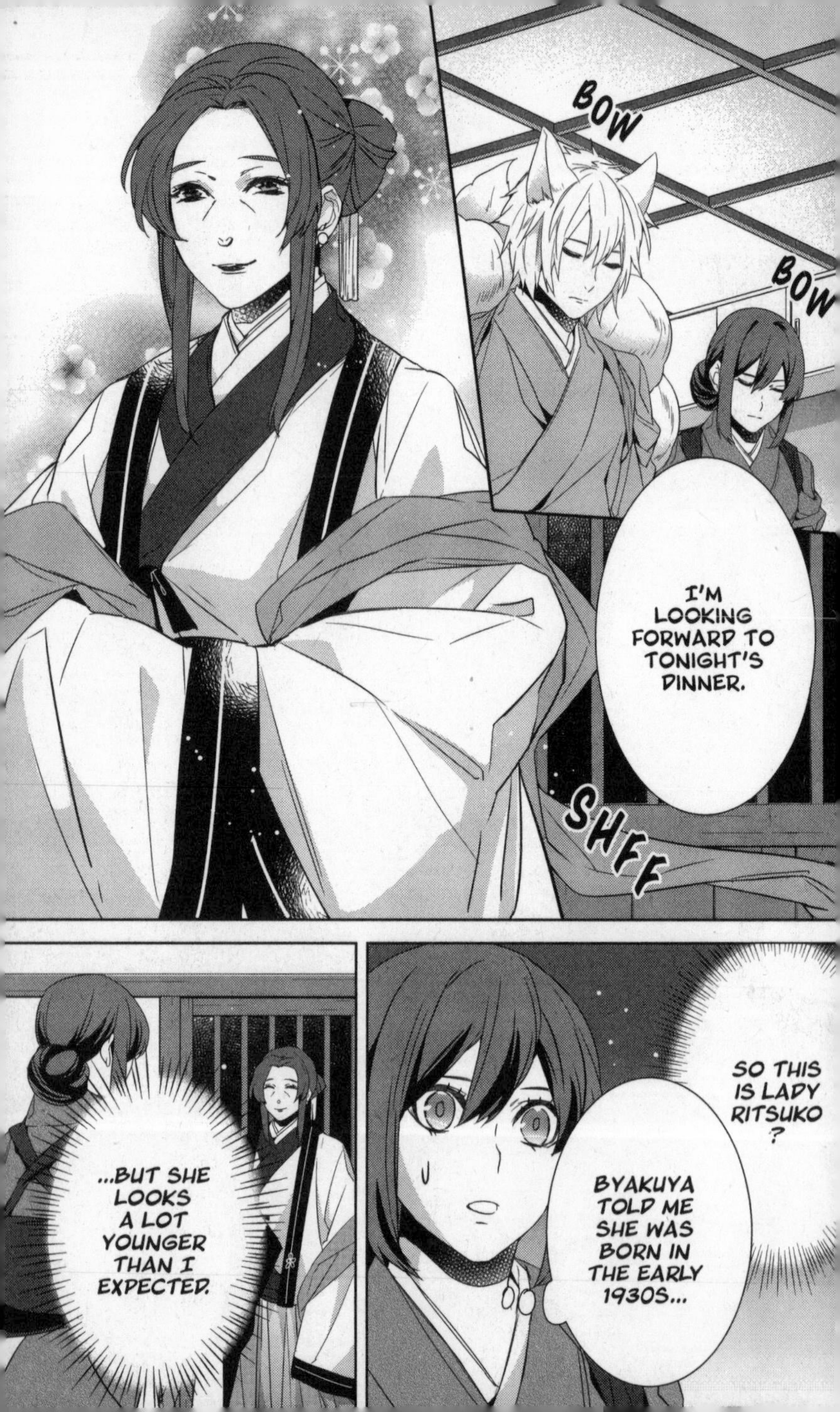
BOW
BOW
I'M LOOKING FORWARD TO TONIGHT'S DINNER.
SHFF
SO THIS IS LADY RITSUKO?
BYAKUYA TOLD ME SHE WAS BORN IN THE EARLY 1930S...
...BUT SHE LOOKS A LOT YOUNGER THAN I EXPECTED.

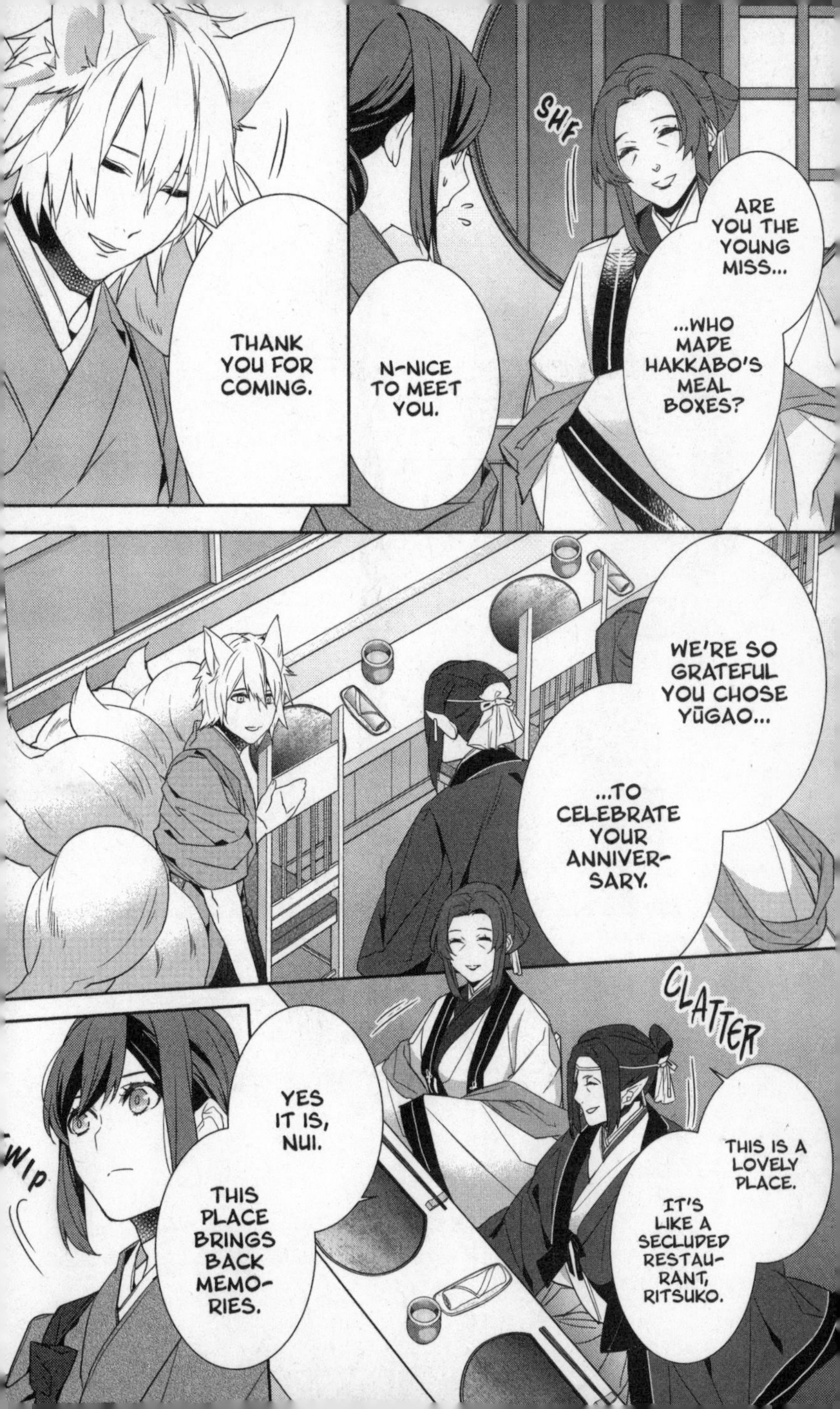
SHF
ARE YOU THE YOUNG MISS...
...WHO MADE HAKKABO'S MEAL BOXES?
N-NICE TO MEET YOU.
THANK YOU FOR COMING.
WE'RE SO GRATEFUL YOU CHOSE YŪGAO...
...TO CELEBRATE YOUR ANNIVERSARY.
CLATTER
THIS IS A LOVELY PLACE.
IT'S LIKE A SECLUDED RESTAURANT, RITSUKO.
YES IT IS, NUI.
THIS PLACE BRINGS BACK MEMORIES.
WIP

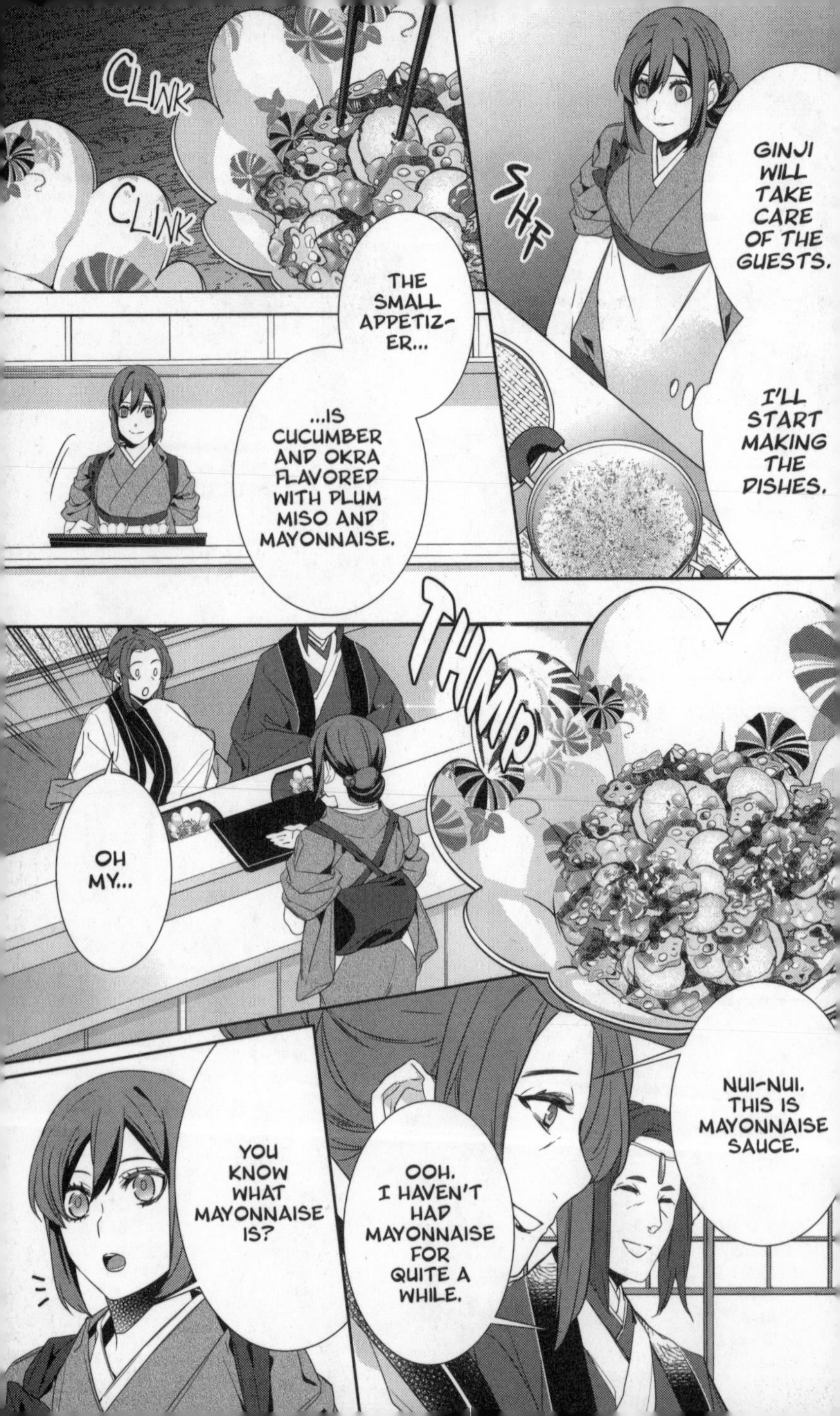
SHF
GINJI WILL TAKE CARE OF THE GUESTS.
I'LL START MAKING THE DISHES.
CLINK
CLINK
THE SMALL APPETIZ-ER...
...IS CUCUMBER AND OKRA FLAVORED WITH PLUM MISO AND MAYONNAISE.
THUMP
OH MY...
NUI-NUI. THIS IS MAYONNAISE SAUCE.
OOH. I HAVEN'T HAD MAYONNAISE FOR QUITE A WHILE.
YOU KNOW WHAT MAYONNAISE IS?

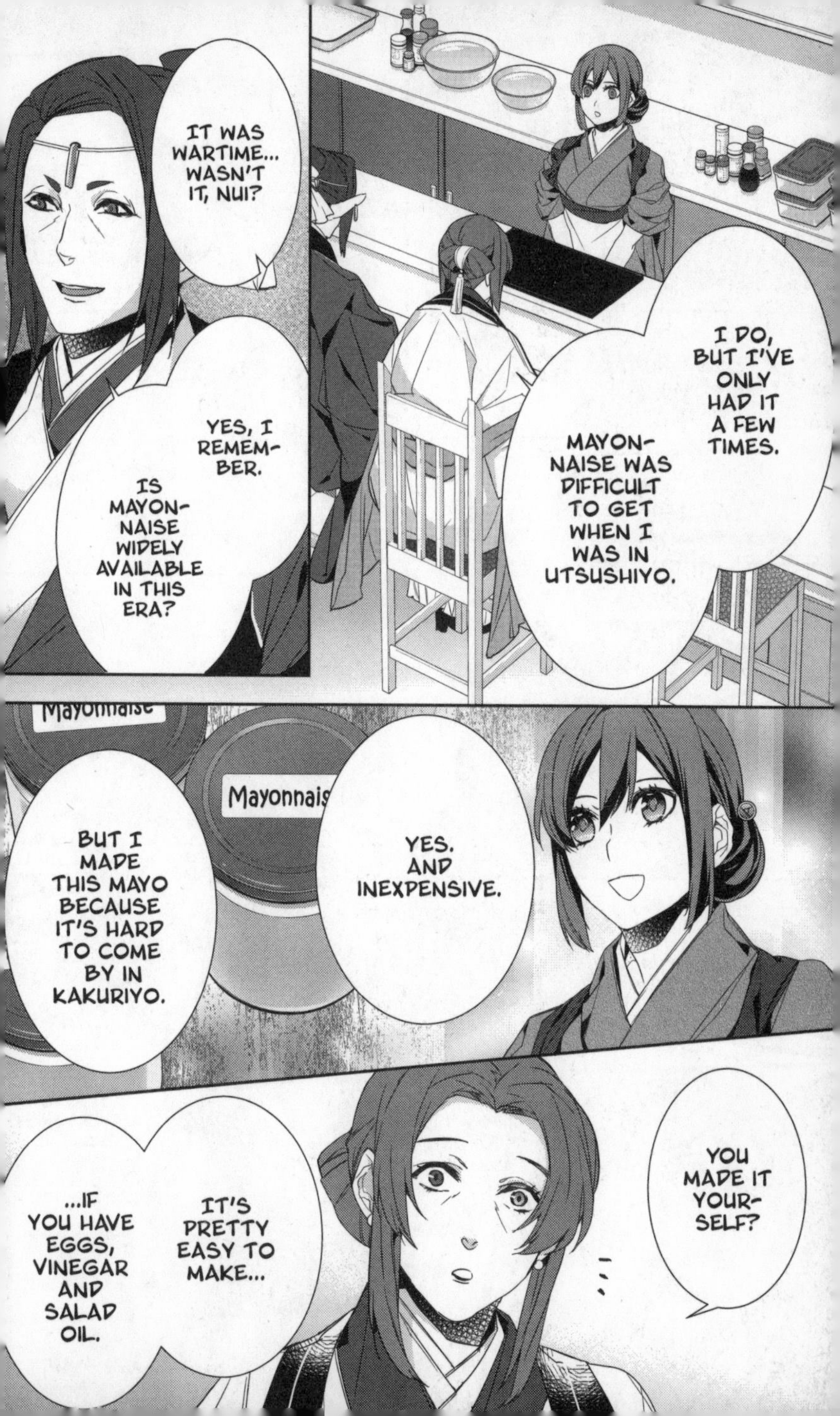
I DO, BUT I'VE ONLY HAD IT A FEW TIMES.
MAYONNAISE WAS DIFFICULT TO GET WHEN I WAS IN UTSUSHIYO.
IT WAS WARTIME... WASN'T IT, NUI?
YES, I REMEMBER.
IS MAYONNAISE WIDELY AVAILABLE IN THIS ERA?
YES. AND INEXPENSIVE.
Mayonnais
BUT I MADE THIS MAYO BECAUSE IT'S HARD TO COME BY IN KAKURIYO.
YOU MADE IT YOURSELF?
IT'S PRETTY EASY TO MAKE...
...IF YOU HAVE EGGS, VINEGAR AND SALAD OIL.

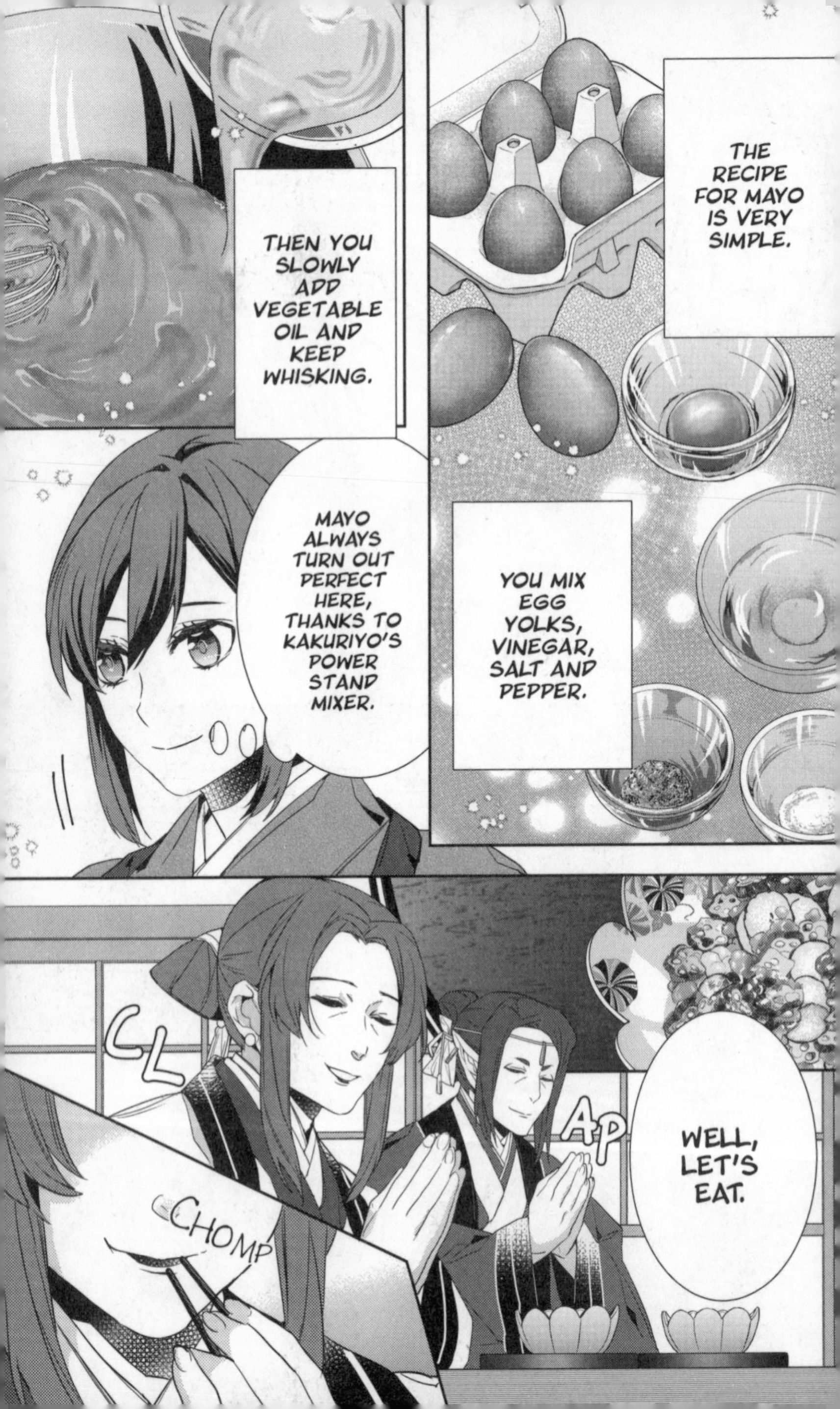
THE RECIPE FOR MAYO IS VERY SIMPLE.
YOU MIX EGG YOLKS, VINEGAR, SALT AND PEPPER.
THEN YOU SLOWLY ADD VEGETABLE OIL AND KEEP WHISKING.
MAYO ALWAYS TURN OUT PERFECT HERE, THANKS TO KAKURIYO'S POWER STAND MIXER.
WELL, LET'S EAT.
CL
AP
CHOMP

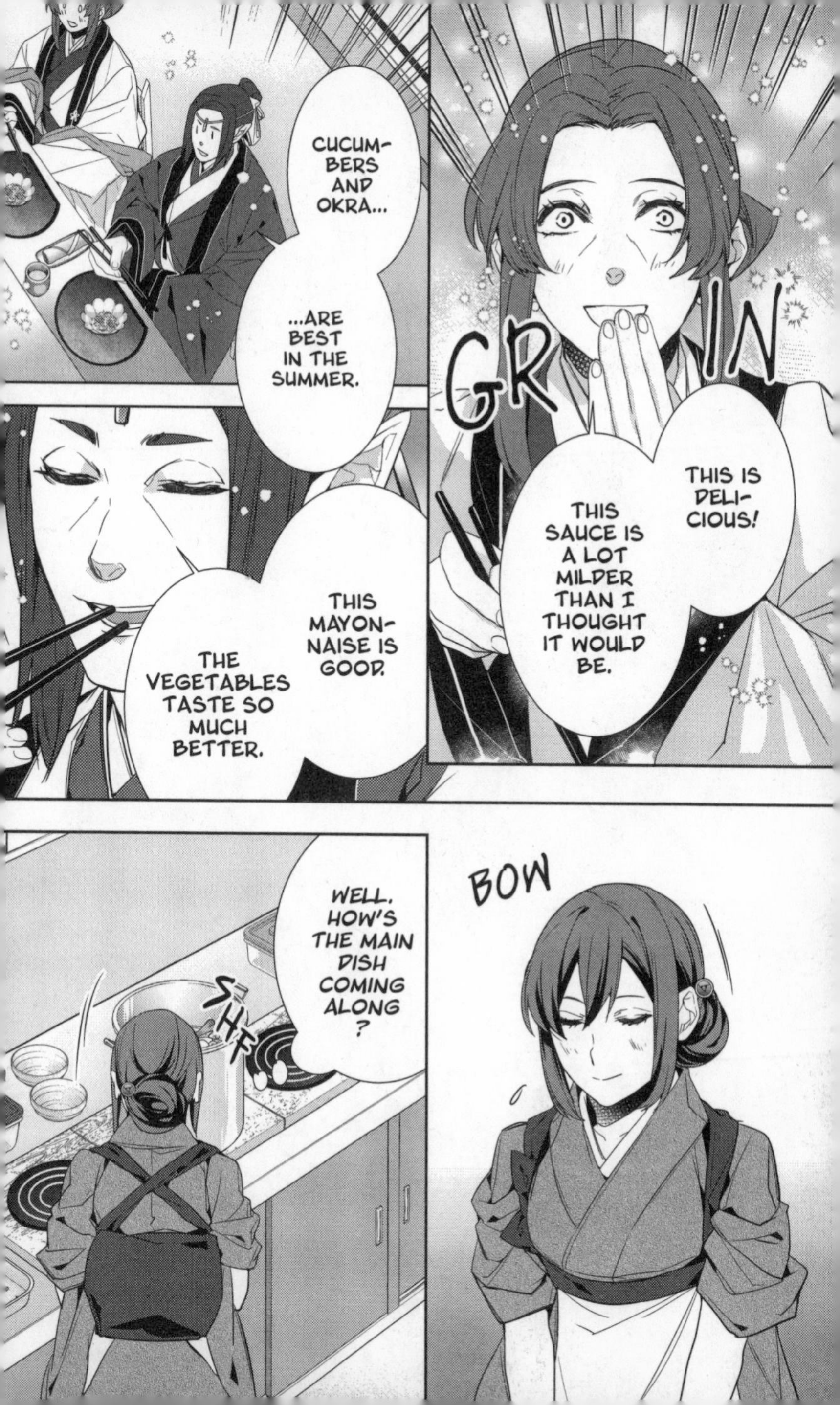
GRIN
THIS IS DELI- CIOUS!
THIS SAUCE IS A LOT MILDER THAN I THOUGHT IT WOULD BE.
CUCUM- BERS AND OKRA...
...ARE BEST IN THE SUMMER.
THIS MAYON- NAISE IS GOOD.
THE VEGETABLES TASTE SO MUCH BETTER.
BOW
SHF
WELL. HOW'S THE MAIN DISH COMING ALONG ?

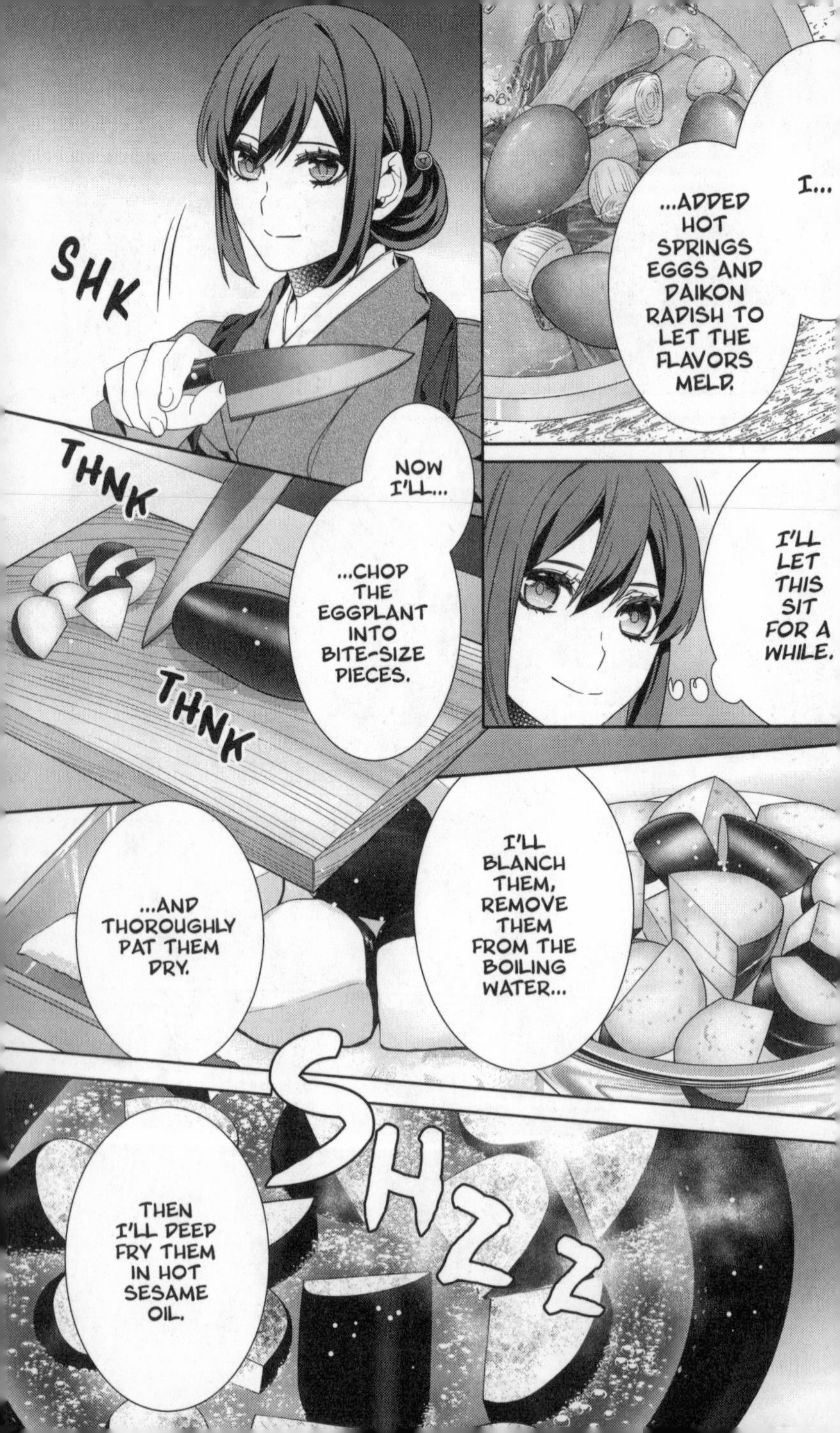
I...
...ADDED HOT SPRINGS EGGS AND DAIKON RADISH TO LET THE FLAVORS MELD.
SHK
I'LL LET THIS SIT FOR A WHILE.
THNK
NOW I'LL...
...CHOP THE EGGPLANT INTO BITE-SIZE PIECES.
THNK
I'LL BLANCH THEM, REMOVE THEM FROM THE BOILING WATER...
...AND THOROUGHLY PAT THEM DRY.
SHZZZ
THEN I'LL DEEP FRY THEM IN HOT SESAME OIL.

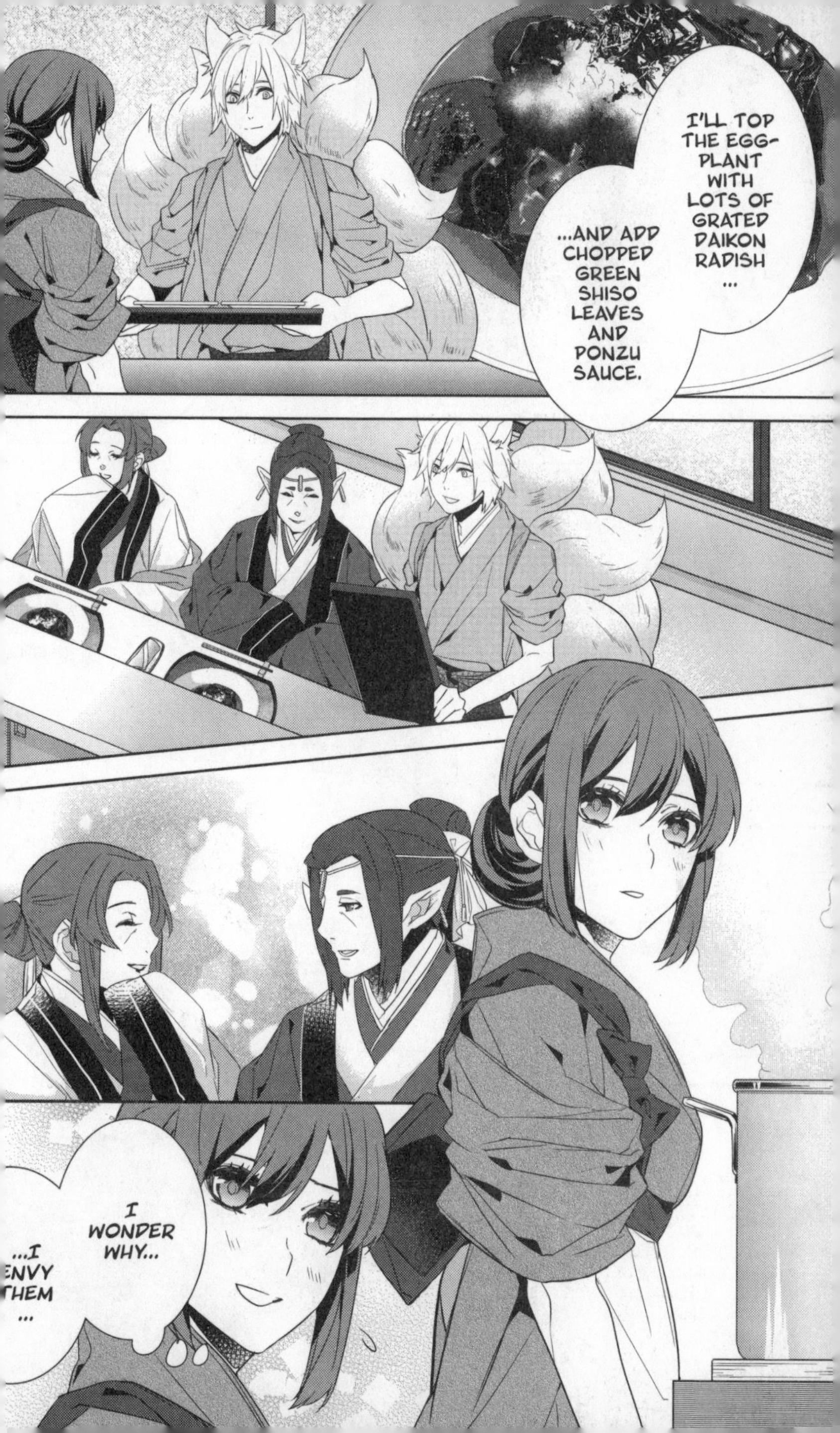
I'LL TOP THE EGG-PLANT WITH LOTS OF GRATED DAIKON RADISH ...
...AND ADD CHOPPED GREEN SHISO LEAVES AND PONZU SAUCE.
I WONDER WHY...
...I ENVY THEM ...

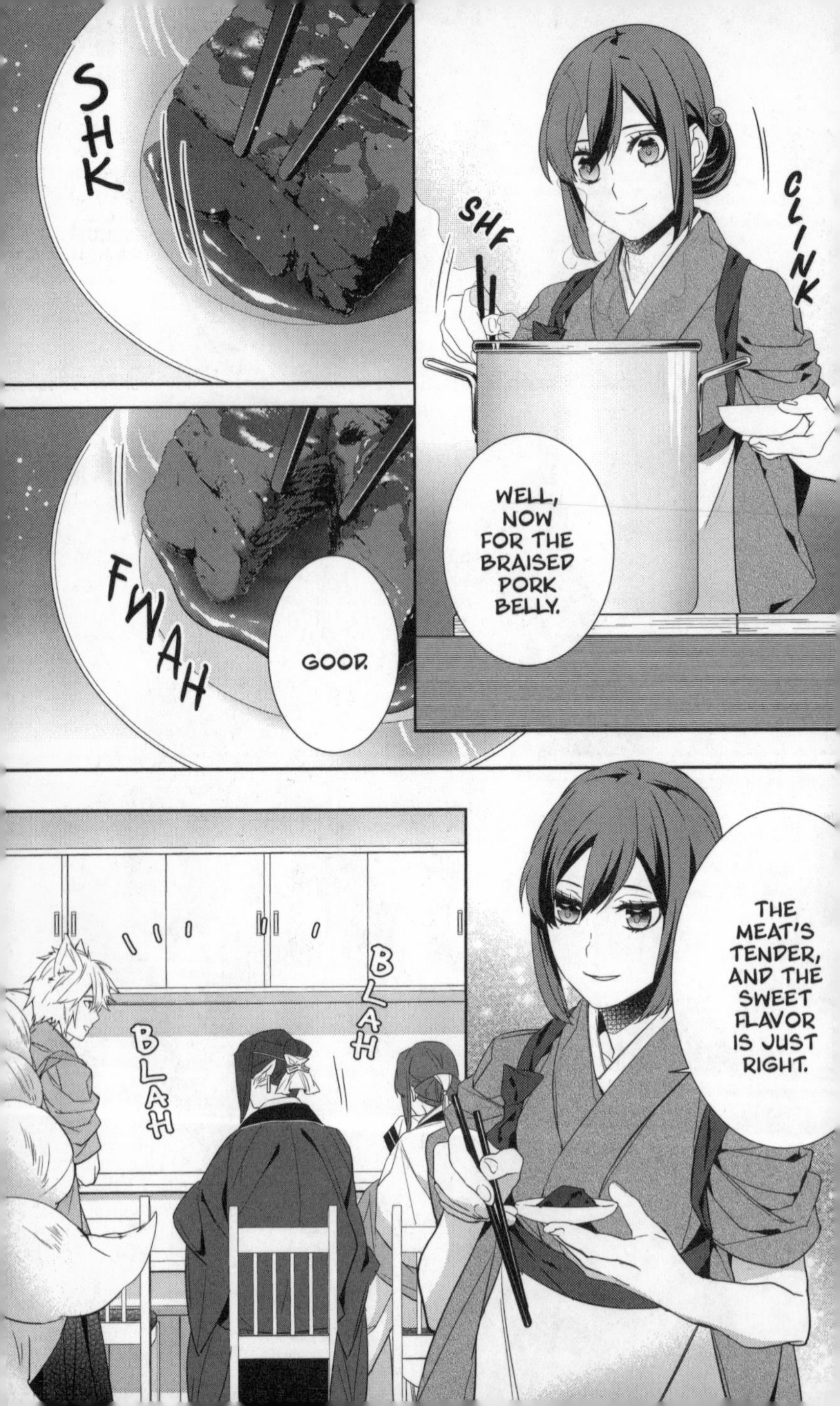
CLINK
SHF
WELL, NOW FOR THE BRAISED PORK BELLY.
SHK
FWAH
GOOD.
THE MEAT'S TENDER, AND THE SWEET FLAVOR IS JUST RIGHT.
BLAH
BLAH

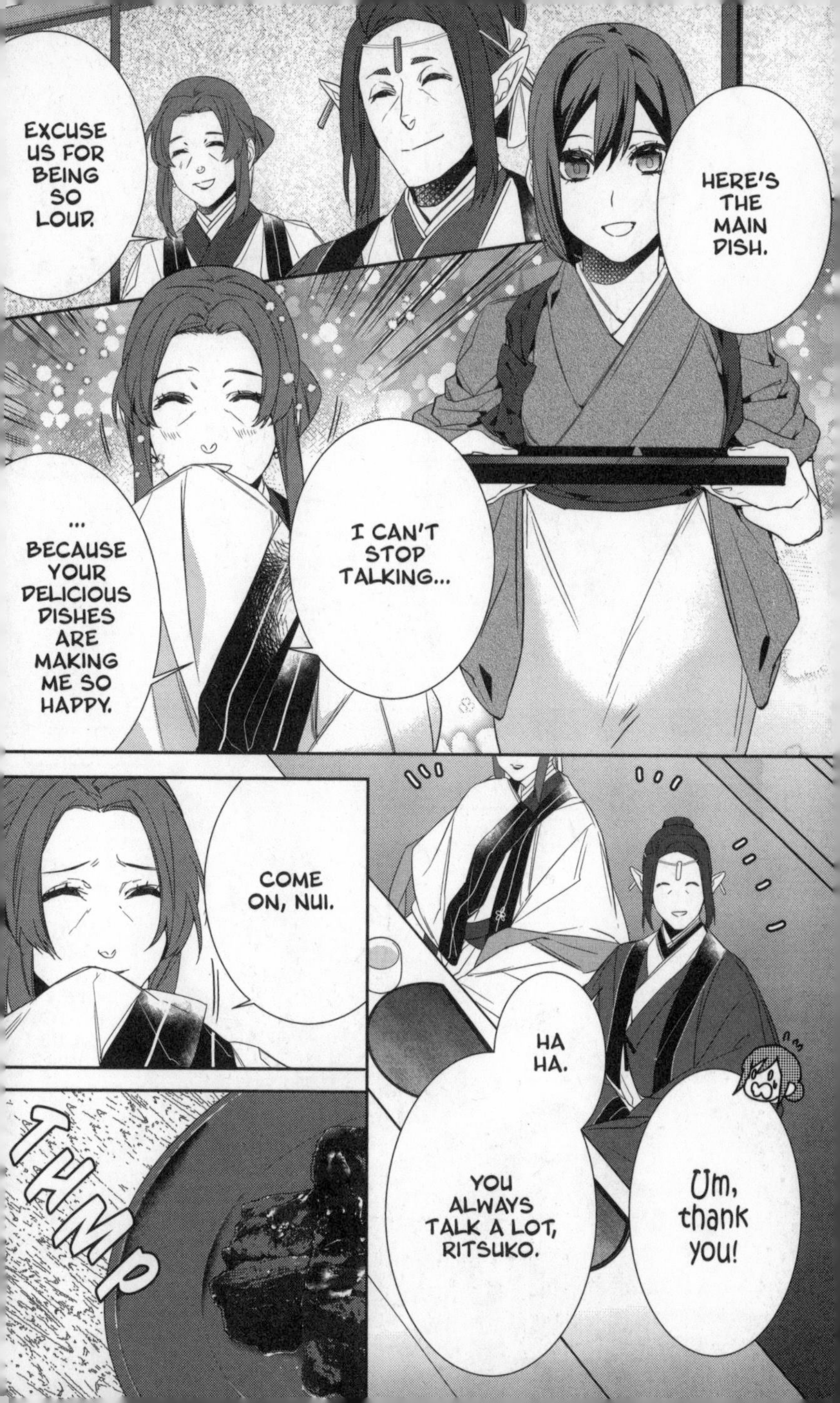
HERE'S THE MAIN DISH.
EXCUSE US FOR BEING SO LOUD.
I CAN'T STOP TALKING...
...BECAUSE YOUR DELICIOUS DISHES ARE MAKING ME SO HAPPY.
Um, thank you!
HA HA.
YOU ALWAYS TALK A LOT, RITSUKO.
COME ON, NUI.
THUMP

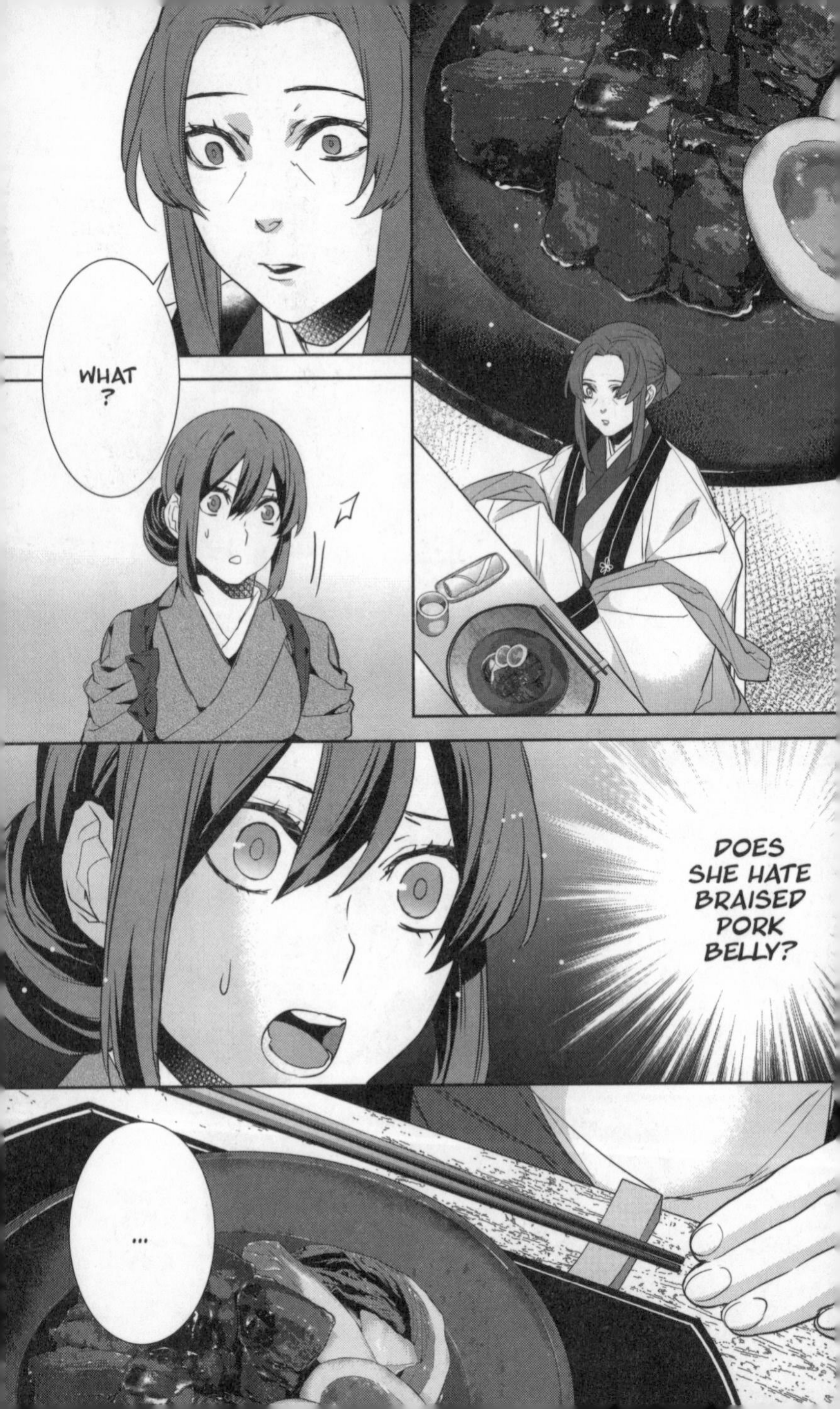
WHAT?
DOES SHE HATE BRAISED PORK BELLY?
...

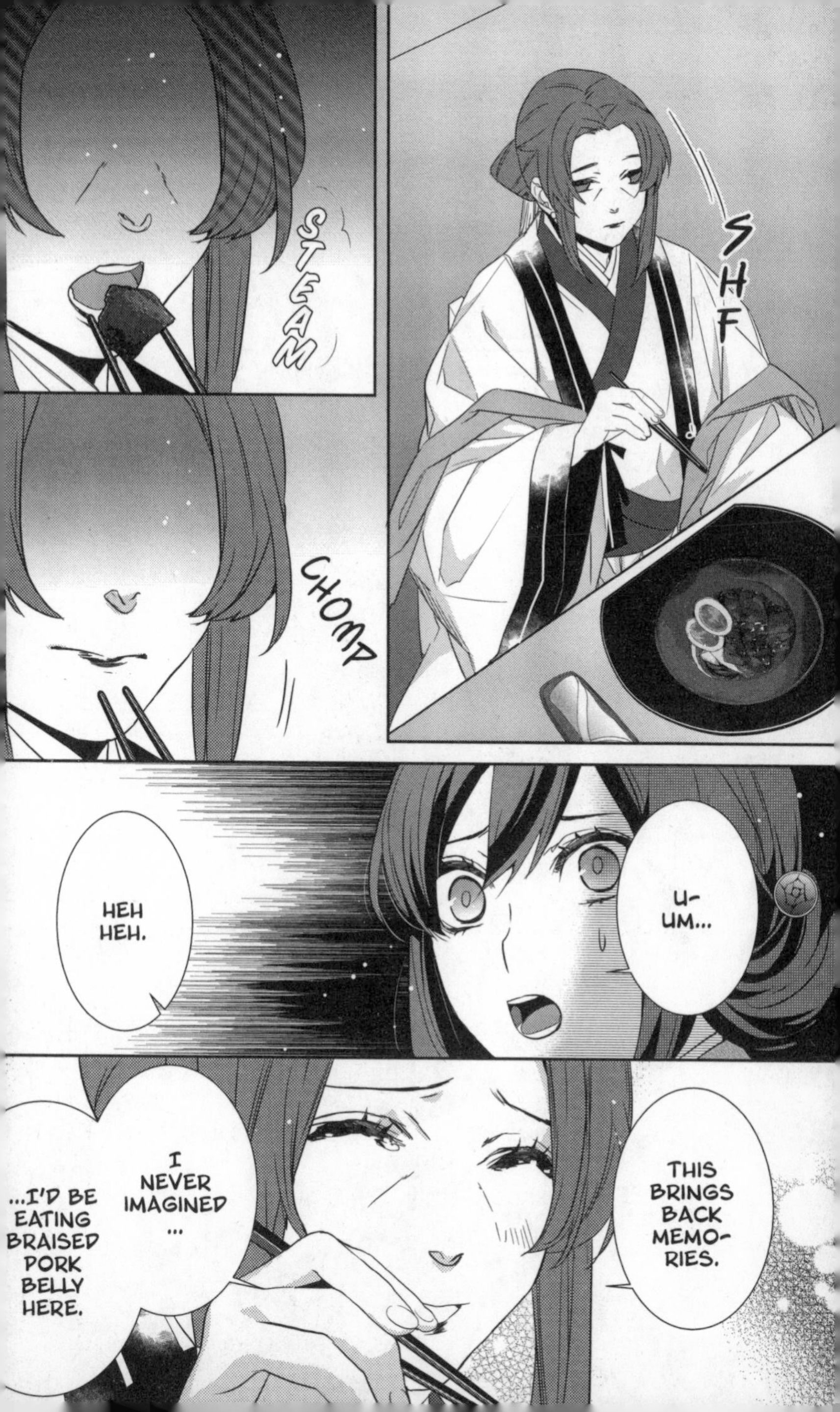
SHF
STEAM
CHOMP
U-UM...
HEH HEH.
THIS BRINGS BACK MEMORIES.
I NEVER IMAGINED...
...I'D BE EATING BRAISED PORK BELLY HERE.

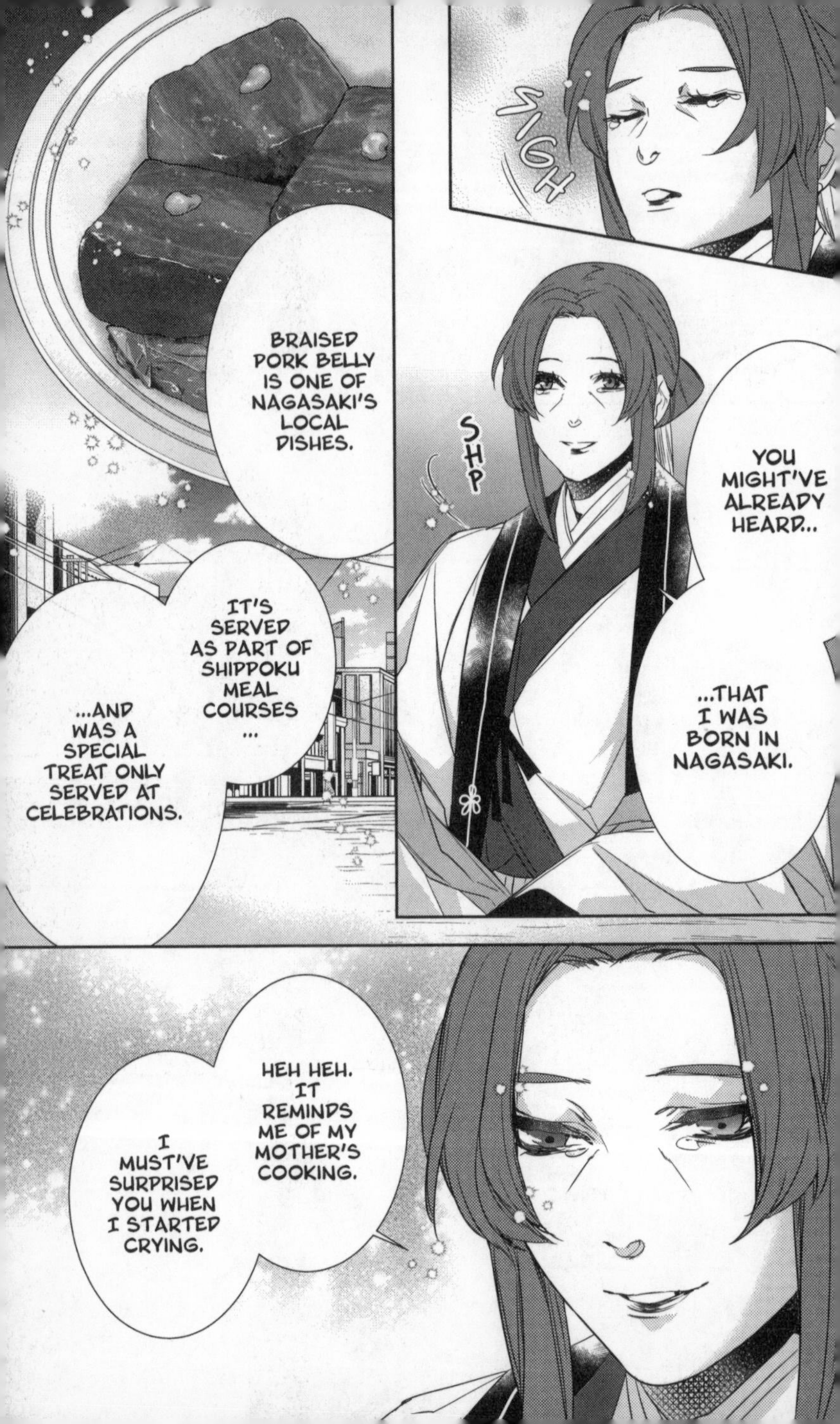
SIGH
SHP
YOU MIGHT'VE ALREADY HEARD...
...THAT I WAS BORN IN NAGASAKI.
BRAISED PORK BELLY IS ONE OF NAGASAKI'S LOCAL DISHES.
IT'S SERVED AS PART OF SHIPPOKU MEAL COURSES...
...AND WAS A SPECIAL TREAT ONLY SERVED AT CELEBRATIONS.
HEH HEH. IT REMINDS ME OF MY MOTHER'S COOKING.
I MUST'VE SURPRISED YOU WHEN I STARTED CRYING.

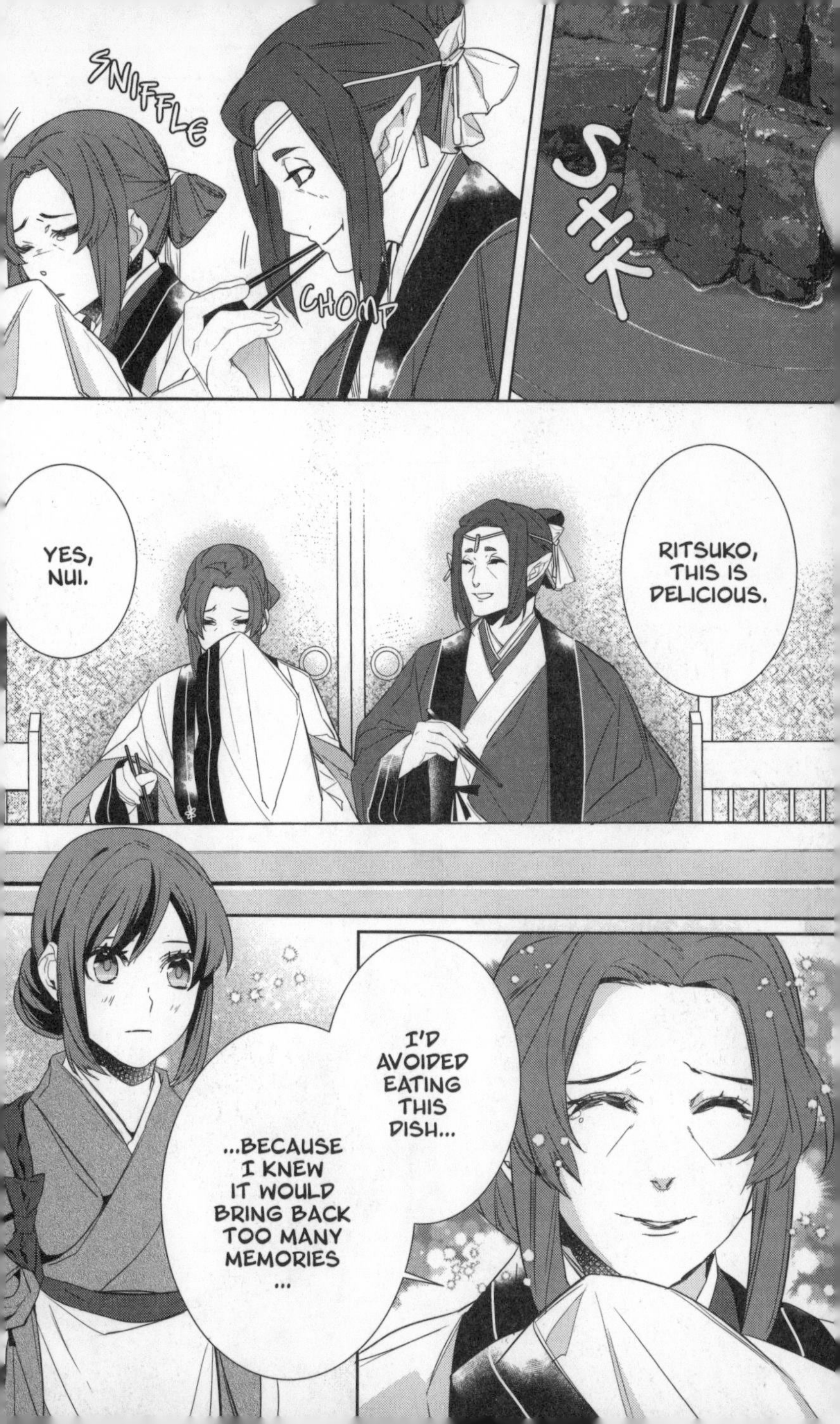
SHK
SNIFFLE
CHOMP
RITSUKO, THIS IS DELICIOUS.
YES, NUI.
I'D AVOIDED EATING THIS DISH...
...BECAUSE I KNEW IT WOULD BRING BACK TOO MANY MEMORIES ...

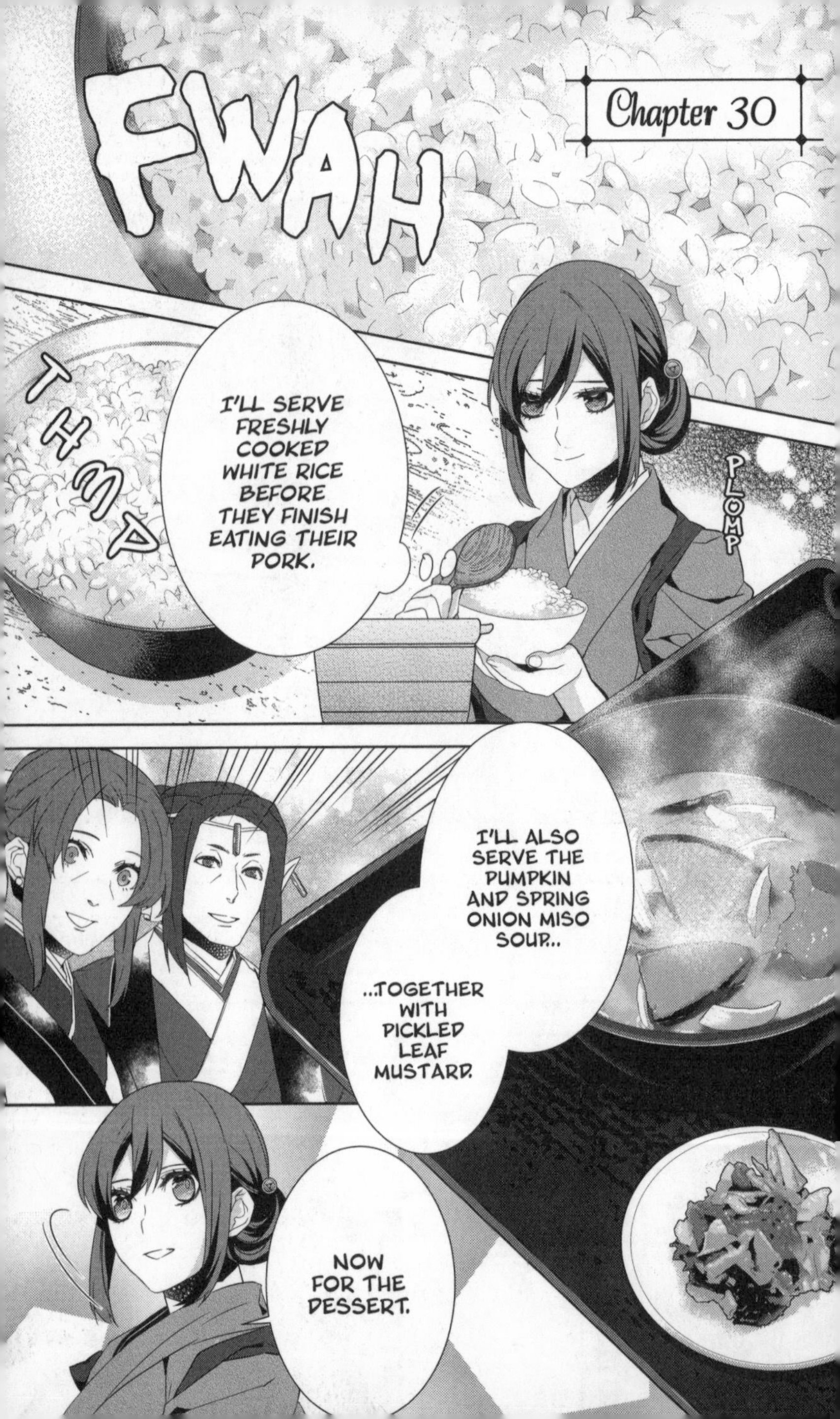
Chapter 30
FWAH
PLOMP
I'LL SERVE FRESHLY COOKED WHITE RICE BEFORE THEY FINISH EATING THEIR PORK.
THMP
I'LL ALSO SERVE THE PUMPKIN AND SPRING ONION MISO SOUP...
...TOGETHER WITH PICKLED LEAF MUSTARD.
NOW FOR THE DESSERT.

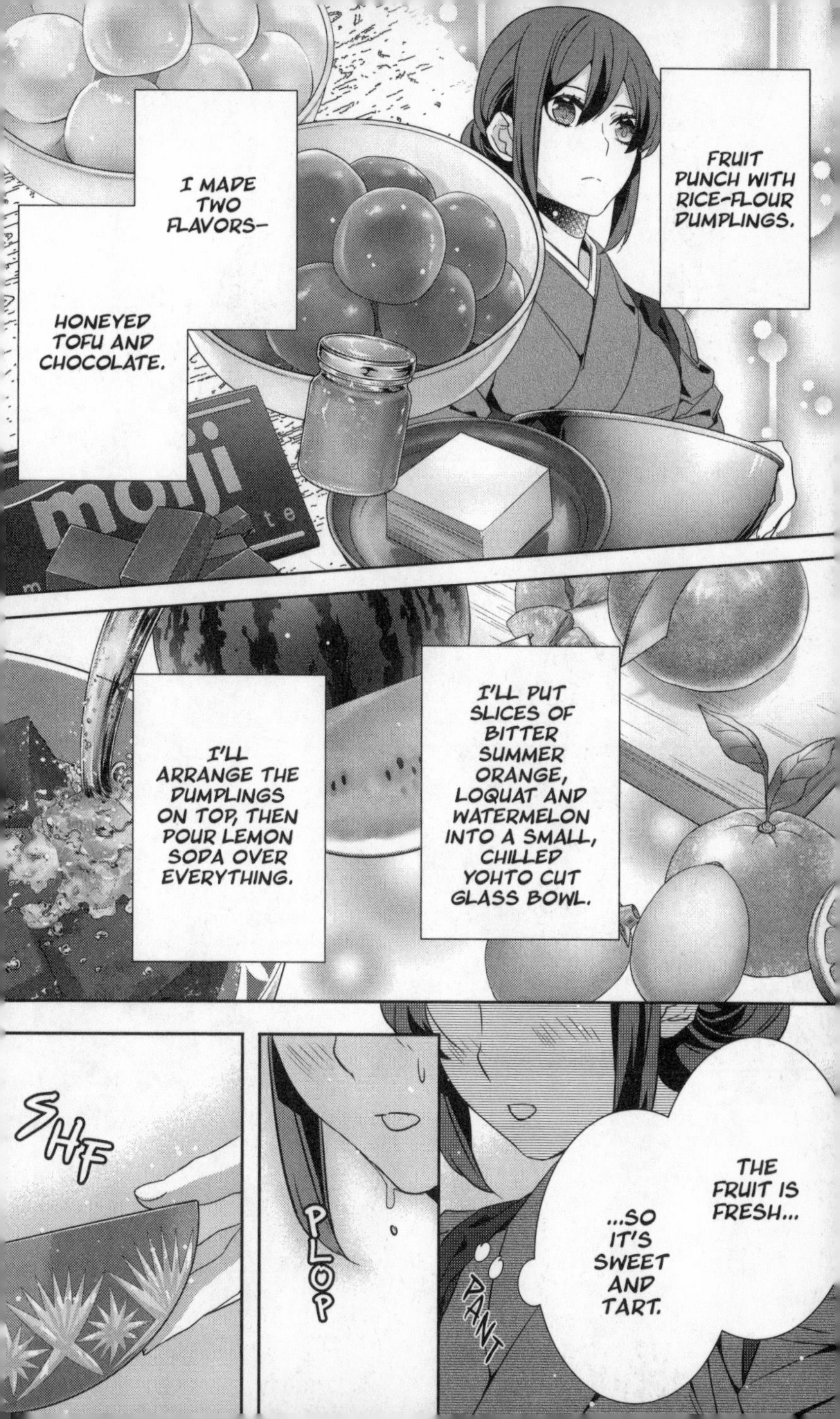
FRUIT PUNCH WITH RICE-FLOUR DUMPLINGS.
I MADE TWO FLAVORS—
HONEYED TOFU AND CHOCOLATE.
I'LL PUT SLICES OF BITTER SUMMER ORANGE, LOQUAT AND WATERMELON INTO A SMALL, CHILLED YOHTO CUT GLASS BOWL.
I'LL ARRANGE THE DUMPLINGS ON TOP, THEN POUR LEMON SODA OVER EVERYTHING.
THE FRUIT IS FRESH...
...SO IT'S SWEET AND TART.
PANT
PLOP
SHF

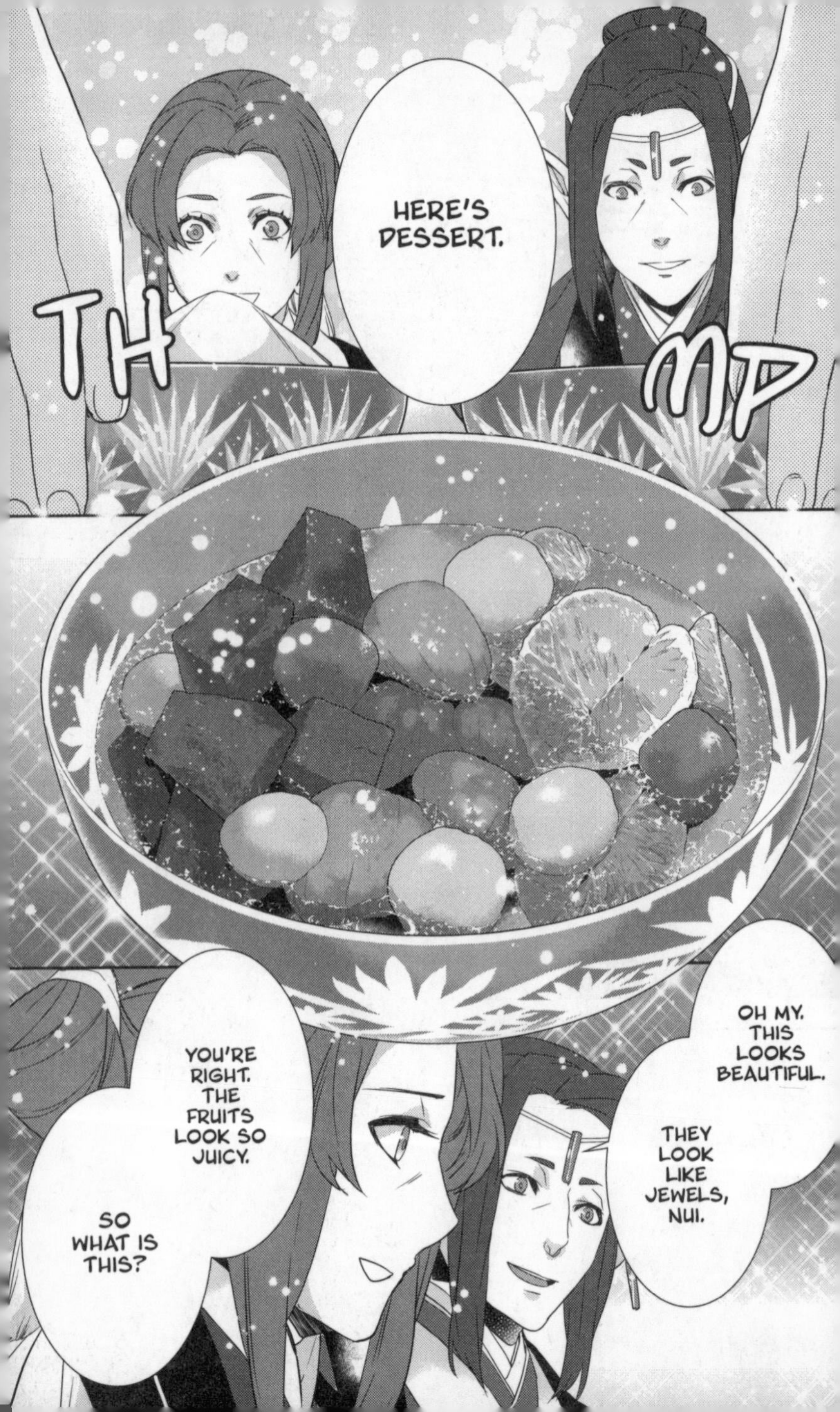
HERE'S DESSERT.
TH
MP
OH MY. THIS LOOKS BEAUTIFUL.
THEY LOOK LIKE JEWELS, NUI.
YOU'RE RIGHT. THE FRUITS LOOK SO JUICY.
SO WHAT IS THIS?

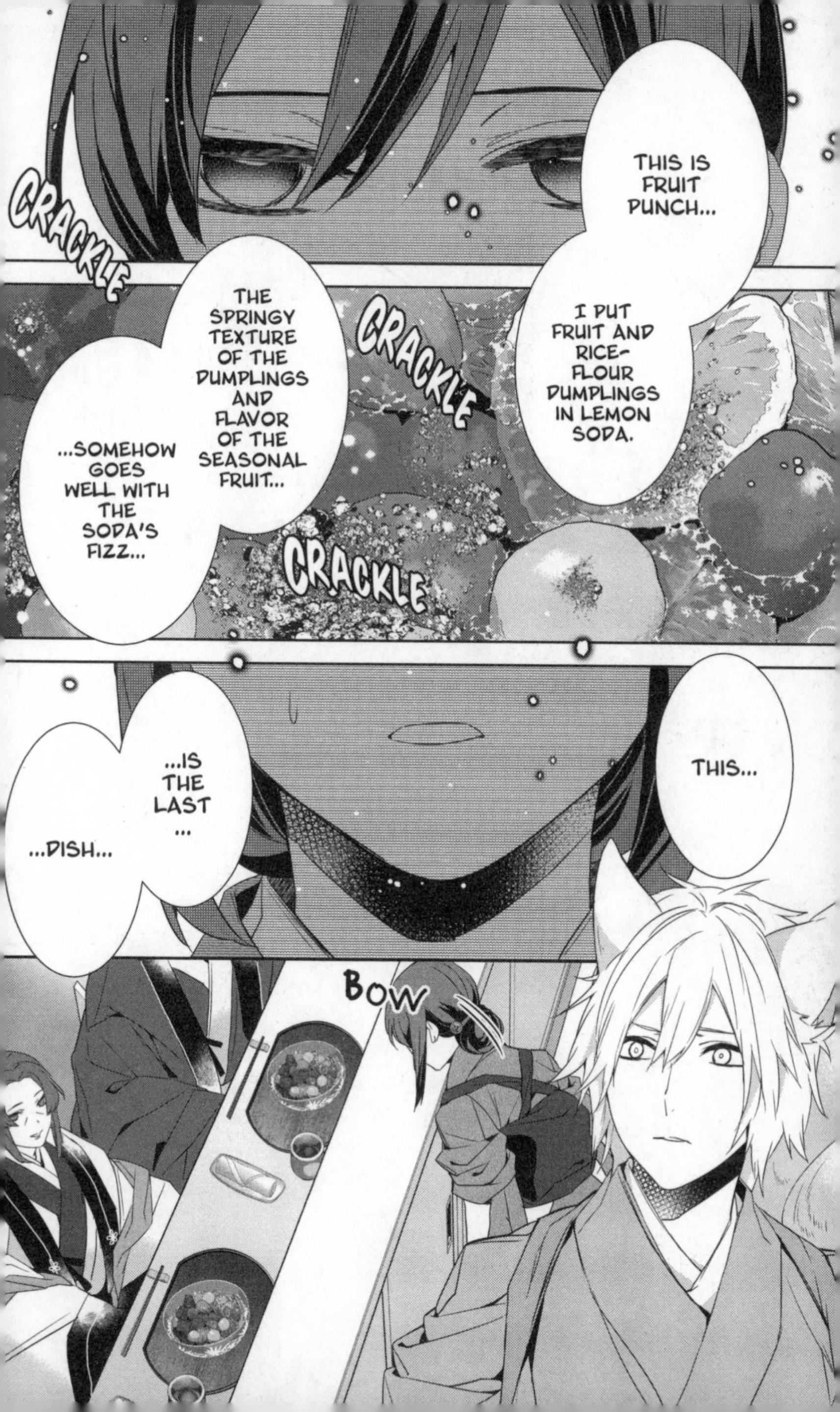
THIS IS FRUIT PUNCH...
CRACKLE
I PUT FRUIT AND RICE-FLOUR DUMPLINGS IN LEMON SODA.
CRACKLE
THE SPRINGY TEXTURE OF THE DUMPLINGS AND FLAVOR OF THE SEASONAL FRUIT...
...SOMEHOW GOES WELL WITH THE SODA'S FIZZ...
CRACKLE
THIS...
...IS THE LAST ...
...DISH...
BOW

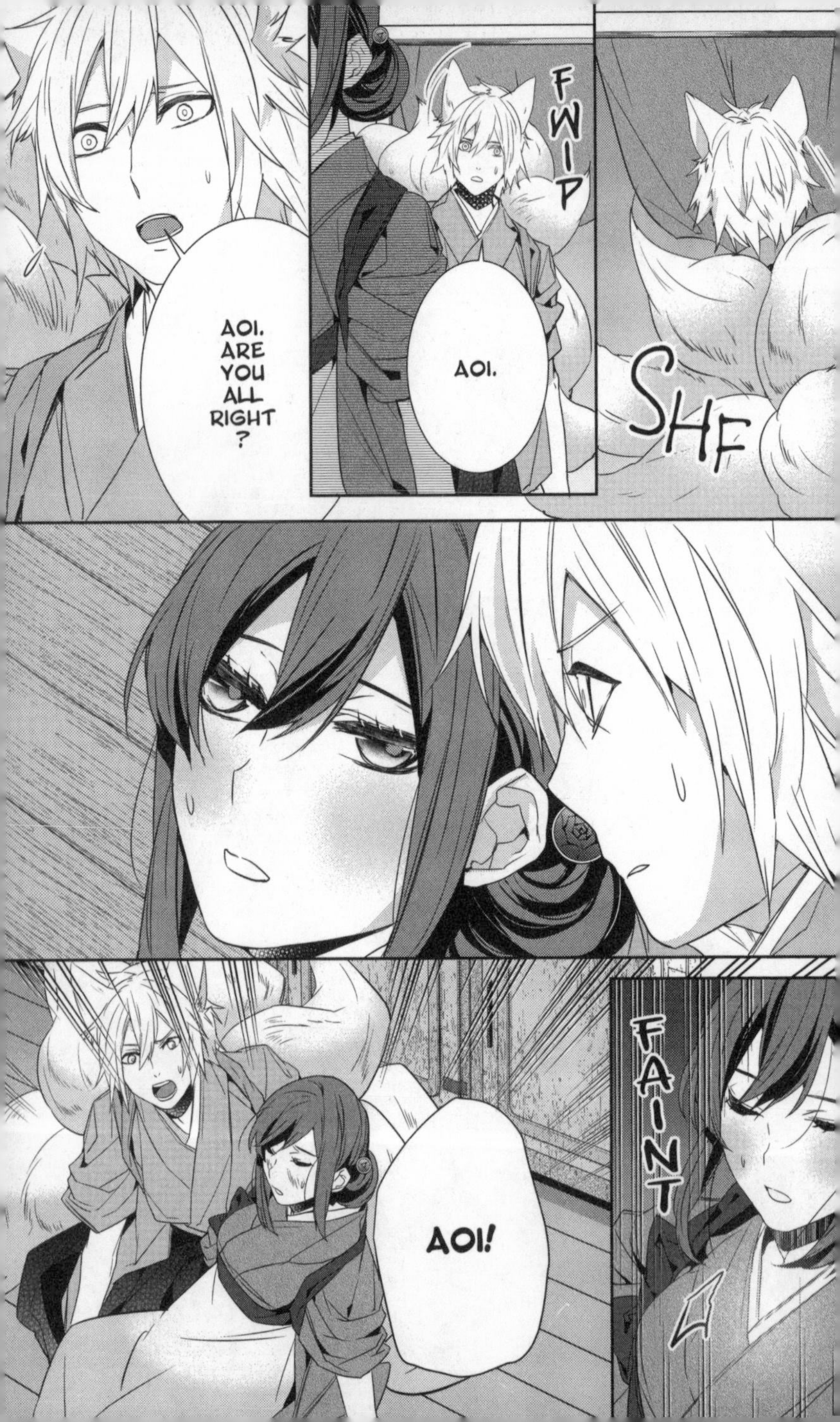
SHF
FWIP
AOI.
AOI. ARE YOU ALL RIGHT?
FAINT
AOI!

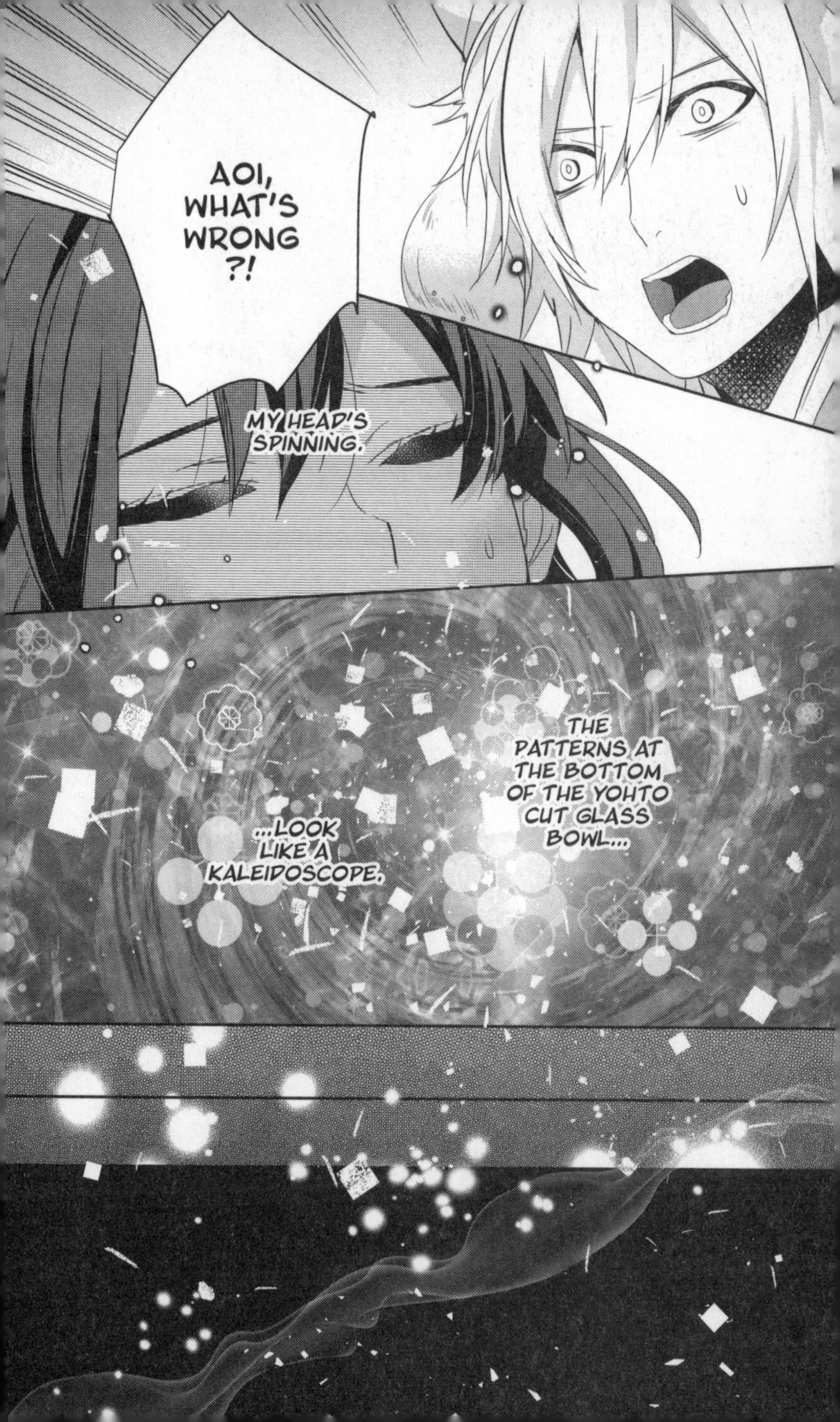
AOI, WHAT'S WRONG ?!
MY HEAD'S SPINNING.
THE PATTERNS AT THE BOTTOM OF THE YOHTO CUT GLASS BOWL...
...LOOK LIKE A KALEIDOSCOPE.

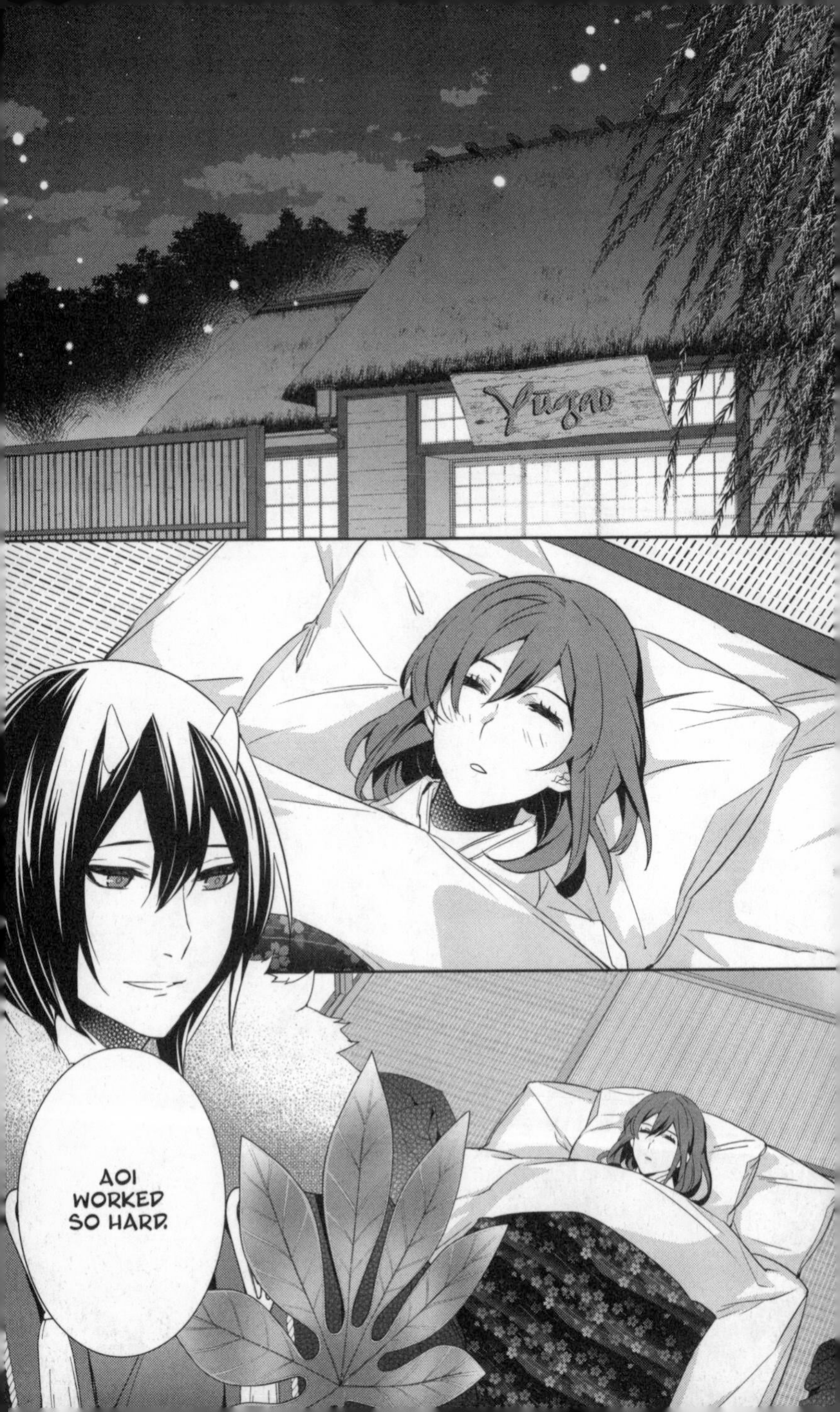
Yugao
AOI WORKED SO HARD.

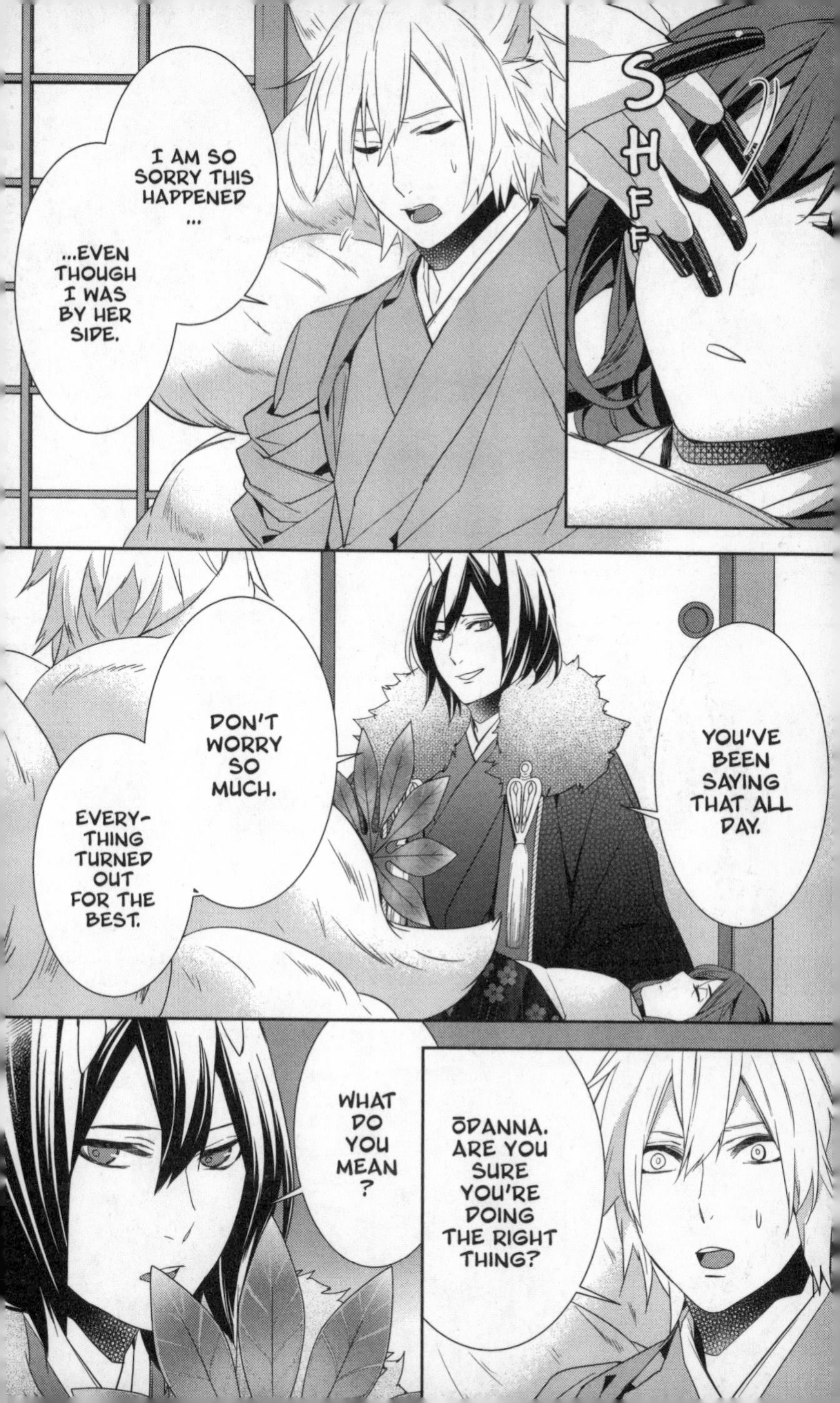
SHFF
I AM SO SORRY THIS HAPPENED...
...EVEN THOUGH I WAS BY HER SIDE.
YOU'VE BEEN SAYING THAT ALL DAY.
DON'T WORRY SO MUCH.
EVERY-THING TURNED OUT FOR THE BEST.
ŌDANNA. ARE YOU SURE YOU'RE DOING THE RIGHT THING?
WHAT DO YOU MEAN?

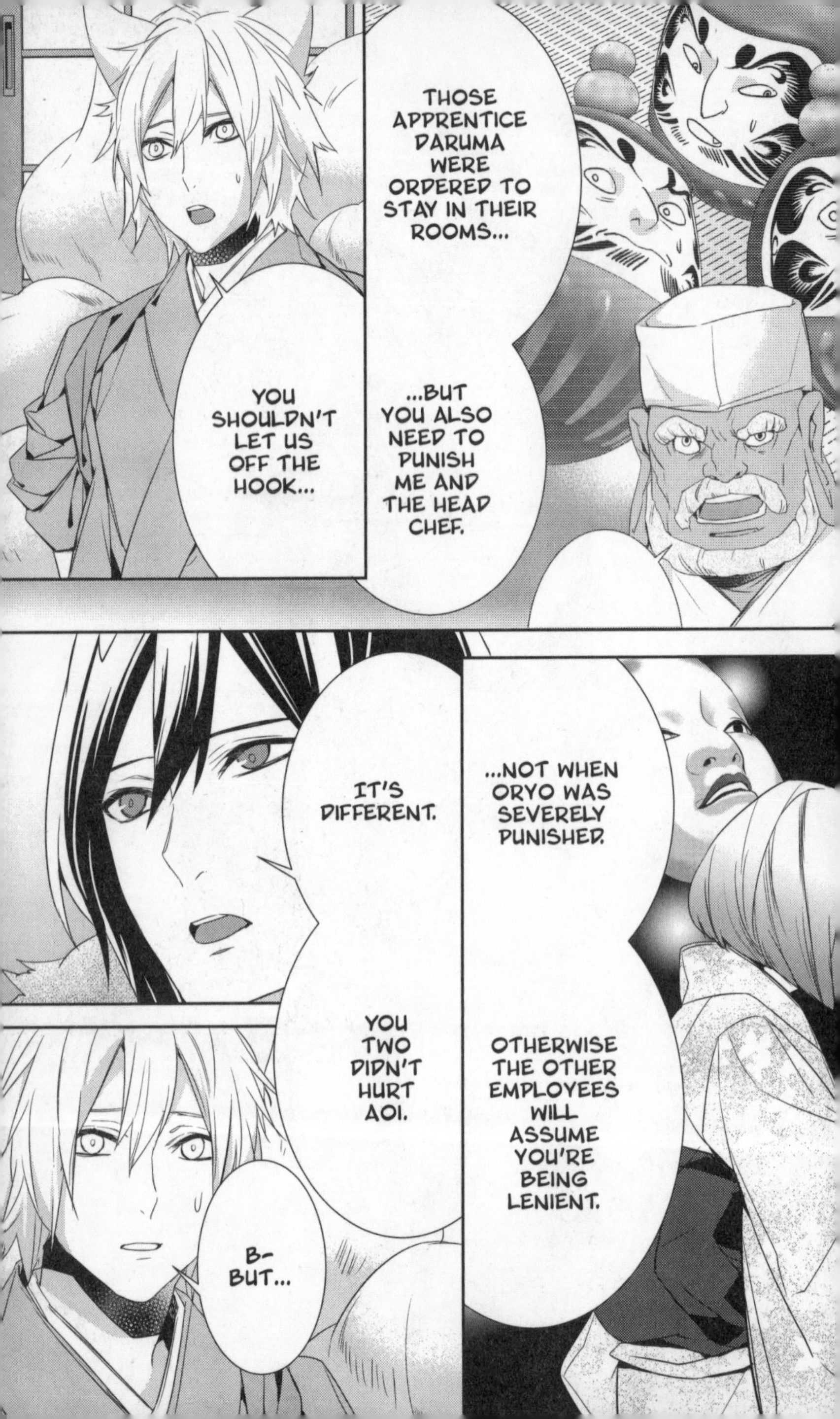
THOSE APPRENTICE DARUMA WERE ORDERED TO STAY IN THEIR ROOMS...
...BUT YOU ALSO NEED TO PUNISH ME AND THE HEAD CHEF.
YOU SHOULDN'T LET US OFF THE HOOK...
...NOT WHEN ORYO WAS SEVERELY PUNISHED.
OTHERWISE THE OTHER EMPLOYEES WILL ASSUME YOU'RE BEING LENIENT.
IT'S DIFFERENT.
YOU TWO DIDN'T HURT AOI.
B-BUT...

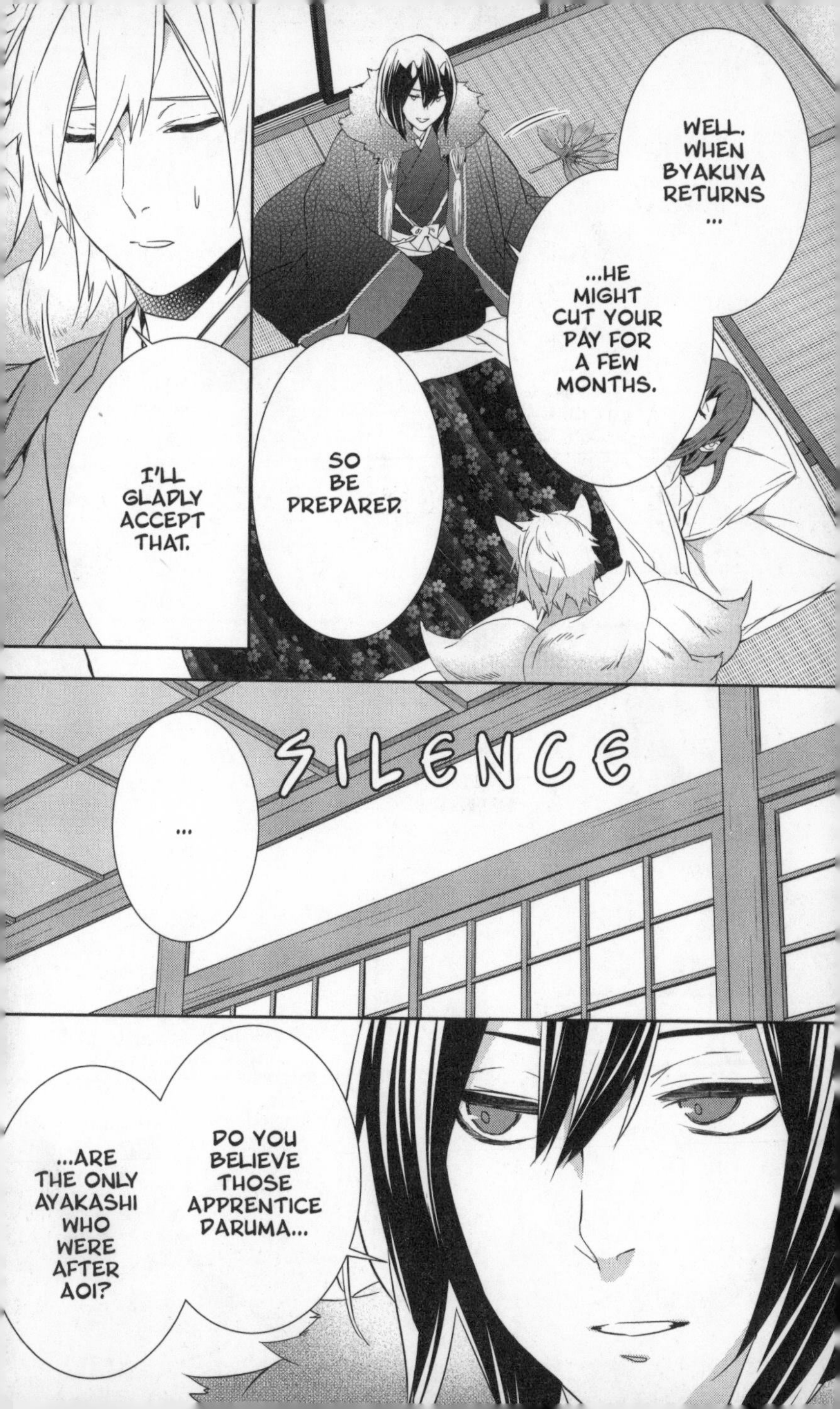
WELL. WHEN BYAKUYA RETURNS...
...HE MIGHT CUT YOUR PAY FOR A FEW MONTHS.
SO BE PREPARED.
I'LL GLADLY ACCEPT THAT.
SILENCE
...
DO YOU BELIEVE THOSE APPRENTICE DARUMA...
...ARE THE ONLY AYAKASHI WHO WERE AFTER AOI?

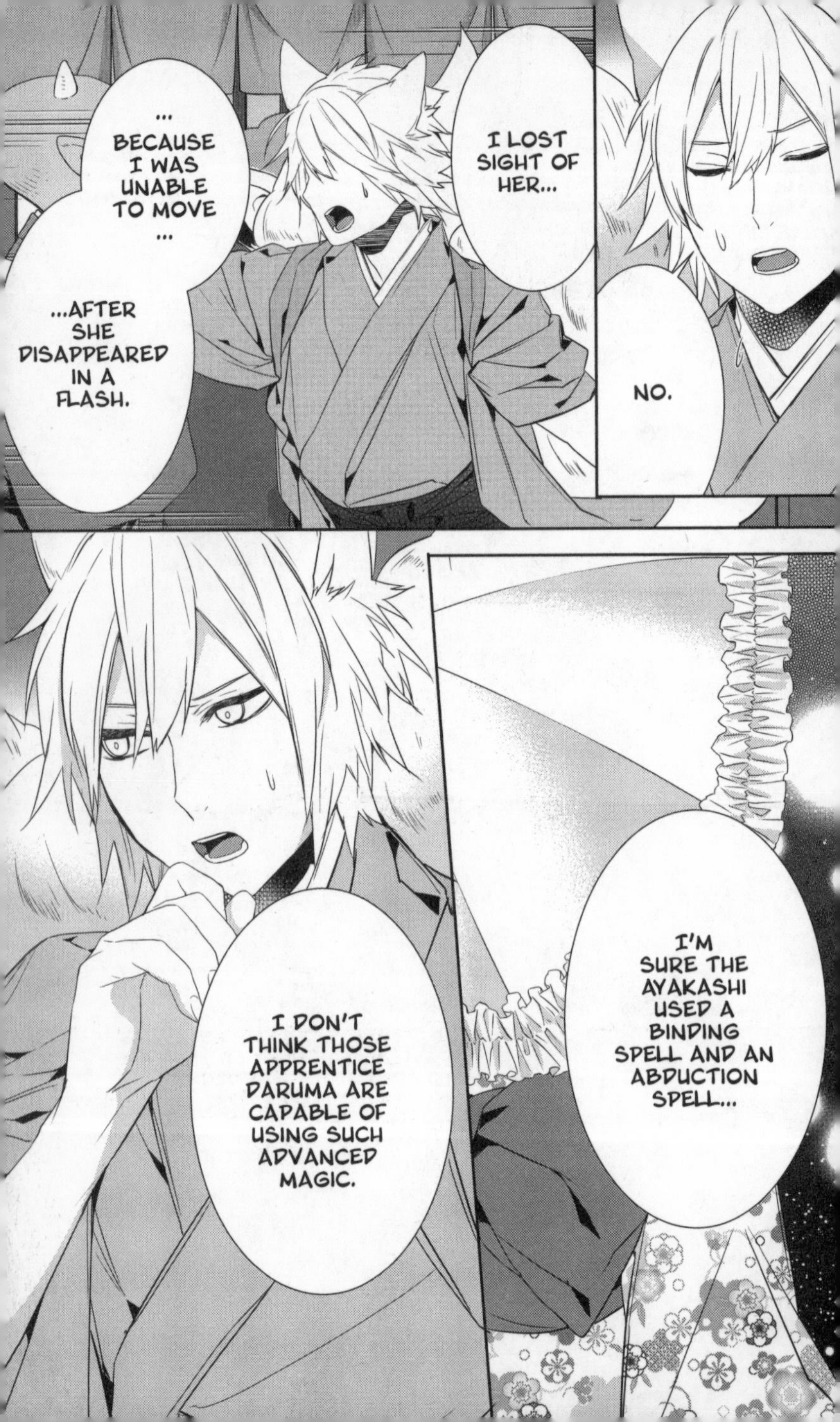
NO.
I LOST SIGHT OF HER...
... BECAUSE I WAS UNABLE TO MOVE ...
...AFTER SHE DISAPPEARED IN A FLASH.
I'M SURE THE AYAKASHI USED A BINDING SPELL AND AN ABDUCTION SPELL...
I DON'T THINK THOSE APPRENTICE DARUMA ARE CAPABLE OF USING SUCH ADVANCED MAGIC.

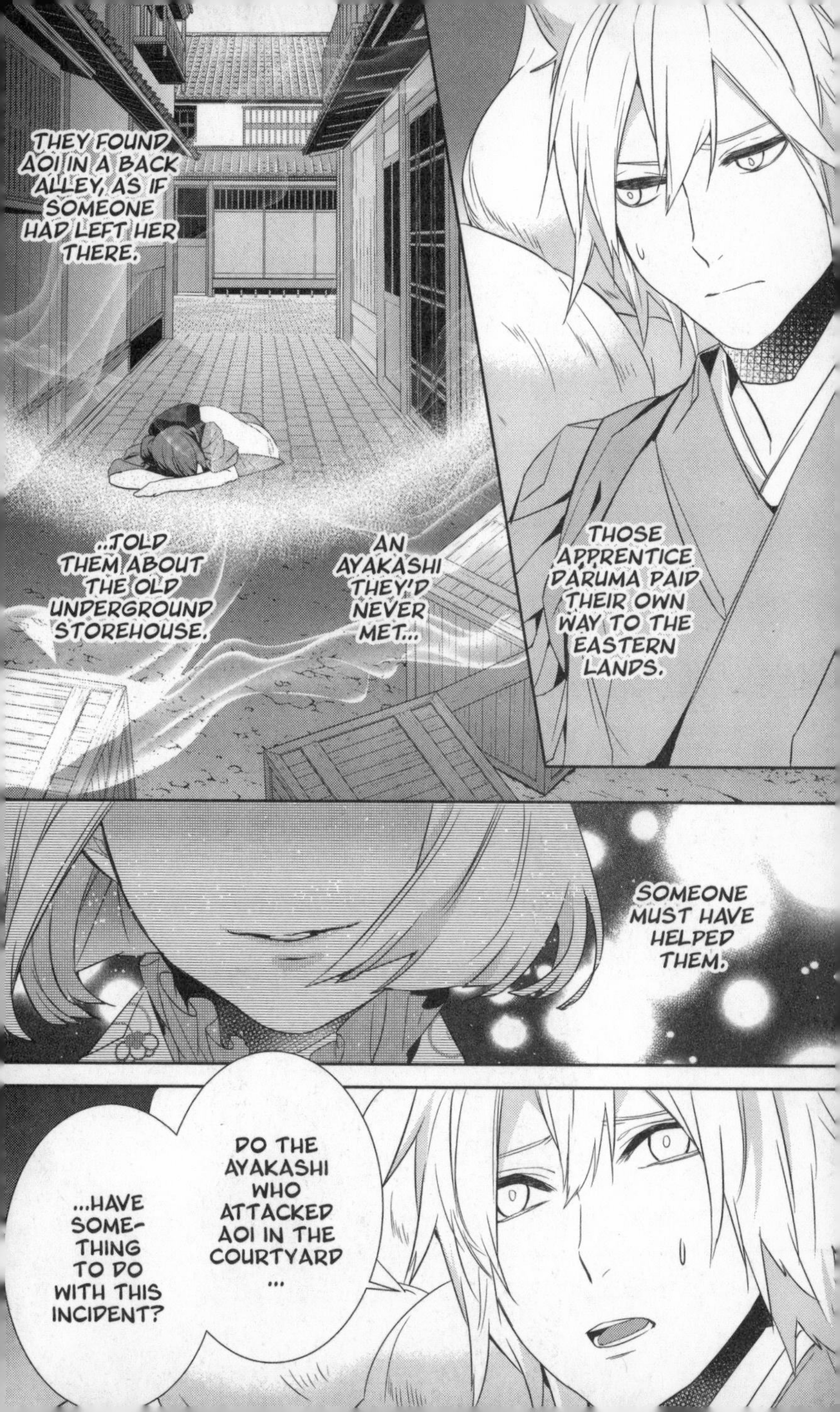
THOSE APPRENTICE DARUMA PAID THEIR OWN WAY TO THE EASTERN LANDS.
AN AYAKASHI THEY'D NEVER MET...
...TOLD THEM ABOUT THE OLD UNDERGROUND STOREHOUSE.
THEY FOUND AOI IN A BACK ALLEY, AS IF SOMEONE HAD LEFT HER THERE.
SOMEONE MUST HAVE HELPED THEM.
DO THE AYAKASHI WHO ATTACKED AOI IN THE COURTYARD...
...HAVE SOME-THING TO DO WITH THIS INCIDENT?

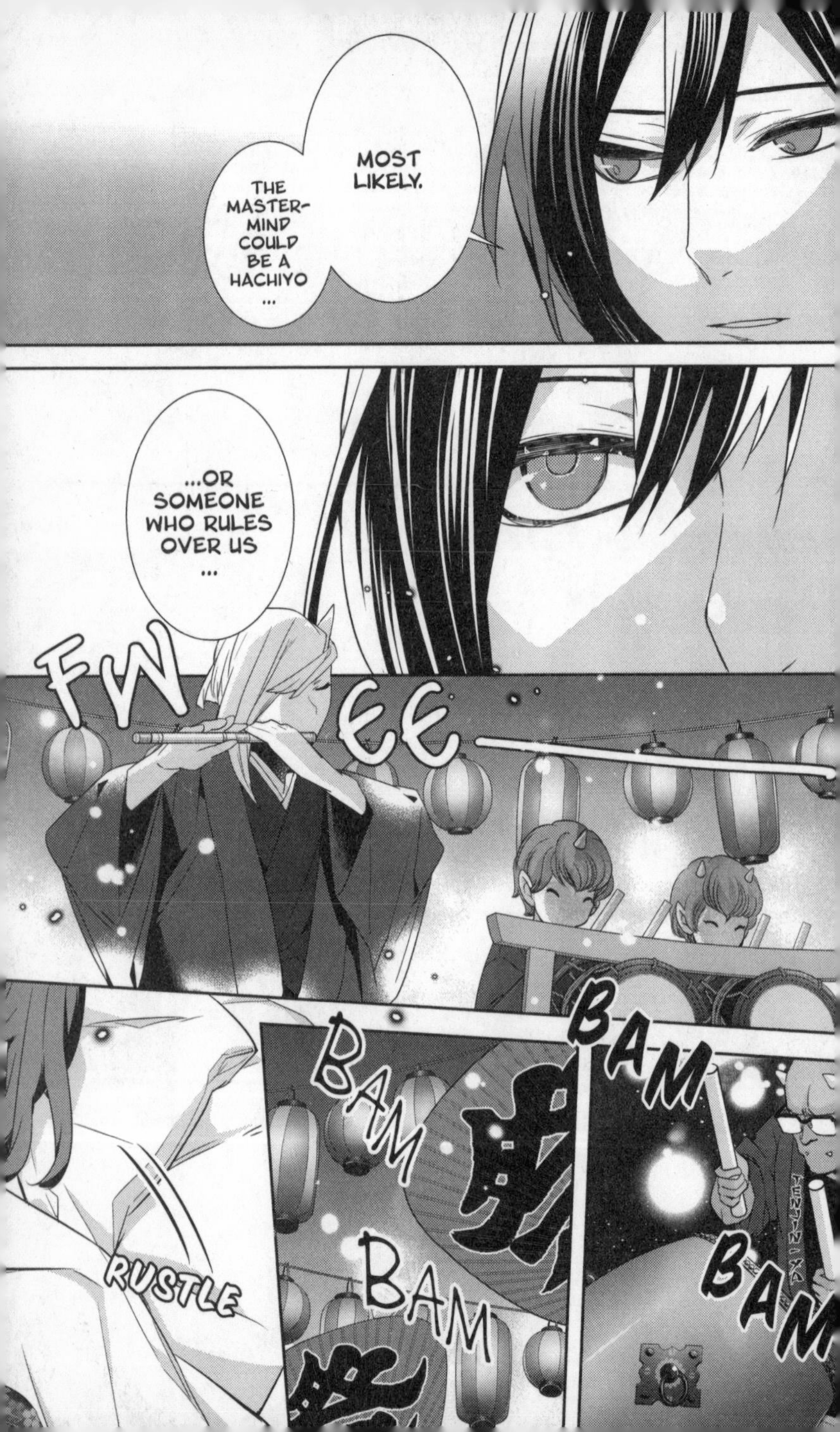
MOST LIKELY.
THE MASTER-MIND COULD BE A HACHIYO ...
...OR SOMEONE WHO RULES OVER US ...
FWEE
BAM
BAM
TENJIN-ZA
BAM
BAM
RUSTLE

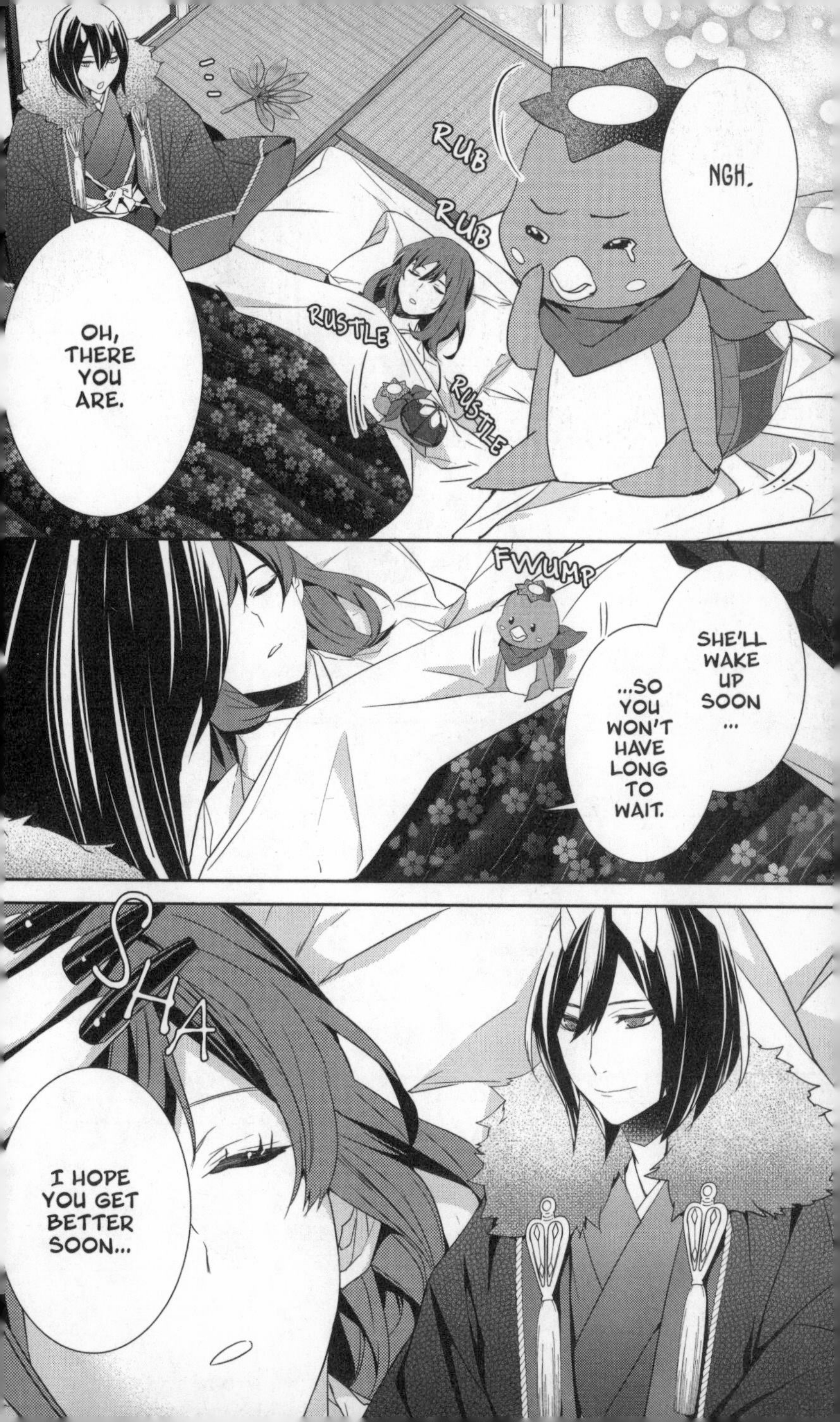
NGH.
RUB
RUB
RUSTLE
RUSTLE
OH, THERE YOU ARE.
FWUMP
SHE'LL WAKE UP SOON...
...SO YOU WON'T HAVE LONG TO WAIT.
SHA
I HOPE YOU GET BETTER SOON...

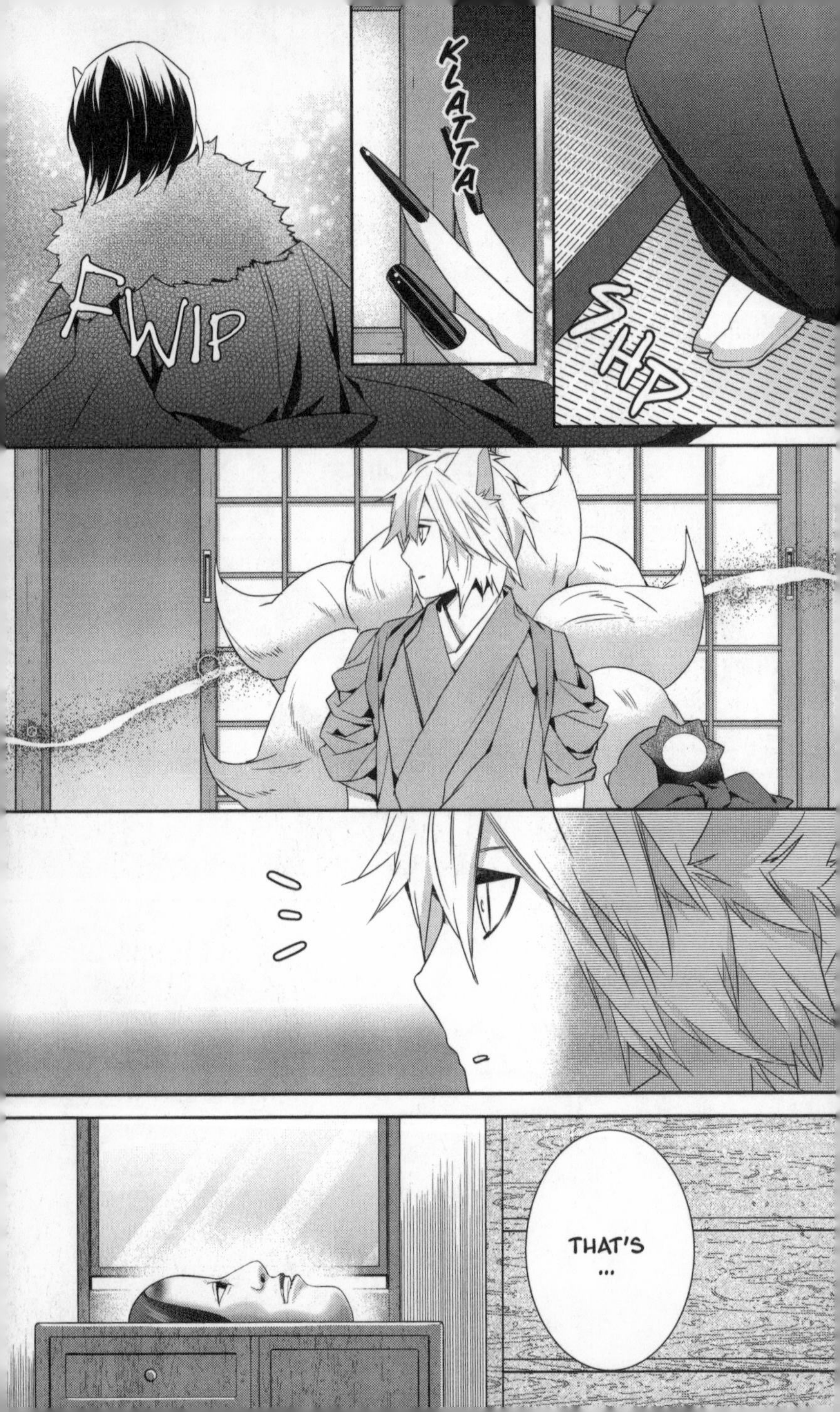
SHP
KLATTA
FWIP
THAT'S ...

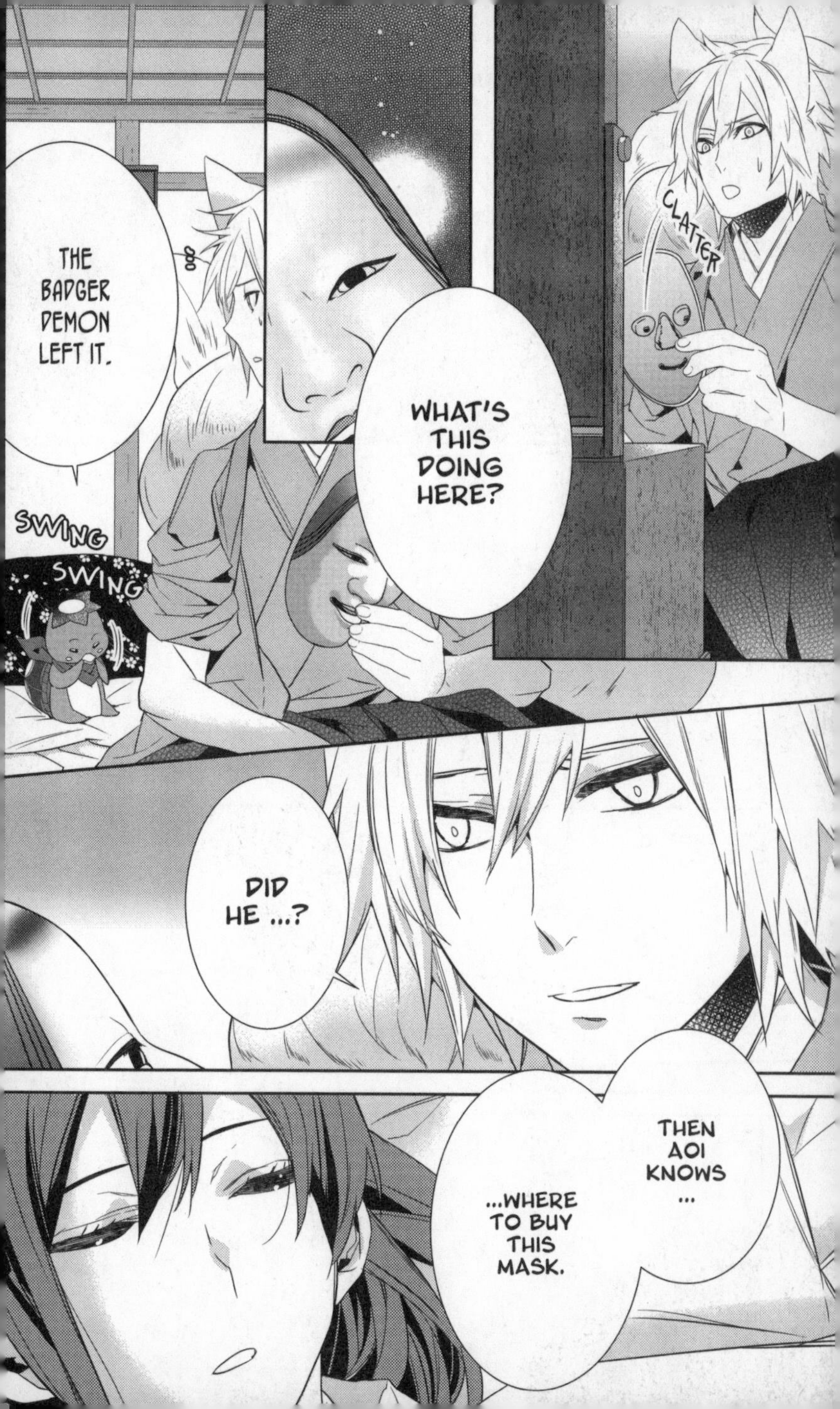
CLATTER
WHAT'S THIS DOING HERE?
THE BADGER DEMON LEFT IT.
SWING
SWING
DID HE ...?
THEN AOI KNOWS ...
...WHERE TO BUY THIS MASK.

FWOOSH

Yugai

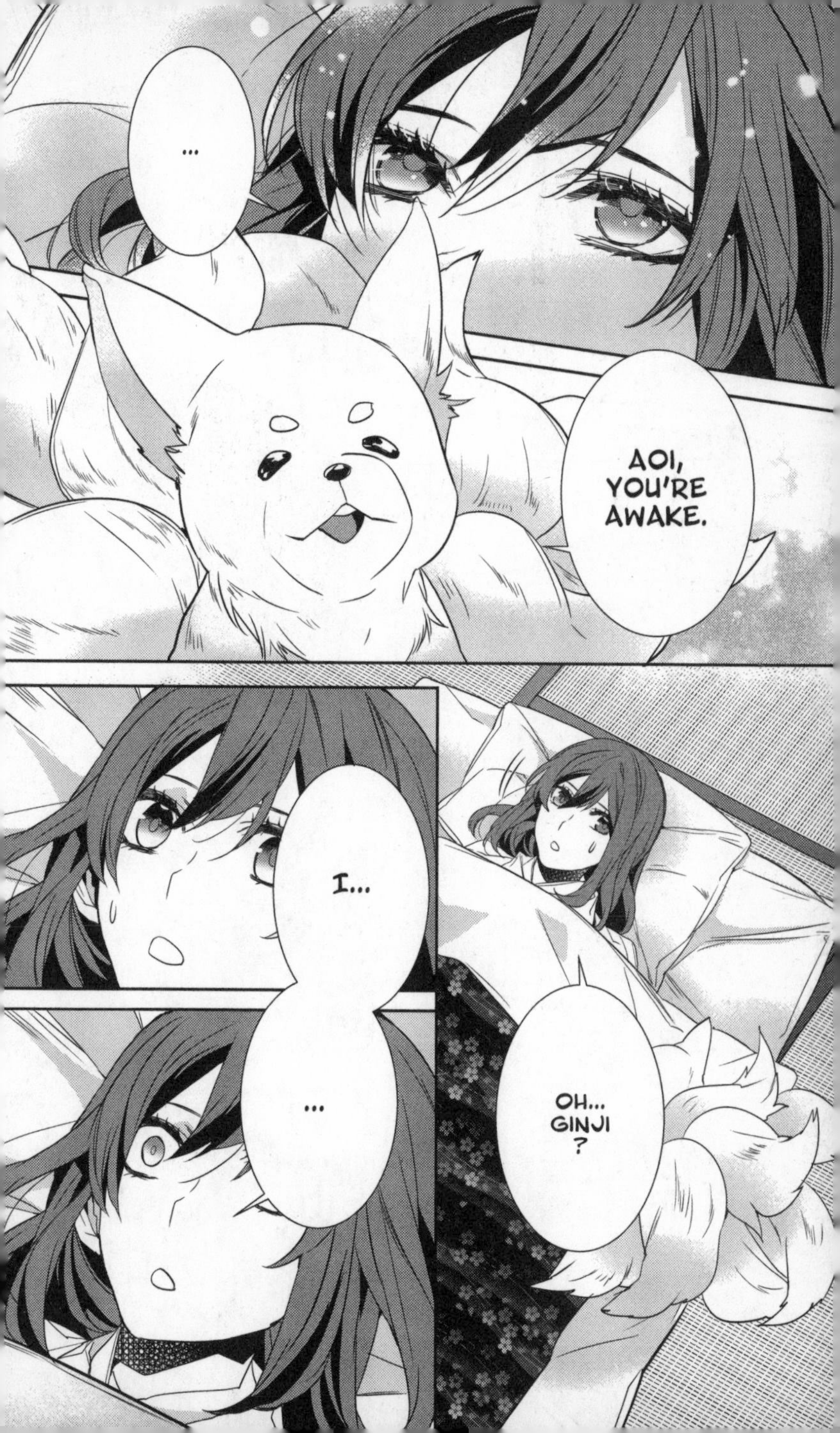
AOI, YOU'RE AWAKE.
...
OH... GINJI?
I...
...

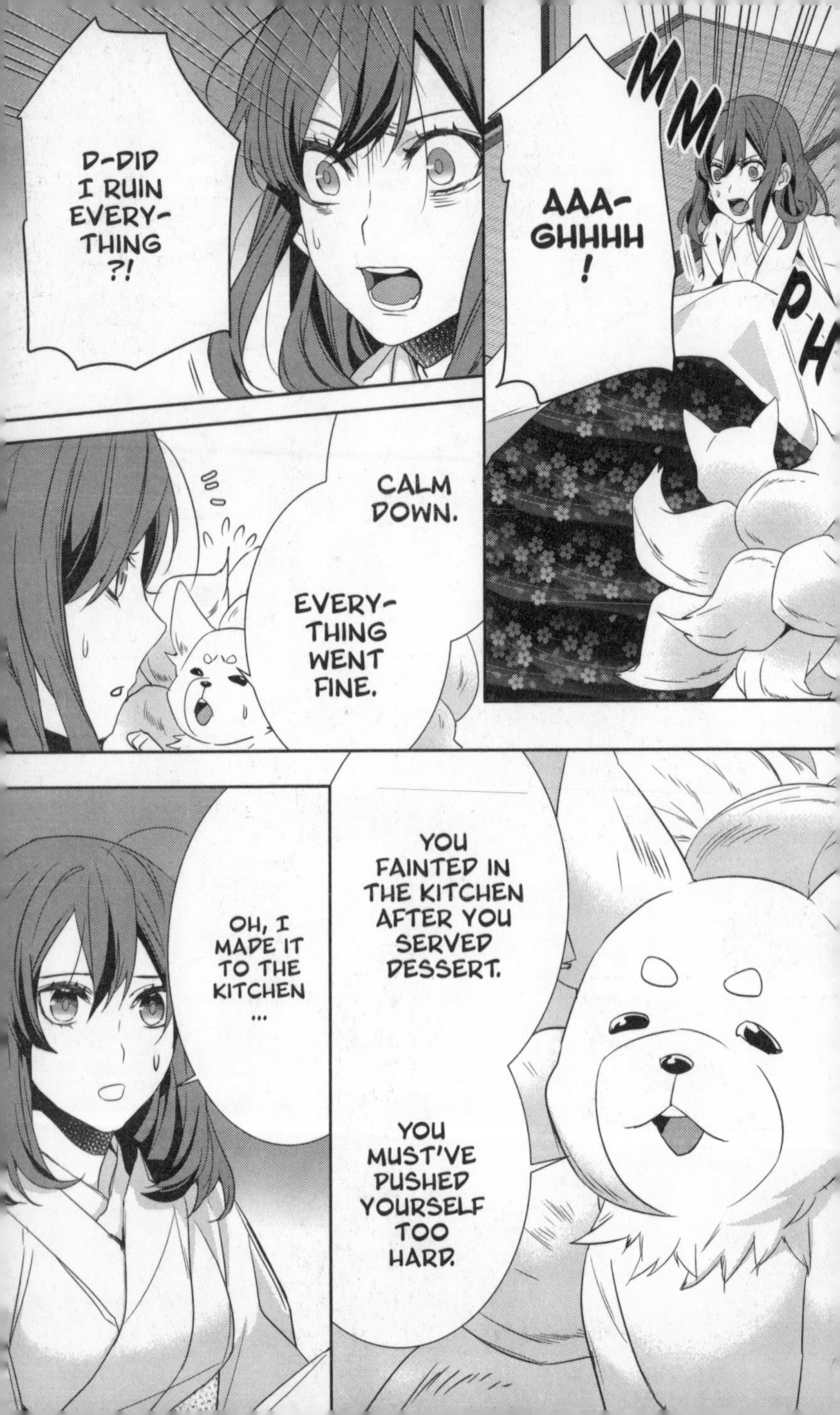
MMMPH
AAA-GHHHH!
D-DID I RUIN EVERY-THING?!
CALM DOWN.
EVERY-THING WENT FINE.
YOU FAINTED IN THE KITCHEN AFTER YOU SERVED DESSERT.
YOU MUST'VE PUSHED YOURSELF TOO HARD.
OH, I MADE IT TO THE KITCHEN...

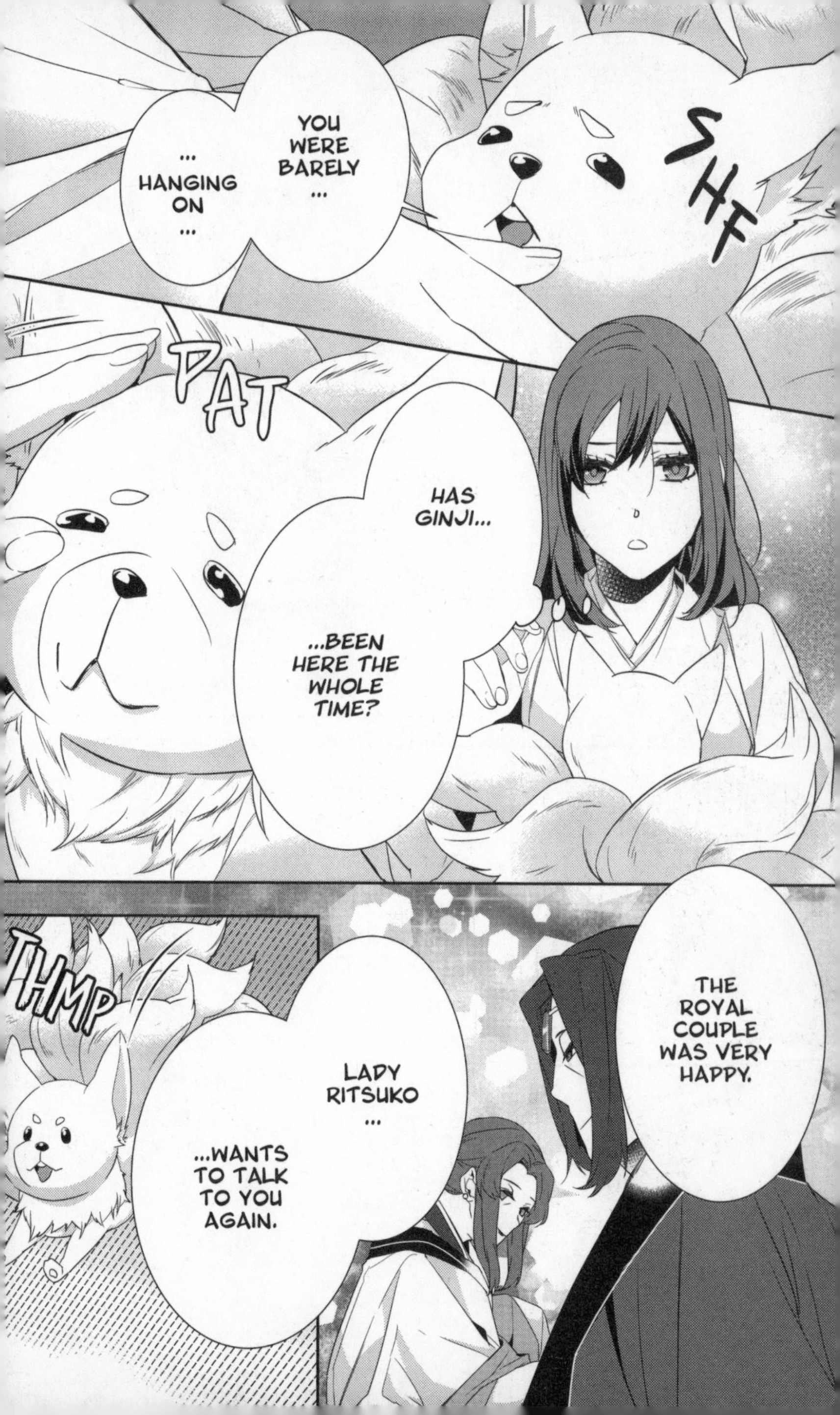
SHF
YOU WERE BARELY ...
... HANGING ON ...
PAT
HAS GINJI...
...BEEN HERE THE WHOLE TIME?
THE ROYAL COUPLE WAS VERY HAPPY.
LADY RITSUKO ...
...WANTS TO TALK TO YOU AGAIN.
THMP

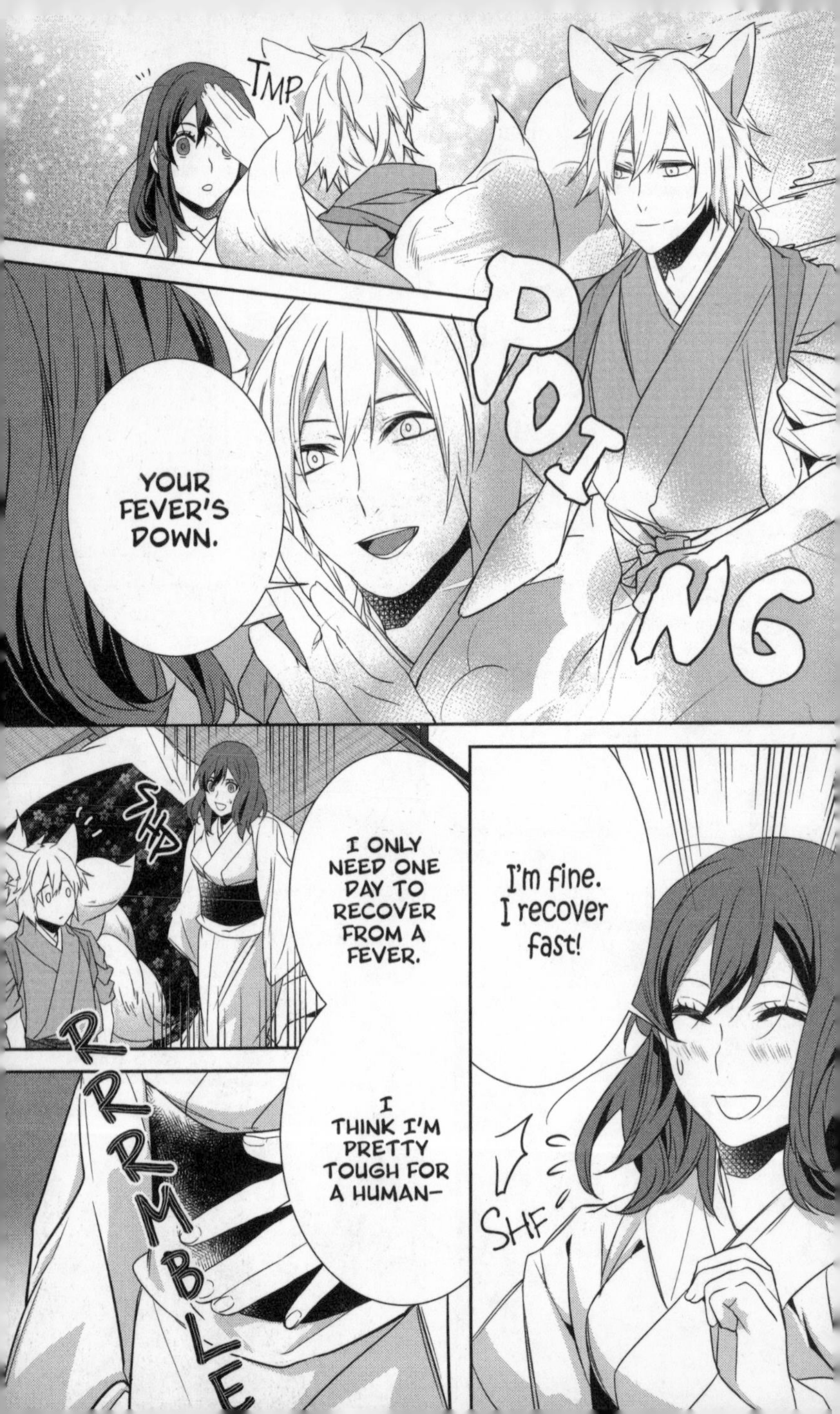
TMP
POING
YOUR FEVER'S DOWN.
I'm fine. I recover fast!
SHF
SHP
I ONLY NEED ONE DAY TO RECOVER FROM A FEVER.
I THINK I'M PRETTY TOUGH FOR A HUMAN–
RRRMBLE

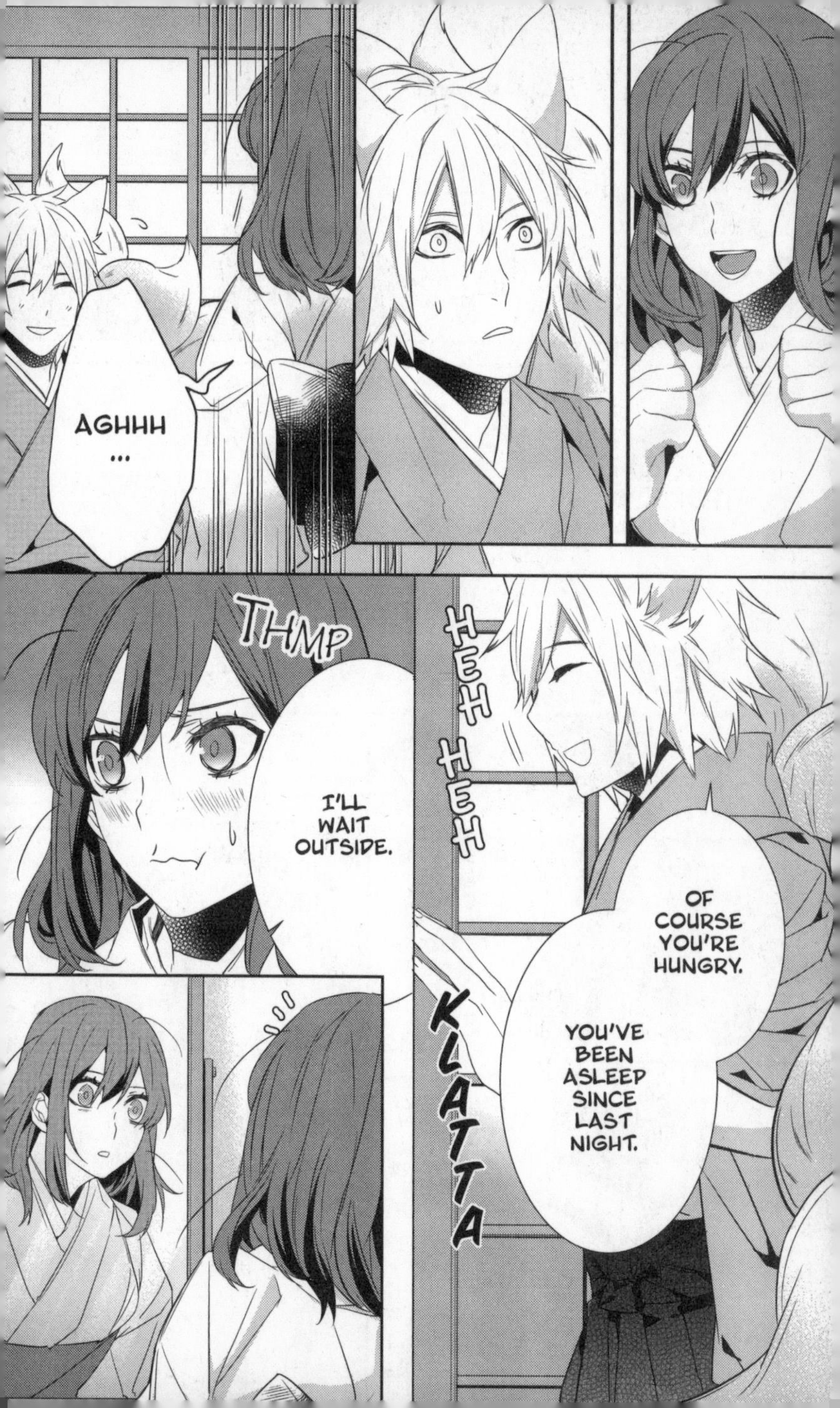
AGHHH ...
HEH HEH
OF COURSE YOU'RE HUNGRY.
YOU'VE BEEN ASLEEP SINCE LAST NIGHT.
KLATTA
THMP
I'LL WAIT OUTSIDE.

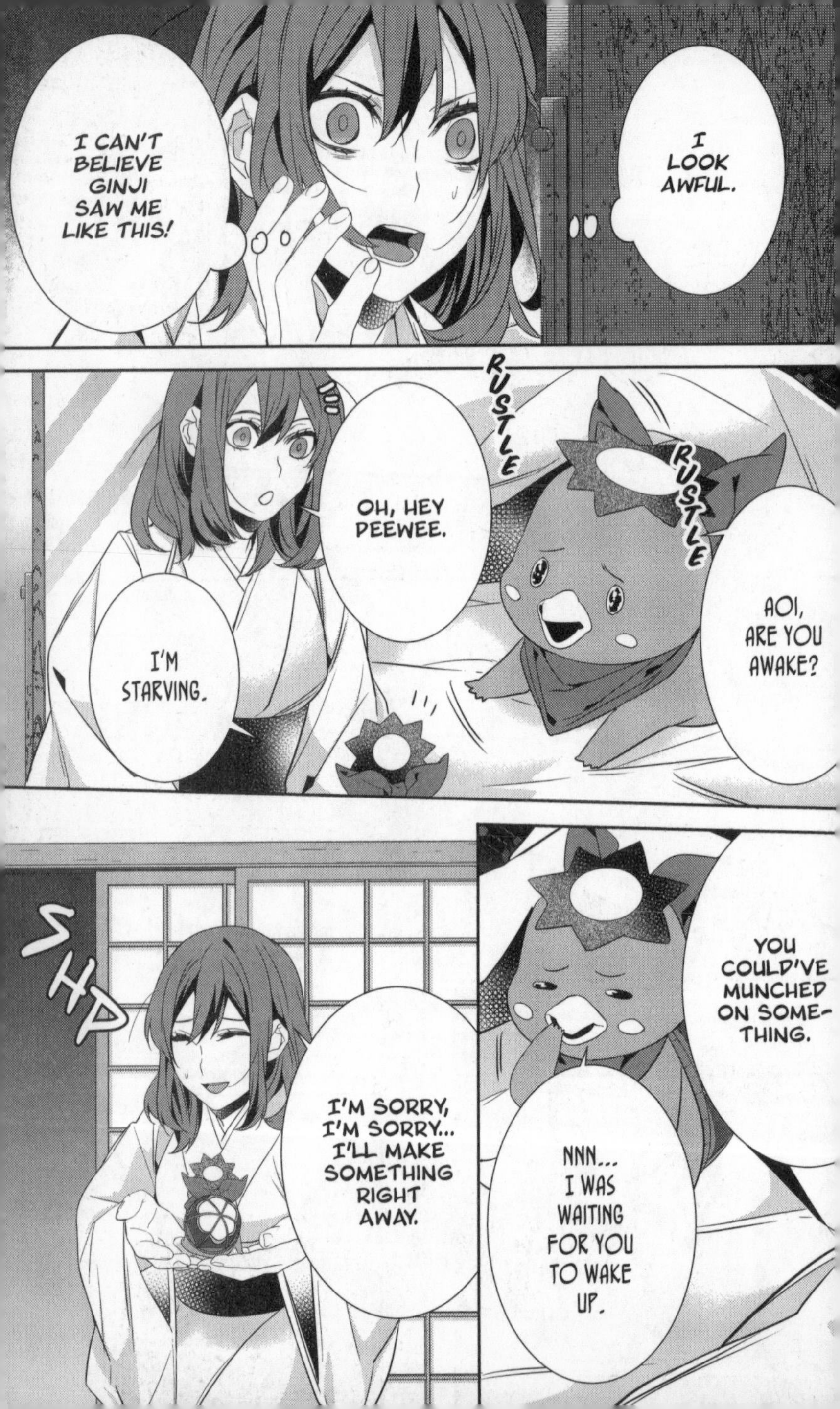
I LOOK AWFUL.
I CAN'T BELIEVE GINJI SAW ME LIKE THIS!
RUSTLE
RUSTLE
AOI, ARE YOU AWAKE?
OH, HEY PEEWEE.
I'M STARVING.
YOU COULD'VE MUNCHED ON SOME-THING.
NNN... I WAS WAITING FOR YOU TO WAKE UP.
SHP
I'M SORRY, I'M SORRY... I'LL MAKE SOMETHING RIGHT AWAY.

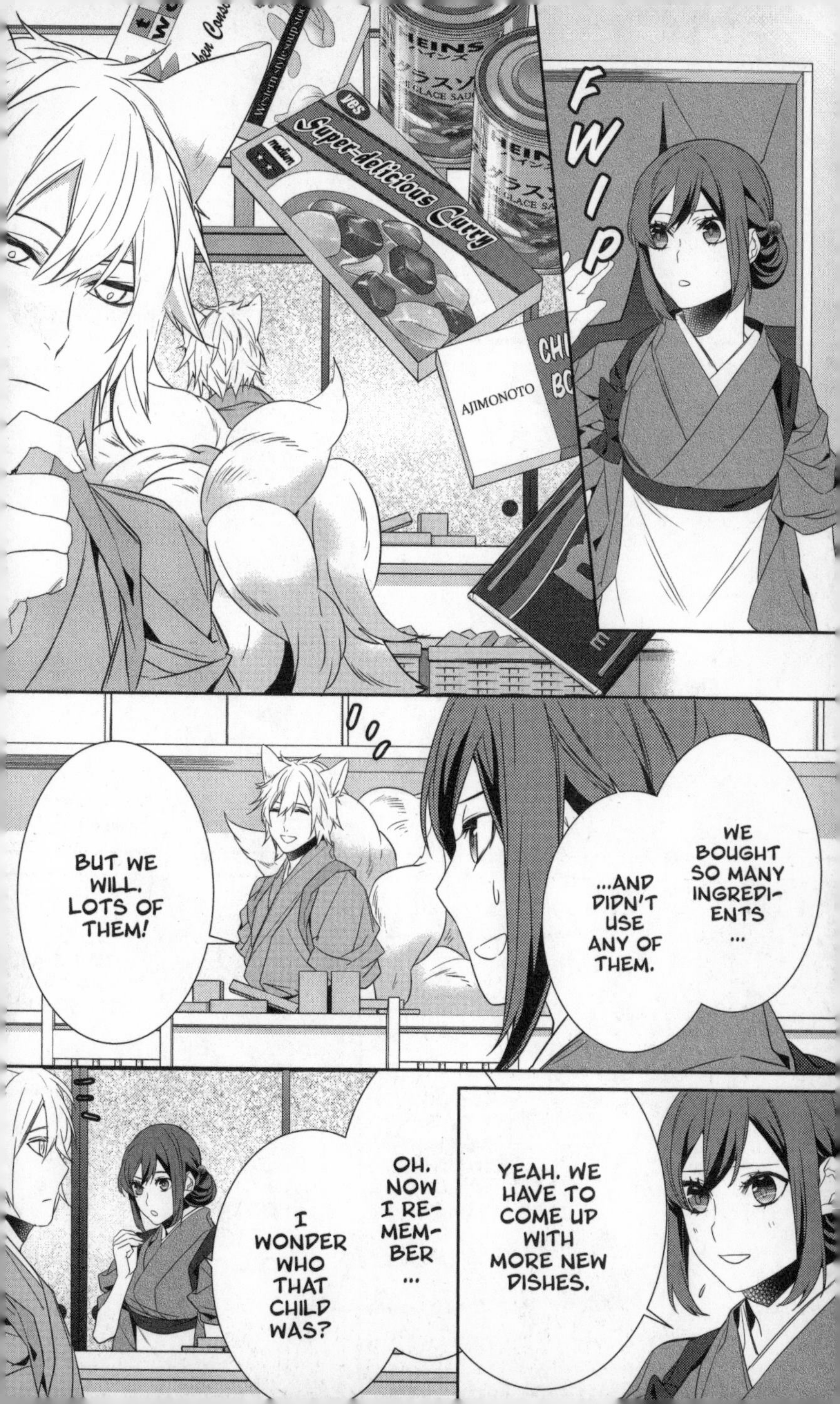
FWIP
HEINS
Super-delicious Curry
medium
AJIMONOTO
WE BOUGHT SO MANY INGREDIENTS...
...AND DIDN'T USE ANY OF THEM.
BUT WE WILL. LOTS OF THEM!
YEAH. WE HAVE TO COME UP WITH MORE NEW DISHES.
OH. NOW I REMEMBER...
I WONDER WHO THAT CHILD WAS?

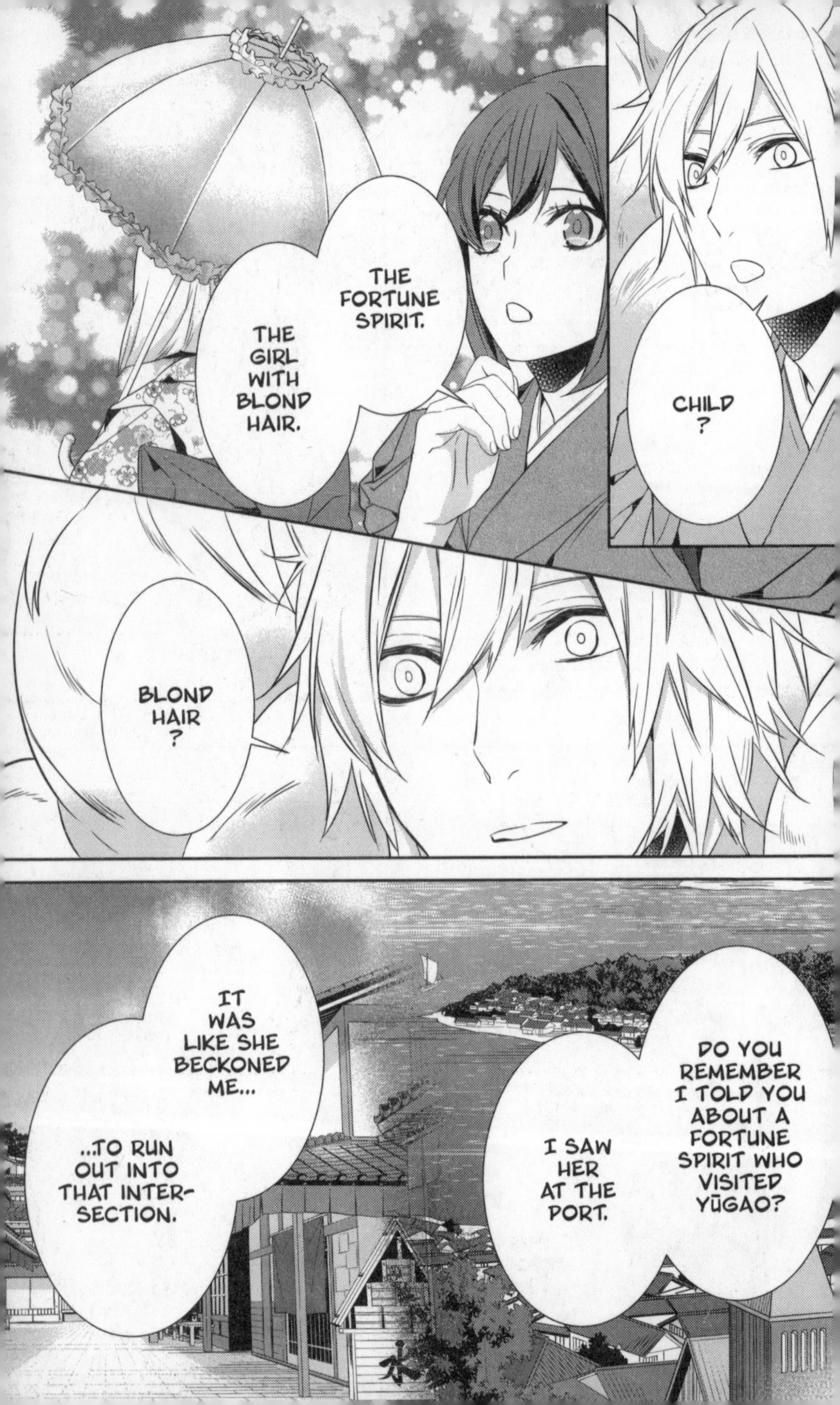
CHILD?
THE FORTUNE SPIRIT.
THE GIRL WITH BLOND HAIR.
BLOND HAIR?
DO YOU REMEMBER I TOLD YOU ABOUT A FORTUNE SPIRIT WHO VISITED YŪGAO?
I SAW HER AT THE PORT.
IT WAS LIKE SHE BECKONED ME...
...TO RUN OUT INTO THAT INTER-SECTION.

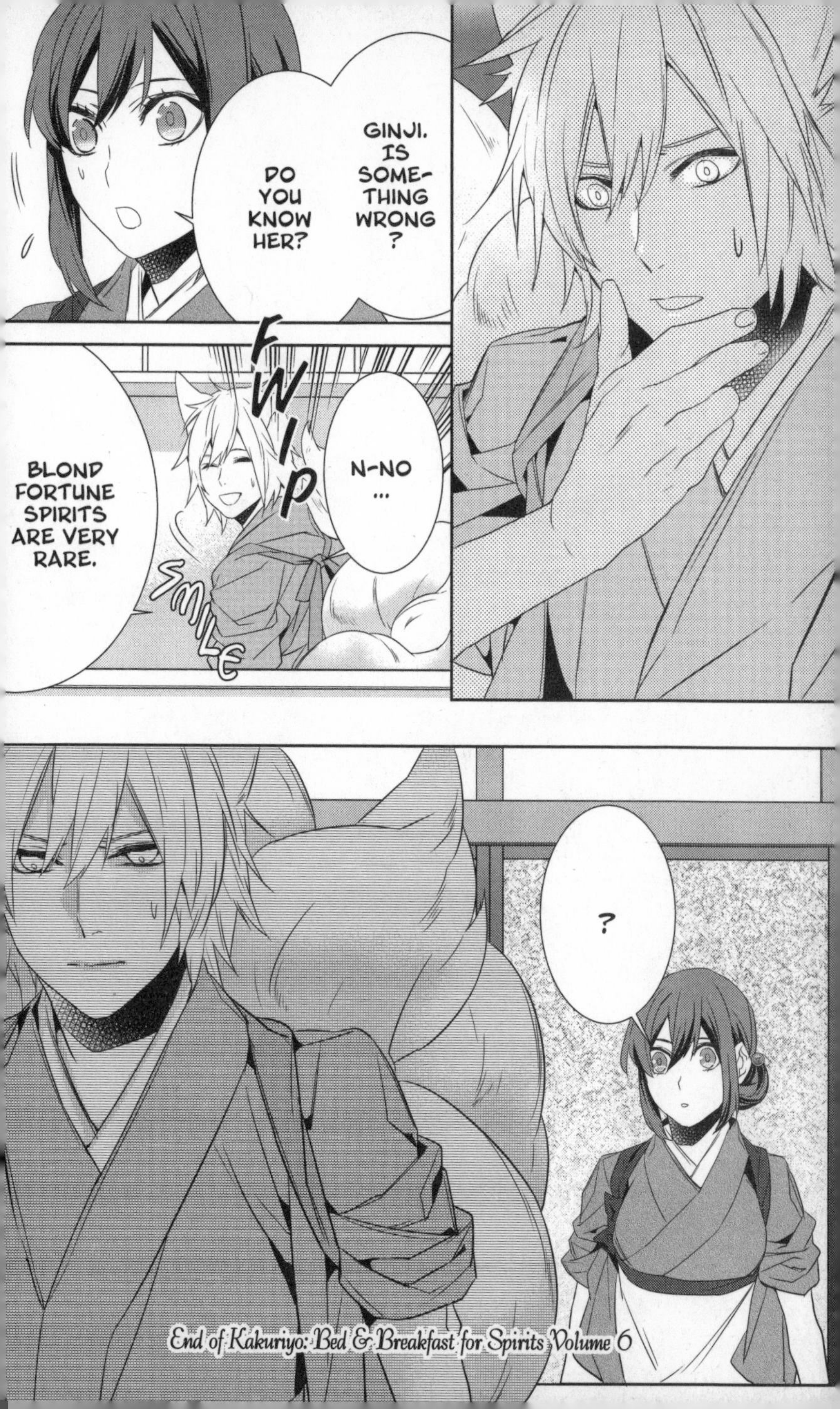
GINJI. IS SOMETHING WRONG?
DO YOU KNOW HER?
FWIP
N-NO ...
BLOND FORTUNE SPIRITS ARE VERY RARE.
SMILE
?
End of Kakuriyo: Bed & Breakfast for Spirits Volume 6

Kakuriyo
Bed & Breakfast
for Spirits

END NOTES

PAGE 96, PANEL 1
Shiso
Also known as perilla or beefsteak plant. It tastes like a cross between mint and basil.

PAGE 96, PANEL 3
Rice-flour dumplings
These particular dumplings are *shirotama,* a type of unfilled mochi.

PAGE 115, PANEL 3
Shippoku Cuisine
This cuisine originated in Nagasaki and the dishes are a mixture of Japanese, Chinese and Western (mostly Dutch) cuisine. Meals are served Chinese-style where guests sit at round tables and dishes are presented on platters. Shippoku course meals are served at celebrations such as wedding receptions.

PAGE 66, PANEL 1
Daruma
Round good-luck dolls made in the shape of the Buddhist monk Bodhidarma. They're usually red.

PAGE 95, PANEL 4
Umeboshi
Extremely sour and salty pickles made from *ume,* a stone fruit similar to a small, hard apricot but often translated as "plum."

PAGE 95, PANEL 5
Ponzu sauce
A citrus-based marinade or dressing.